Also by Joseph M. Belth

A Report on Life Insurance (1963)
Participating Life Insurance Sold by Stock Companies (1965)
The Retail Price Structure in American Life Insurance (1966)
Life Insurance: A Consumer's Handbook (1973, 1985)
The Insurance Forum (1974-2013)
Blog at www.josephmbelth.com (2013-)

The Insurance Forum:

A Memoir

the INSURANCE FORUM®:
A Memoir

Joseph M. Belth

The Insurance Forum
Ellettsville, Indiana

Published by

The Insurance Forum
Post Office Box 245
Ellettsville, Indiana 47429-0245

ISBN: 0-941173-18-6

Designed by Jeffrey E. Belth

1 3 5 4 2

To
Marge, Ann, Mike, and Jeff
The Great Team I Brought to Indiana in 1962

Table of Contents

Foreword

$\mathcal{P}$rofessor Joseph M. Belth has crafted an immensely enjoyable memoir validating his firm belief that "any business built on the nondisclosure of information vital to its customers will not survive—and will not deserve to survive—over the long term." This book presents his courageous life's work and fascinating behind-the-scenes backstories of battles with adversarial insurance executives and regulators. The author always follows his basic belief in fairness for life insurance consumers in ways that no other investigative journalist has been so well equipped to master by education, experience, and inclination. Our trailblazing friend and colleague published what we consider to be the most influential insurance monthly newsletter ever, *The Insurance Forum*, "for the unfettered exchange of ideas about insurance." He did this for 40 years, using first-rate investigative journalism along with his sharp pen to fight, sometimes successfully, sometimes not, for a more level playing field for consumers in the life insurance market.

The memoir is a compelling "must read" for industry insiders, insurance regulators, reporters, lawmakers, and any others considering insurance issues. People outside the field who are interested in the history and future of the life insurance industry also will be intrigued. Through reflections on development of and responses to articles in the *Forum*, the memoir illustrates why and how more meaningful disclosure and stronger regulatory oversight would benefit consumers, and, simultaneously, how past and present industry practices thwart these noble goals. In addition to chapters about intriguing insurance issues, readers are treated to autobiographical insights into Belth's formative years. These personal stories offer insight into his inquisitive interest in and respect for the important role life insurance plays in our financial well-being. You will find his courageous, indefatigable personality jumping out from the pages.

Economics is the bedrock for most of what appears in this memoir. Indeed, a fundamental assumption made by economists about a competitive market is that consumers are informed when contemplating the purchase of a product or service. We know that this assumption is rarely valid for some purchases, especially insurance. The book describes clearly and specifically, using sound methods published in respected journals, how the life insurance industry would be strengthened and improved by a rigorous system that discloses product prices and rates of return, all in the public interest. Yet life insurers and their regulators continue systematically to deny information critical to informed consumer decision making.

At the time Belth retired from Indiana University, his esteemed colleague, Professor John Douglas Long, recognized him as "the most prominent life insurance scholar in the world." We agree. Belth's scholarly work stands alone in its high degree of creativity, forward thought, innovation, and challenge to the status quo. While Belth's work is grounded in the deep knowledge of a world-class scholar, it is much more. He understands the practical elements of insurance. This fact allowed him to use the *Forum* to communicate to those outside the academic community his often controversial views on deceptive industry practices and recommendations for reform. Always full of detail and keen observations, Belth's analyses and opinions in the *Forum* and condensed in this memoir are as unquestionably objective and credible as his scholarly work. As you read the memoir you, like we, cannot help but be both entertained and amazed at what was accomplished through the *Forum* over its 40-year existence.

Anyone who knows Belth well, as we do, realizes he grew up with a strong internal sense of right and wrong along with the toughness to resist peer pressure. In fact, he may be the most ethical and objective person we know. His writings in the *Forum* and this memoir leave no doubt that he has filled a critical role as the "conscience of the life insurance industry." A cartoon sketch early in the book portrays him as a courageous warrior in armor seeking justice and protection for life insurance consumers. Persistence is exemplified by, for example, his 50 articles from 1981 to 1990 about the indiscriminate replacement of existing life insurance policies by the A. L. Williams organization. In 1981, the North Carolina insurance commissioner, with seemingly close ties to ALW, banned a *Forum* article critical of some ALW practices from being distributed by North Carolina insurance agents. Belth sued the commissioner, resulting in a summary judgment for Belth and payment of Belth's legal fees and expenses by the commissioner. The backstory described in the book is simply spellbinding.

Belth and his work, as summarized in this book, have received many prestigious awards. Among them are six awards for outstanding articles in *The Journal of Risk and Insurance* (the world's leading academic journal in its field), the 1966 Elizur Wright Award, a 1990 George Polk Award, and the American College's 1999 Huebner Gold Medal.

The memoir presents mesmerizing accounts of the enormously positive influence Belth has had on the life insurance business. A sampling includes:

- Prohibition of the "traditional net cost method" of price measurement that was so misleading that it often showed negative costs of insurance over 20 years or so,
- requirements that interest be paid on death benefits from the date of the insured's death,
- opposition—often successful—to the creation of mutual holding companies,
- calling attention to the weaknesses of surplus notes issued by insurers in an effort to make themselves appear more financially secure, and
- strong and continuing criticism of the nefarious practices

associated with stranger-originated life insurance, where insurable interest and other important insurance principles are violated.

Even a total list of changes prompted by Belth would understate his substantial impact on life insurance industry performance over the last 40 years. We say this because many industry decision makers undoubtedly avoided certain anti-consumer actions because no executive wanted his or her company to be the subject of a scathing article in the *Forum*.

For every victory, there were several defeats. Perhaps the one that Belth most regrets is the failure of policy makers to enact meaningful life insurance disclosure. For the first 18 years of his career, he was devoted to generating a system in which life insurance consumers would be assured of access to meaningful measures of insurance prices and rates of return. Appearances before congressional and state regulatory committees were frequent. Belth shares with his readers intriguing stories of how the political power of the life insurance industry prevented the enactment of meaningful price and rate of return disclosure. For example, at the federal level in the late 1970s, U.S. Senator Philip Hart introduced truth-in-life-insurance legislation. The life insurance lobby blocked the bill. A less significant yet meaningful consolation prize was a requirement that the time value of money be recognized in a new price measure. The Federal Trade Commission released a staff study critical of life insurance from the consumer point of view. Belth served as a consultant to the staff. Life insurance executives were furious at the recommendations and mounted a successful effort to enact federal legislation barring the FTC from studying insurance without a formal request from a congressional committee.

At the state level in 1980, a task force of the National Association of Insurance Commissioners (NAIC), after long negotiations, proposed a new model regulation to require meaningful disclosure of prices and rates of return. Belth describes the anger of the industry and how it led to the firing of the head of the NAIC central office. The Indiana insurance commissioner (a past president of the NAIC), who chaired the task force, was also fired. No regulators have since proposed disclosure of prices and rates of return. Following that experience, Belth essentially abandoned this signature consumer objective.

As aspiring insurance professors, two of us (Pritchett and Schmit) began to view Belth as a mentor while we were students in his graduate courses and through almost daily interactions as his graduate assistants at Indiana University (Pritchett in the 1960s; Schmit in the 1980s). Admiration by the other author of this foreword (Skipper) began while a graduate student at the University of Pennsylvania, where Belth had earlier finished his Ph.D. studies. This respect intensified in the 1970s when Skipper, as a young professor, examined Belth's early books and academic articles in greater depth, propelling Skipper to specialize in the area of life insurance and public policy. The result of these early experiences by the three of us has been lasting friendship with and admiration for a true scholar's scholar. Belth's personal integrity and demanding standards of excellence as reflected in this memoir serve as an inspiration to us and the reader, showing what one dedicated individual can accomplish.

S. Travis Pritchett
> Distinguished Professor Emeritus of Finance and Insurance
> Holder of the W. Frank Hipp Chair of Insurance, prior to retirement
> University of South Carolina—Columbia
> Charleston, South Carolina

Joan T. Schmit
> American Family Distinguished Chair in Risk Management and Insurance
> Wisconsin School of Business
> University of Wisconsin—Madison
> Madison, Wisconsin

Harold D. Skipper
> Professor Emeritus of Risk Management and Insurance
> Holder of the C.V. Starr Chair of International Insurance, prior to retirement
> Coauthor of *Life Insurance,* 15th edition, Lucretian, LLC, 2015
> Georgia State University
> Atlanta, Georgia

June 2, 2015

Preface

The Insurance Forum—referred to in this memoir as the *Forum*—began in late December 1973, a few days before the U.S. Postal Service raised the price of a first-class postage stamp from five cents to eight cents. I dated the introductory four-page issue January 1974, sent it to some people I thought would be interested, and invited them to subscribe for $15 per year. More than a hundred accepted the invitation, and my experiment in insurance journalism was off the ground.

After 40 years, 463 issues (including 17 double issues), and 4,810 pages, I mailed the December 2013 final issue to subscribers. Thus ended the experiment.

My experience with the *Forum* was extraordinary. The purpose of this memoir is to share the experience with those interested in consumer insurance protection issues in general and consumer insurance disclosure issues in particular.

The introductory chapter 1 explains why and how the *Forum* began, and briefly describes several significant events that occurred during the four decades of operation. Chapters 2 and 3 are purely autobiographical; they describe my pre-Indiana years (1929–1962) and my Indiana years (1962–2015). Chapters 4 through 15 examine numerous aspects of life insurance, which has been the primary focus of my research efforts throughout my academic career and during my retirement years. Chapters

16 through 18 discuss three forms of health insurance. Chapters 19 through 21 explore annuities. Chapters 22 through 28 cover several aspects of insurance company operations. Chapters 29 through 31 discuss state regulation of the insurance industry. The concluding chapter 32 presents personal observations about life insurance. A glossary is included to assist with terminology, and an index is also included.

There are many references to issues of the *Forum*. When an issue is mentioned, the month and year are followed by "of the *Forum*" when needed to avoid possible confusion with issues of other periodicals. At the end of each chapter is an indication of the issues of the *Forum* mentioned in that chapter.

Our website (www.theinsuranceforum.com) lists the titles of all articles in all issues. Hard copies of all issues are available. For ordering information, please visit our website or write to us at P.O. Box 245, Ellettsville, Indiana 47429.

After I ended work on the *Forum* by turning over the final issue to the printer, I began a blog (www.josephmbelth.com). There is no cost for access, and readers may sign up to receive each new item automatically by e-mail. This memoir contains references to specific blog items. At the end of each chapter is an indication (by number and date) of blog items, if any, mentioned in that chapter.

Thoughts are welcomed concerning this memoir, the *Forum*, and the blog items. Please write to me at the address above or at jmbelth@gmail.com. I will try to acknowledge all comments.

Joseph M. Belth
Ellettsville, Indiana

June 12, 2015

1

Introduction

$\mathcal{T}$he road to the *Forum* began with a chance encounter involving Herbert Denenberg, Ralph Nader, and me. Denenberg and I were graduate school classmates at the University of Pennsylvania in the late 1950s. He was a year behind me, but we were in some classes together.

In 1965, when Denenberg was a member of the insurance faculty at Penn, he was elected vice president of the American Risk and Insurance Association (ARIA), an organization of insurance professors and others interested in insurance education and research. He had been nominated by petition rather than by ARIA's nominating committee. At the time he was—and today remains—the only person in the 83-year history of ARIA elected to an ARIA leadership position without the recommendation of the nominating committee. (As mentioned briefly in this chapter, and as discussed in chapter 29, Denenberg later served as the Pennsylvania insurance commissioner.) As ARIA vice president, he chaired the program committee for the ARIA annual meeting to be held in August 1966.

Nader became a household name in 1965 with the publication of his landmark book, *Unsafe at Any Speed: The Designed-In Dangers of the American Automobile*. To stimulate attendance at the annual meeting, Denenberg invited Nader to be a guest speaker, and Nader accepted the invitation. Denenberg announced the program several weeks prior to the meeting. I had been planning to attend the meeting, and made it a point to read Nader's book. He and I met for the first time during the course of the meeting, and I commended him on the book.

Nader then startled me by saying he liked my book, *The Retail Price Structure in American Life Insurance,* which had been published earlier that year. I had heard he was a voracious reader, but I never dreamed he would be familiar with my relatively obscure book.

During our conversation Nader turned to the subject of naming names. He had identified automobile manufacturers and many individuals and organizations in his book, and he said correctly that I had not identified insurance companies in my book. Nor had I identified insurance companies in my other writings up to that time, with two exceptions. One exception was my 1961 doctoral dissertation at the University of Pennsylvania. The other exception was my report to Consumers Union, which I had published in book form in 1963, and which is discussed in chapter 3. Nader said that failing to name names results in books, articles, and reports being relegated to dusty shelves, while naming names makes the material more interesting, more widely read, and more effective in addressing important social issues.

Nader is persuasive, as anyone who has met him knows. I soon began identifying companies in many of my articles, other writings, and speeches, with predictable results. Over the next eight years, I encountered 31 incidents where my work was subjected to censorship. The experience eventually led to my decision to publish the *Forum* "for the unfettered exchange of ideas about insurance."

The beginning of the *Forum* is described in chapter 3. The discussion there includes an explanation of how I connected with Harry Privette, a talented cartoonist whose work is shown in several appropriate places in this memoir.

The remainder of this introductory chapter mentions, roughly in chronological order, a few of many important developments that occurred during the *Forum* years. As indicated, most of them are discussed more fully later in this memoir.

The FTC Staff Report

In July 1979, at a hearing before the U.S. Senate Committee on Commerce, the Federal Trade Commission (FTC) released a staff report entitled *Life Insurance Cost Disclosure*. The report focused on the need to disclose to consumers rates of return on the savings component in cash-value life insurance policies. During the preparation of the report, I served as one of several consultants to the FTC staff.

The staff report enraged the life insurance industry. The report also angered state insurance regulators, who viewed the report as an intrusion on their regulatory turf. The life insurance industry arranged for the report to be shelved permanently. Also, as discussed in chapter 6, the industry persuaded Congress to enact legislation permanently barring the FTC from even studying, let alone reporting on, insurance without a specific request from a congressional committee.

The NAIC Task Force Report

In November 1980 a special task force of state insurance commissioners that had been appointed by the National Association of Insurance Commissioners (NAIC) released a report prepared by members of the staff in the NAIC's central office, which was then located in Milwaukee. The report recommended that the states adopt regulations requiring life insurance companies to provide rigorous disclosure of price information to life insurance prospects and policyholders.

The task force report enraged the life insurance industry, which arranged for the report to be shelved permanently. The industry also took draconian steps. It persuaded the NAIC to fire Jon Hanson, an attorney who headed the NAIC's central office staff and was a coauthor of the report. What is now the American Council of Life Insurers, the major life insurance company trade association, hired Carolyn Cobb, a young attorney who was the other coauthor of the report, away from the NAIC's central office. Indiana Governor Robert Orr fired H. Peter Hudson, the Indiana insurance commissioner and a former president of the NAIC. Hudson had chaired the NAIC task force. See chapter 6.

Churning

I used the word churning, which is explained in chapter 4, in the April 1981 issue of the *Forum*. The four-page issue was devoted in its entirety to an article about the activities of the A. L. Williams organization (ALW), a large national insurance agency that indiscriminately replaced existing cash-value life insurance policies.

My use of the C-word enraged ALW, which began a national campaign to discredit the *Forum* and me. Ronald Raxter was a staff attorney in the North Carolina Department of Insurance. Barry Clause was an ALW executive who had worked previously in the Department and had been a Raxter colleague. Clause persuaded Raxter to ban dissemination of my April 1981 article. They took the outrageous position that dissemination of the article constituted an unfair trade practice under North Carolina laws and regulations.

John Ingram was the North Carolina insurance commissioner at the time. My attorney demanded that Ingram publicly rescind the Raxter ban. When Ingram failed to do so, we filed a lawsuit against Ingram in the federal district court in Raleigh. We won the case. The judge ordered Ingram to rescind the ban publicly. A three-judge panel of the federal appellate court in Richmond, Virginia unanimously affirmed the decision from the bench without my attorney saying a word. The state of North Carolina paid my legal expenses. We sold more reprints of the April 1981 issue than of any other issue in the previous or subsequent history of the *Forum*. The controversy made the *Forum* widely known among life insurance companies and agents. See chapter 5.

The Legal Battles Over Access to Data

In March 1985 I began trying to obtain access to the data generated in an early warning system developed by the NAIC to identify insurance companies that needed enhanced regulatory scrutiny because of possible financial trouble. The NAIC treated the information as confidential.

I fought several legal battles seeking access to the data in accordance with public records laws. Eventually I obtained a court order requiring the District of Columbia insurance commissioner to release the data to me. I published the data in the December 1987 issue. However, I was not able to update the material later because the NAIC stopped providing the data to the District of Columbia commissioner. See chapter 30.

The Collapse of Executive Life

In 1986 I began writing about Executive Life Insurance Company, a large California-based company. During the next five years I wrote several major articles about the company's financial problems. At one point I mentioned the possibility that the company was insolvent.

In April 1991 Executive Life's parent company filed for bankruptcy protection, and its life insurance company subsidiaries were taken over by state insurance regulators. The collapse was the largest failure in the history of American life insurance. See chapter 7.

The Failed Reorganization of Provident Mutual

In January 1998, long after Denenberg's tenure as the Pennsylvania insurance commissioner, the board of directors of Provident Mutual Life Insurance Company of Philadelphia adopted a plan to reorganize through the creation of a mutual holding company (MHC). The plan would have provided a financial windfall for Provident Mutual's executives, but it would have been a bad deal for the company's policyholders. Three months later, the Pennsylvania Insurance Department held a public hearing on the plan in Philadelphia. The hearing, which I attended, was a farce.

In February 1999 Provident Mutual's policyholders approved the MHC plan in a vote that followed distribution of a flawed policyholder information statement. Two days later, in a stunning development, a Pennsylvania judge issued a preliminary injunction barring the company from implementing the plan. Six months later the judge made the injunction permanent. The company scrapped the plan and later converted from the mutual form of organization into a shareholder-owned company under the sponsorship of Nationwide Corporation.

I wrote several major articles in the *Forum* about Provident Mutual's flirtation with the MHC plan. However, credit for defeat of the plan goes to a pair of intrepid opponents of the plan and a small group of policyholders who brought legal action against the company. See chapter 26.

The Attempted Bribery of an Elderly Widow

In October 1998, Paul Schneider, a certified public accountant in Florida, sent an amazing letter to a 79-year-old widow in Pennsylvania. She showed the letter to a friend who by coincidence was one of my subscribers, and he shared it with me.

The letter described a frightening scheme later called stranger-originated life insurance or speculator-initiated life insurance. The scheme involves bribing a person to buy a large, unneeded life insurance policy for the purpose of selling the policy to investors (I call them speculators in human life) who thereby acquire a strong financial interest in the early death of the person whose life is insured.

The Schneider letter prompted me to devote the entire March 1999 issue of the *Forum* to a 12-page article about the scheme. I later wrote dozens of articles about it. See chapter 9.

The Legal Battles in New Mexico

I devoted the entire December 1998 issue of the *Forum* to a 12-page article about fractional (modal) premium charges. They are the extra charges that insurance companies impose on policyholders who pay their insurance premiums more often than once a year.

Immediately after the issue was published, two attorneys from New Mexico came to see me in Bloomington. They said they were planning to file class action lawsuits against several life insurance companies for failing to disclose the annual percentage rates (APRs) associated with fractional premium charges. The attorneys asked me to be an expert witness. Initially I declined, but eventually agreed to work with them. Unfortunately all but one of the lawsuits were settled without requiring the companies to disclose APRs to prospects and policyholders. See chapter 8.

The Default at General American

In 1999 the Missouri director of insurance placed General American Life Insurance Company under supervision because of a severe liquidity problem that arose from a devastating run on the company. The company was later acquired by Metropolitan Life Insurance Company. I wrote several articles about developments at General American. See chapter 22.

The Legal Battle in New York

In May 2000 I began a legal battle over access to executive compensation data publicly filed with what was then the New York Department of Insurance by life insurance companies doing business in the state. The data were filed in accordance

with a 1906 state law requiring companies to disclose data to the Department showing the compensation of highly paid life insurance company executives. The data always had been available to the public until the Department decided, in a ruling adopted in 2000 without notice to the public and without debate, to end public access to most of the data.

I won a court victory allowing me to obtain the data I needed for my tabulations. Later the Department, by then under new management, rescinded the ruling at my request.

Those developments enraged the Life Insurance Council of New York (LICONY), an association of life insurance companies doing business in the state. LICONY quietly persuaded the New York legislature to enact an amendment that decimated the century-old disclosure law. I say quietly because there were no debates in either house of the legislature on the proposed amendment, no hearings, and no press coverage. I learned of the amendment through a tip from a "Deep Throat" informer after the amendment had sailed through both houses of the legislature and had been sent to New York Governor David Paterson for his signature. I tried without success to persuade him to veto the amendment. See chapter 24.

The O'Connell Ban

In the late 1990s Robert O'Connell became the chief executive officer of Massachusetts Mutual Life Insurance Company. The company was a defendant in one of the New Mexico lawsuits relating to the failure to disclose fractional premium charges as APRs. In September 2000 O'Connell testified by deposition in the case. The plaintiffs' attorney gave him a rough time. A few weeks later O'Connell banned the *Forum* from the company's home office. I learned about the ban when several executives abruptly canceled their subscriptions. One told me about the ban but did not cancel his subscription; he said he would not allow anyone to tell him what he could or could not read. Others asked me to change the addresses on their subscriptions to their home addresses.

In June 2005 Massachusetts Mutual's board of directors announced it had fired O'Connell because of allegedly serious financial irregularities. I wrote several articles in the *Forum* about the firing because of the extraordinary nature of the developments that prompted the board's action and because of the legal dispute that arose over O'Connell's severance compensation. The firing was not related to the banning of the *Forum*.

A Pair of Profiles

In January 1978, four years after I launched the *Forum*, Paul Ingrassia, a reporter for *The Wall Street Journal*, profiled me on the front page of the newspaper. The article drew considerable attention to my early campaigns relating to the need for life insurance price disclosure and the need to pay interest on the life insurance death benefit from the date of the insured's death to the date of the benefit check. The article also brought widespread attention to the *Forum*. The campaigns referred to in the article are discussed in chapters 6 and 12.

In April 1990, Eric Berg, a reporter for *The New York Times*, profiled me in the newspaper. The article mentioned some of my campaigns and brought attention to the *Forum*.

The George Polk Award

George Polk was a CBS correspondent who was murdered in 1948 while covering the civil war in Greece. The George Polk Awards were established in 1949 by the journalism department at Long Island University and are among the most coveted in journalism. Among those who have received George Polk Awards (listed alphabetically with the year in parentheses) are R. W. Apple, Jr. (1967), Russell Baker (1978), Red Barber (1984), Ed Bradley (1979), Carl Bernstein (1972), Walter Cronkite (1970), Fred Friendly (1990), David Halberstam (1963), Seymour M. Hersh (1969), Chet Huntley (1958), Peter Jennings (1990), Ted Koppel (1981), Charles Kuralt (1980), Don McNeill (1983), Edward R. Murrow (1951), Morley Safer (1965), Eric Severeid (1954), William Lawrence Shirer (1982), I. F. Stone (1970), and Robert Woodward (1972).

In April 1991 I received a George Polk Award in the special publications category, one of 13 categories that year. It was a great honor for the then 17-year-old *Forum* and me.

The following statement was read during the luncheon at which the award was presented:

> The award for Special Publications went to Joseph M. Belth for his "The Insurance Forum." The judges honored Mr. Belth's four-page monthly newsletter for its intense scrutiny of the insurance business since 1974. A one-man operation, it keeps a watchful eye on deceptive sales practices, corporate operations, and consumer interests. While acknowledging the more desirable practices in the business, the newsletter has become a public watchdog commenting relentlessly on its inadequacies and concerned with correcting the unbalanced coverage in the insurance trade press. Intent on reform and informing those in decision-making positions, Mr. Belth carries on despite the continuing hostility of many in the industry.

2

The Pre-Indiana Years: 1929-1962

J was born on Tuesday, October 22, 1929, in Syracuse, New York. One week later, on what became known as "Black Tuesday," the stock market crashed.

My Grandparents

My paternal grandparents were Joseph Morton Belth, after whom I was named, and Rebecca Belth. My maternal grand-parents were Isaac Bright and Dorothy Bright. They all came to America around 1900 from eastern Europe, passed through Ellis Island, and settled in New York City. The Bright family later moved to Syracuse.

I often think of how my grand-parents uprooted themselves from their homes and endured the rigors of travel to America so that their descendants would have the opportunity to live in this great country. My indebted-ness to them influences my views on immigration matters.

Joseph Morton Belth, *c.* 1920

My Parents

My father was Irving Belth. He was born in 1893 in Poland and was the second oldest of six children. He came to Amer-

ica with his family as a small child. He served in the infantry in the Great War and fought in France. After the war, he moved from New York City to Syracuse. For many years he owned a Syracuse millinery store where he sold ladies' hats and other accessories. He earned a comfortable living until World War II, when most women stopped wearing hats. Shortly after the war, he closed the millinery store. He then opened a

Irving Belth, 1923

china shop, but it was not financially successful. By 1947, when I finished high school, he had financial problems and health problems. My father died in 1952 at age 58.

My mother was Helen Rose Bright Belth. She was born in 1904 in New York City and was the oldest of four children. Her family later moved from New York City to Syracuse. After my father died, my mother went to work for the Syracuse Board of Education as a clerk. She and her widowed mother and I continued to live in our house until I married and later left Syracuse. After her mother died, my mother lived alone in our house until she sold it and moved into a small apartment. She did not want to move to Indiana, and fortunately a sister lived nearby in Syracuse. My mother lived as a widow for 26 years and died in 1978 at age 73.

As mentioned, my father was in the millinery business. Isaac Bright, my maternal grandfather, was also in the millinery business. That is how my parents met. They were to be married on June 29, 1924. However, Joseph Morton Belth, my paternal grandfather, died in an automobile accident while traveling

Helen Rose Bright, 1923

from New York City to Syracuse for the wedding. The wedding was postponed until July 15, 1924. It was conducted as a private ceremony without any celebration. I never asked my parents for details about the accident, because I knew the subject was painful for them. My wife and I eventually inherited from my mother a pair of beautiful silver candlesticks that my paternal grandparents had given to my parents as a wedding gift. The original wedding date is inscribed on the base of each candlestick. We use the candlesticks every Friday evening in welcoming the Sabbath and are reminded of the family tragedy that delayed my parents' wedding.

Our Syracuse Home

After the wedding my father bought a house in Syracuse at 245 Cambridge Street, two miles east of the city's main business district. It was a comfortable bungalow. I am an only child. The house was my home for 25 years, until my marriage. To please my mother, and for sentimental reasons, I chose Post Office Box 245 as the mailing address when I launched the *Forum* in Ellettsville, Indiana, at the end of 1973.

Our house was a short walk from a small neighborhood business district. It included two grocery stores, two drug stores, several other small stores, a small branch of the Syracuse Public Library where I was a frequent patron, and a small neighborhood movie theater where I was a regular customer.

My Schools

My first day of school was at a kindergarten in Orlando, Florida. My parents sometimes spent time in Florida during the worst part of the long and harsh Syracuse winters.

I attended Syracuse public schools. Sumner, an elementary school, was an easy walk. Edward Smith, a junior high school, was a little more than a mile away; I sometimes walked and sometimes rode a bicycle. Nottingham High School was an easy walk. I never rode a school bus.

Early Sunday afternoon, December 7, 1941, I heard on the RCA radio at the north end of our living room the news of the Japanese attack on Pearl Harbor. During the war, because of gasoline rationing, we used our car very little. My mother did the driving; my father, like many who grew up in New York City, never learned to drive.

In high school I took three years of English, three years of mathematics, three years of Latin, two years of Spanish, general science, history, geography, social studies, and, at my father's suggestion, typewriting and shorthand. I graduated in 1947 in the top five of my class of more than 200.

The high school teacher with whom I maintained closest contact after graduation was Marion Golley. She taught typewriting and shorthand, and she was close to retirement when I met her. She was a stern, no-nonsense teacher. Other students seemed afraid of her, but I found her a grand lady. She seemed to have a soft spot in her heart for me, perhaps because boys rarely enrolled in her classes. After I left Syracuse, whenever I went back for a visit, I invited her to join my mother and me for a restaurant dinner.

Because of my father's health and financial problems, I did not immediately go to college. Instead, I found a job with a locally owned wholesaler that sold automobile and refrigerator parts. I started as a secretary, thanks to my father's suggestion that I study typewriting and shorthand, and subsequently I became an assistant parts manager.

Our Synagogue

My parents belonged to Temple Adath Yeshurun, a conservative synagogue about a mile west of our house. Our religious leader was Rabbi Irwin Hyman. Our musical leader was Cantor Samuel Arluck; his son, Hyman Arluck, who changed his name to Harold Arlen, composed "Over the Rainbow" and received an Oscar for the music in the great 1939 movie, *The Wizard of Oz*. I am reminded of Arlen and his father whenever I see the great 1927 movie, *The Jazz Singer*. My Hebrew teacher was Reverend Isaac Simon, who was also assistant rabbi at the synagogue.

Joseph Morton Belth, 1942

I celebrated my bar mitzvah on Saturday, October 10, 1942. The next day's issue of *The New York Times* did not report the event. Nor did it say anything about the plight of the European Jews. It was filled with stories about what was happening at a place then named Stalingrad.

My First Life Insurance

Reverend Simon was a part-time agent for Equitable Life Assurance Society of the United States. In 1941 and 1944, my father bought from him two small (they seemed large in those days) cash-value policies on my life. The face amounts were $8,500 and $5,000.

When I went to work in 1947, the gross amount (before deductions) of my first weekly paycheck was $22, at the rate of 50 cents per hour for 44 hours (five eight-hour days and four hours on Saturday). At that point my father turned over the policies to me. He said now that I was gainfully employed it was time for me to take responsibility for paying the premiums. I bought another $5,000 policy from Reverend Simon in 1948. Those policies were my first exposure to the use of life insurance as a vehicle for systematic savings, and the loan values of those policies provided an important source of funds later on.

In 1952, when my father died, we discovered that, because of his serious financial problems, he had surrendered much of his life insurance for its cash value. However, the life insurance that was still in force when he died allowed my mother and me to stay in our home. That experience began my intense interest in life insurance, later prompted me to enter the life insurance business as an agent, and eventually led me to embark on an academic career in insurance.

Baseball

Baseball was one of only two sports in which I did more than dabble. The other was table tennis, which is discussed in chapter 3.

I often visited Syracuse's Municipal Stadium, which later became MacArthur Stadium, to watch the Syracuse Chiefs of the Triple-A International League. My parents and I sometimes traveled to New York City to visit the family. I recall attending a baseball game at Yankee Stadium before World War II and seeing Joe DiMaggio and the other famous Yankees of the era.

By the time I got to high school, I was serious about baseball. I tried out for the team and earned a starting position at second base. I was proficient at catching pop flies, fielding ground balls, and turning ground balls into double plays. I was not a high percentage hitter because I never learned to hit a good curve ball. I think our coach, "Doc" Manor, put up with my problems at the plate because of my proficiency in the field. Despite my poor hitting, the team photograph in our class yearbook shows me with a bat on my shoulder.

The Syracuse Chiefs, at the time a farm club for the Cincinnati Reds, caused me to become a Reds' fan early on. One of my most vivid memories was seeing Jackie Robinson when he played in 1946 for the Montreal Royals, at the time a farm club

"Slugger" and teammates, 1947

for the Brooklyn Dodgers. He was obviously a very special talent. Consequently I was not surprised when he broke the color line in major league baseball the following year. I remained a Reds' fan when I moved to Indiana, and often took our sons to see the Reds at Crosley Field and later at Riverfront Stadium.

Nonsmoking

My father never smoked cigarettes, but he loved to smoke White Owl cigars. My mother did not smoke, hated smoking, and strongly urged me not to smoke. I think she understood the serious health hazards of smoking long before they were highly publicized. I have never smoked, and I credit my mother for my freedom from that terrible addiction. When anyone offered me a cigarette, my habitual response was: "Thanks, but I don't smoke." People soon stopped offering me cigarettes.

My wife has never smoked, and our three children have never smoked. I have never seen our grandchildren smoke, and I hope neither they nor their children will ever smoke.

National Guard

My father performed the patriotic but thankless task of serving on the local draft board during World War II. A few years after the war, when the draft was reinstituted because of mounting tensions on the Korean peninsula, my father ordered me to join the New York National Guard to avoid the draft. I obeyed his order and joined the headquarters battery of the

249th field artillery battalion of the 27th infantry division, which later became an armored division. The armory was a mile west of our house. I spent one night each week there, and two weeks each summer at what was then Pine Camp near Watertown in northern New York State.

Richard Kenyon and Tyler Stewart were with me in the National Guard. They were cousins who lived near one another less than a mile from our house. They were amateur radio enthusiasts who introduced me to the amazing world of ham radio. That became my main hobby for several years. I engaged exclusively in continuous-wave telegraphy rather than voice communication. My call letters were W2COU.

During the spring of 1951, I served three months of active duty for training in the Artillery School at Fort Sill, Oklahoma. While there I heard radio newsman Walter Winchell report that the 27th division was about to be nationalized. He was wrong; the 27th was not nationalized during the Korean War. Some of my classmates at the school were not so fortunate; their units back home were nationalized, and my classmates found themselves in the midst of some of the worst of the fighting while I was comfortably back home in Syracuse.

I remained in the National Guard for eight years. By the time I left the Guard, I had reached the rank of first lieutenant. I had completed an officer candidate training school program in Syracuse, and later I taught in the program. That was my first taste of formal teaching.

The Life Insurance Business

As mentioned earlier, when my father died I learned the value of the financial protection afforded to beneficiaries by life insurance. The experience prompted me to enter the life insurance business as an agent.

I approached the Syracuse agency of Penn Mutual Life Insurance Company. The manager asked me to take an aptitude test of the type then used in the life insurance industry to judge whether an individual had a good chance to become a successful agent. I flunked the test.

Robert O'Neill was an old friend of the family; he had

served on the draft board with my father during World War II. O'Neill was the manager of the Syracuse agency of Continental American Life Insurance Company, which had its home office in Wilmington, Delaware. He allowed me to retake the aptitude test. By then I knew how to answer the questions, and I passed the test. I joined the agency in March 1953.

I was not a large producer; the results of my first aptitude test probably were correct. I was more interested in studying the business than doing what was necessary to be a financially successful agent. I remember O'Neill's frustration with the time I spent studying instead of selling and prospecting. I completed the two parts of the LUTC (Life Underwriter Training Council) program. I also completed the first of the five parts of the CLU (Chartered Life Underwriter) program. Several years later, after I completed my graduate work, I received the CLU and CPCU (Chartered Property and Casualty Underwriter) designations.

Continental American was a shareholder-owned company that sold only participating (dividend-paying) life insurance. In the 1990s, long after I had left the company, it was acquired by and later merged into Provident Mutual Life Insurance Company of Philadelphia. In 2002 Provident converted from a mutual company into a shareholder-owned company and became part of Nationwide Corporation.

Our Marriage

I married Marjorie Helen Lavine (Marge) on June 12, 1955, in Syracuse. Her parents were Abraham Lavine, a general surgeon, and Aldia Lavine, a former nurse. Marge has a younger brother, Charles Lavine. The Lavines belonged to the Temple Society of Concord, a reform synagogue two blocks from our synagogue. The Lavines lived about a mile from our house, but Marge and I did not meet during our school years. We attended different elementary and junior high schools. We both attended Nottingham High School, but she started there just after I finished. It was by accident that I met the love of my life.

My mother and Lillian Lavine Sack, a sister of Marge's father, were close friends in high school. Consequently my mother attended the funeral when Lillian's mother died. My

Marge and Joe, 1955

mother asked me to pick her up at the Lavines' house after the funeral. When I arrived, Marge answered the door. I had never seen her before, and I was smitten. My mother was not there; someone had driven her home from the funeral, and no one had told me about the change in plans. When I got home, I asked my mother about the young woman who had answered the door; my mother said it was probably Marge. A day or two later I mustered the courage to call Marge and ask for a date. We were engaged a few months later. I am forever grateful for the mix-up that brought us together.

After the wedding, we moved into an apartment in Camillus, a few miles west of Syracuse. Marge, who had earned her bachelor's degree just before we were married, taught general science in the junior high school in Camillus, and I continued to work in the life insurance business.

Our three children—Ann, Michael (Mike), and Jeffrey (Jeff)—were born in 1958, 1959, and 1962. Mike married Jeanne, and Jeff married Sandra (Sandy). Today we have two granddaughters (Rachel and Rebecca), two grandsons (Alan and Caleb), and a stepgrandson (Whitney Swain).

Undergraduate School

One day in the spring of 1956, less than a year after Marge and I were married, and while driving to a sales appointment, I made the spontaneous decision to attend college. I cannot explain how or why I made the decision; the idea simply hit me. Like accidentally meeting Marge, joining the National Guard, and entering the life insurance business, starting college nine years later than my high school classmates was a pivotal event in my life.

I checked out Syracuse University, but thought the tuition of about $500 per semester was too much for me. Through a friend I learned of the two-year Auburn Community College (ACC) in Auburn, New York, about 20 miles west of the Camillus apartment where Marge and I lived. ACC, which is now Cayuga Community College (CCC), was three years old at the time. It was and remains a unit of the State University of New York. The tuition was about $100 per semester.

I called ACC and made an appointment to visit. When I arrived, for some unexplainable reason they rolled out the red carpet. I met the president and some professors, and was given a tour. ACC was housed at the time in an abandoned elementary school; I remember having to bend way down to get a drink of water from the drinking fountains, which were designed for elementary school children. Now CCC consists of several buildings on a beautiful campus. I enrolled at ACC and began my studies there in September 1956. I graduated from ACC in June 1958 with a two-year associate degree in business.

One of my professors at ACC was John Syrjala, who taught freshman English and was the faculty adviser for the student newspaper. He was a great teacher. I learned more about the structure of the English language than I had learned in high school English, although some of it was familiar because of my high school classes in Latin and Spanish. Not long after I started at ACC, Syrjala asked me to serve as a reporter for the student newspaper. Later he asked me to be the editor. I have no idea what prompted him to offer me that important position. It was my first experience as an editor.

During my second year at ACC, I scheduled classes so that I could travel to Auburn on some days each week and to Syracuse University on other days. I had arranged to transfer to Syracuse the credit hours I had earned at ACC, and I had met the cost of enrolling at Syracuse by borrowing against my life insurance. I took heavy course loads, and also enrolled in summer classes at Syracuse.

In August 1958, at the end of the second summer session, I graduated with a bachelor's degree in accounting *summa cum laude* from Syracuse's College of Business Administration. By completing a total of four years of work at ACC and Syracuse in two years, I had made up two of the nine years by which I was behind my high school classmates.

A Major Turning Point

During my final summer session at Syracuse, I experienced a major turning point in my life. I was taking a course in production management, a subject in which I had no interest. However, at the time it was a requirement for a bachelor's degree in business administration at Syracuse.

The instructor was Herbert Sim, an economics professor at the University of Notre Dame. He was visiting that summer and teaching part-time while completing work on his doctoral dissertation at Syracuse. He was teaching that summer because he needed the money to live on. Also, he needed to finish the dissertation and receive his doctorate that summer to retain his faculty position at Notre Dame.

Some of my classmates were current or recently discharged members of the military. They and I were older and perhaps a bit more serious about our class work than many college-age undergraduate students. Several of those classmates and I had concerns about how Sim was conducting the course. In July 1958 I met with him by appointment in his office. I told him that I did not like the way students were talking behind his back, and that I felt he should be made aware of our concerns. I described those concerns. Instead of reacting angrily, he smiled, acknowledged the concerns, explained the situation, and changed the subject.

Sim asked about my grade point average and career plans. I said I was about to graduate *summa cum laude,* and told him of my interest in life insurance. He asked if I had considered insurance teaching and research. I said I was selling life insurance part-time while in school, was planning to enroll part-time in a master's degree insurance program at Syracuse, and hoped to teach insurance some day at the college level.

Sim asked if I was aware of the S. S. Huebner Foundation for Insurance Education administered at the University of Pennsylvania in Philadelphia. I said that I was familiar with the writings of Professor Solomon Huebner—he was the author of the first college textbook on insurance and was known as "The Father of Insurance Education"—but that I was not aware of the foundation. Sim said the foundation offered fellowships for a program of study leading to a doctoral degree for persons who intended to pursue the field of insurance teaching and research at the collegiate level.

Sim said he knew some foundation officials, including Professors Dan Mays McGill and Harry Loman. He said he would write a letter of introduction if I would pay them a visit. I told him that Marge and I were planning to drive to New York City in August for a brief celebration of my graduation, and that we could easily stop off in Philadelphia on the way back to Syracuse. So I accepted his offer to set up an appointment.

When I visited Penn, I received red-carpet treatment. (I have never seen Sim's letter, and have always suspected he made the arrangements by telephone instead.) First I met with McGill, the executive director of the foundation. He then sent me to meet with Loman, who then sent me back to McGill's office. I had the feeling that Loman called McGill on the telephone while I was walking back to McGill's office.

McGill offered me a fellowship on the spot. He said it was five months past the application deadline, but he waived the deadline and said I could enroll for the 1958 fall semester, which started in two weeks, or the 1959 fall semester. He said the fellowship was for a three-year program leading to a Ph.D. degree in applied economics with a concentration in insurance. He said the foundation would cover the cost of tuition, fees, and books, and would provide a small monthly stipend to cover some of our living expenses. The first two years of the program were for course work and the third year was for work on the required doctoral dissertation.

I asked McGill what would happen if I spent one year in the master's program at Syracuse and enrolled at Penn in the fall of 1959. He smiled, and said I would still have to complete

Dan Mays McGill, 1978

two years of course work at Penn and write the dissertation. What he was telling me ever so tactfully was that spending the year at Syracuse would be a waste of time. I asked him whether it would be acceptable if I started in the fall semester of 1958 one week late. He said it would be no problem. I then told him Marge and I would discuss the matter on our drive back to Syracuse and I would call him. After she and I discussed the matter, I decided to accept the offer to enroll immediately. I called McGill, thanked him profusely, and told him I would start classes one week late.

Thus my visit to Sim's office to tell him about his students' concerns became a pivotal event in my life. Sim and I remained in contact for the rest of his life. He completed his dissertation and received his doctorate at Syracuse in that summer of 1958. He subsequently taught many more years at Notre Dame. At one point he invited me to South Bend to present a guest lecture. He retired in 1992 and died in 2011. The final time I saw him was when we got together for lunch not far from where he was living in Florida during his retirement. The restaurant was near Marge's parents, who lived in Florida during their retirement years.

Graduate School

I wound down my part-time insurance business in Syracuse and dealt with other loose ends. I borrowed $2,000 under the student loan program of the New York State Higher Education Assistance Corporation, borrowed $3,000 under the federal student loan program, and again tapped the loan values of my life insurance. We left our eight-month-old daughter Ann with Marge's parents in Syracuse, and went apartment hunting in Philadelphia. In the process, we learned a lesson in real estate.

We found a nice apartment in a Philadelphia suburb, signed a lease agreement, gave the landlady a check for one month's rent in advance, and planned to move there in a few weeks. Marge flew back to Syracuse, and I rented a hotel room in Philadelphia. A few days later I received in the mail at the foundation office a letter from the landlady. She said she had rented the apartment to a retired military officer and his wife who had no children living with them. I assumed she felt that an older couple without an infant underfoot would cause less wear and tear on her apartment. With her letter she returned our check and the lease agreement. I was furious, and spoke with a business law professor at Penn. He said that lease agreements are stacked against the tenant, and that we had no cause of action.

We found another apartment and moved our meager belongings to Philadelphia in a U-Haul trailer. Because we could not get occupancy for a few weeks, Marge and I had the memorable experience of living in a hotel room with a crib for Ann and a Murphy bed that came out of the wall.

Our new apartment was in a garden type development in southeast Philadelphia near the airport. There were several two-story buildings, each of which had two apartments on the ground floor and two apartments on the second floor. The development was a considerable distance from the Penn campus, but only a few short blocks away I was able to board a subway-surface trolley car that had a subway stop directly under the foundation office. I was the first Huebner fellow to live there, but several others followed. We greatly enjoyed what became a closely knit community of insurance doctoral students and their families. Our second child Mike was born during that time.

While at Penn I had the privilege of studying under several great insurance professors. Among them, in addition to McGill and Loman, were John Adams, Clyde Kahler, Charles McCaffrey, and Wayne Snider. Among the students in my class and adjacent classes were Robert Crowe, Herbert Denenberg, William Glendenning, Robert Goshay, George Granger, George Green, Charles Hall, J. D. Hammond, Ronald Horn, Vane Lucas, Joseph Melone, William Nye, Dennis Reinmuth, George Rejda, Gary Stone, Steven Weisbart, Royall Whitaker, and Frank Wirig.

I completed the program in the prescribed three years. Only a few previous Huebner fellows had been able to do that. I spoke with several former fellows and discovered that their practice was to wait until they completed the two years of course work before they tackled the dissertation project. I also learned that many fellows experienced difficulty nailing down a dissertation topic, spent their third year searching for a topic, and had to leave Penn with the proverbial ABD (all but the dissertation) degree. They then would take a full-time faculty position, and would have to write the dissertation at a time when they should have been working on scholarly articles for publication in academic journals.

Because of my delay in starting college, I wanted to move through the program quickly. I devised a plan to start working on the dissertation during the second year of course work. As mentioned earlier, Continental American, for which I had been an agent, was a shareholder-owned company that sold only participating (dividend-paying) life insurance. I knew that New York State had enacted a law limiting the extent to which shareholders could benefit from participating business. The law intrigued me. I prepared a dissertation proposal on the subject and discussed the proposal with McGill. He was delighted with it and agreed to chair my dissertation committee. By the time I finished the two years of course work, I was well along on the dissertation. I completed it and defended it successfully in April 1961, even before the end of the third year. I received my doctorate from Penn's Graduate School of Arts and Sciences at the spring 1961 commencement.

I am deeply indebted to McGill. He offered me a fellowship, taught the life insurance course, and chaired my dissertation committee. During his course I had the unique privilege of using a mimeographed preliminary version of *Life Insurance*, his superb textbook, the first edition of which was published in

1959. Consequently my classmates and I had the rare opportunity to provide input into the published version.

My First Position

In April 1961 I accepted a joint appointment as the first full-time staff member in continuing education at the American Society of Chartered Life Underwriters and the American College of Life Underwriters. They were housed in Huebner Hall at the then new American College campus in the Philadelphia suburb of Bryn Mawr.

Marge and I moved into a rented house in Broomall, near Bryn Mawr. Our third child Jeff was born while we lived there.

In my joint Society/College position I worked under Paul Mills, the Society's managing director. I also met several other prominent people in insurance education: Herbert Graebner, dean of the College; Davis Gregg, president of the College; Huebner, who had retired from Penn and was occupying an office in Huebner Hall; and Jack Keir of the College staff.

A few staff members occasionally had the pleasure of going out for a restaurant lunch with Huebner. What I remember most vividly was how he would argue a point. He did so by snapping his fingers to emphasize a particular idea.

There were interesting aspects of my Society/College position, but I was not comfortable there. I wanted to teach insurance, but found myself organizing courses instead. Also, I wanted to engage in insurance research, but my position involved primarily administrative work. I often spent evenings in the library at Huebner Hall working on research projects, some of which later resulted in articles published in academic journals. Not the least of my concerns was that I detected some displeasure about the research I was conducting. Although Mills never said anything on the matter, I had the feeling that Graebner and Gregg were concerned about what they perceived as the somewhat controversial nature of my research.

Another Major Turning Point

The Journal of Risk and Insurance (then *The Journal of Insurance*) is published quarterly by the previously mentioned ARIA. My first academic article, "The Cost of Life Insurance to the Consumer—A Single Year Attained Age System," was published in the December 1961 issue of the *Journal*. The article presented a method for calculating, on a year-by-year basis, the price of the protection component of a cash-value life insurance policy from the consumer's point of view.

Publication of the article turned out to be another pivotal event in my life. The article caught the attention of Walter Williams, an economics professor who at the time was teaching insurance in the School of Business at Indiana University in Bloomington, Indiana. The insurance area at the school was chaired by Professor J. Edward Hedges, and Professor John Douglas Long was also a member of the insurance faculty.

The School of Business had been approached by Consumers Union (CU), which publishes the monthly magazine *Consumer Reports*. CU had been subjected to criticism for a recent series of articles about automobile insurance. Those articles had been prepared by two freelance writers. CU wanted a study of life insurance, but wanted it prepared by someone with academic credentials. CU offered to finance an academic study of life insurance from the consumer's point of view, but no one at Indiana University wanted to handle the project. Williams invited me to Bloomington to discuss the possibility of my conducting the study.

I was hesitant about the idea. I was familiar with a series of life insurance articles CU had published about 25 years earlier. CU had hired Mort and E. A. Gilbert to write the articles. They were the authors of a 1936 book entitled *Life Insurance: A Legalized Racket*. The book and the CU articles were highly critical of the life insurance business and suggested no one should buy anything other than term life insurance. I believed then and still believe that term life insurance and cash-value life insurance are two different types of financial medicine, and that the choice between them should be made only after a careful examination of the consumer's financial situation. I wondered whether CU had preconceived views on the subject, and I visited CU's headquarters in Yonkers, New York. Officials there flatly denied they were wedded to the views expressed in the earlier articles, and they insisted they wanted an academic study. I was relieved by their response to my concerns.

When I visited Bloomington, Hedges offered me an appointment as visiting assistant professor of insurance to conduct the study. Half of my salary for that year was to come from the research grant, and half was to come from the school. I was to teach half a normal load during that year. The offer was for a one-year appointment with no guarantee of a permanent position, but there were hints I might be offered a regular appointment the following year. I accepted the offer, resigned my Society/College position in Bryn Mawr, moved my family to Bloomington, and joined the Indiana University faculty effective July 1, 1962.

Shortly before I left Bryn Mawr, I ran into Sim, who had played such a pivotal role in my life. He was attending a meeting of the American College's CLU examination committee. I told him about my upcoming move to Indiana. He questioned my sanity in resigning my Society/College position with only a one-year visiting appointment at Indiana, and he wondered what I would do if the appointment was not renewed. I said that taking a leave of absence from my Society/College position would be inappropriate because there was no way I would return. I said that, if the appointment at Indiana was not renewed, I felt I would be able to find a position somewhere. In jest, I also mentioned unemployment insurance.

Not long after I arrived at Indiana University, Williams announced he was resigning and leaving the school. In 1963, I received a regular appointment as assistant professor of insurance. I became associate professor of insurance in 1965, and professor of insurance with tenure in 1968. On my retirement in 1993, I became professor emeritus of insurance, a title I still hold. Thus the one-year visiting appointment began my 53-year connection with Indiana University.

3

The Indiana Years: 1962-2015

*W*hen I told my mother in 1962 that we were moving to Indiana, her reaction consisted of a one-word exclamation and question: "Indiana!?" I think she was aghast because she had never been farther west than Niagara Falls and may have thought Indiana was an unsettled territory. Indeed, my only prior trip west was in 1951 for the three-month course at Fort Sill, Oklahoma, as mentioned in chapter 2. When we arrived in Bloomington, our young family of five found a welcoming community.

Home Life

Because of my one-year visiting appointment, we rented a small house four miles west of the campus. After our unhappy real estate experience in Philadelphia, I asked Logan Howard, the landlord, about a lease. He said he was willing to enter into a lease, but he also said he did not want us to continue living in the house if we were not comfortable with it. We looked each other in the eye and closed the deal on a handshake. It worked out well. We lived in the house for seven years, during which he never increased the rent, even when we began to receive Bloomington city water and no longer had to rely on our well. He was an ideal landlord.

Marge and Ann were interested in horses. Indeed, they were

passionate on the subject. I often kidded Marge's parents about the situation, because they had refused to allow Marge to own a horse. What I said was that their refusal had kindled Marge's keen interest, which she passed along to Ann. Marge bought a horse that she stabled at a local saddle club, and we watched for a suitable piece of property. Eventually we found the ideal spot six miles west of our rented house—ten miles west of the campus—and two miles outside Ellettsville, a Bloomington suburb.

The property consisted of seven acres with a five-year old ranch house and a small horse barn. We moved there in August 1969 and have lived there ever since. Several years later we purchased an adjoining 13 acres that had become available.

Synagogue

Shortly after we arrived in Bloomington during the July 4th weekend in 1962, we were welcomed by Irving and Rose Fell, a charming couple who had lived in Bloomington for many years. We also met Sidney and Riette Smith and Eugene and Frances Weinberg, but there was no organized Jewish community. Marge and I became active in efforts to organize. We participated in creating what is today Congregation Beth Shalom, the largest center of Jewish activity between Indianapolis and Louisville.

Our first modest building opened in 1970. In August 1983, three weeks before the beginning of the High Holy Days, our building was firebombed by members of a neo-Nazi group. Our response was to use the insurance money and additional contributions to repair and significantly expand the building. We were the beneficiaries of an outpouring of support from the general community, most significantly from the St. Thomas Lutheran Church next door. We had originally purchased our land from the Lutherans, and we shared and still share the combined parking lot. Immediately after the firebombing, the Lutherans essentially turned over their church to us. We conducted our High Holy Day services, weekly Sabbath services, and other activities there for almost a year until completion of the repair and expansion of our building. The Lutherans demonstrated the meaning of true friendship.

Exercise

Upon settling in Indiana, I got busy with various forms of exercise. I had been a fairly good "basement" table tennis player in Syracuse. I found a table tennis club in Indianapolis, and started driving there one night a week. Initially the "club players" there were too much for me, but later I began to hold my own. I participated occasionally in tournaments held in Indianapolis and other midwestern cities. Eventually I earned state rankings in the men's and senior men's divisions. However, the round trip to Indianapolis became too much to handle, and I gave up table tennis.

I was also involved in a daily program of jogging. I kept that up until our family physician told me it was too hard on my knees. At that point I began riding a stationary exercise bicycle for a half hour every day, and have been doing so ever since.

University Life

In 1962 the School of Business occupied what is now Woodburn Hall, but the school had outgrown it. I was housed with other overflow faculty members in Ballantine Hall. A year later we moved into the new Psychology Building, where we were housed for three years.

During that period I experienced an unforgettable incident on Friday, November 22, 1963. I conducted an early afternoon class that day. After the class, when I walked into the hallway, I learned about the assassination of President John Kennedy.

Hedges chaired the faculty committee that oversaw the construction of the new School of Business building. Sadly, after his hard work, he did not live to occupy the building. He suffered an aneurysm and died a few weeks before we moved into the building in the fall of 1966.

Long specialized in property insurance, and I focused on life insurance. I am deeply indebted to him for taking on more than his share of administrative and committee work in the school and at the university level, leaving me more time to devote to my research.

I became active in the previously mentioned ARIA. Hedges and Long had earlier gone through the chairs and served as

ARIA presidents. I did likewise, and served as president in 1973.

We offered undergraduate and graduate courses in insurance. Most students were interested in a general survey of insurance. We also offered additional courses for those interested in the insurance business.

We had little enrollment at the graduate level, but enjoyed working with a small number of students interested in insurance teaching. Several went through the Indiana program during my time there and went on to academic careers: E. J. Leverett, University of Georgia; Cheyeh Lin, University of Cincinnati; Travis Pritchett, Virginia Commonwealth University and University of South Carolina; Joan Schmit, South Carolina and University of Wisconsin (Madison), and William Warfel, Indiana State University (Terre Haute).

Pritchett and Schmit later went through the chairs and served as presidents of ARIA. Pritchett also edited *The Journal of Risk and Insurance* for several years. Pritchett and Schmit today are two of my closest friends.

Research

My first research effort at Indiana involved the study funded by Consumers Union (CU). Contrary to what CU officials had told me on my visit to Yonkers, it turned out that CU did indeed have preconceived views. They did not like my report, which sought to educate readers about how much life insurance to buy, the nature of term life insurance and cash-value life insurance, how to choose between them, and how to identify favorably priced life insurance. CU farmed out to freelance writers most of the new articles, which suggested consumers should consider only term life insurance. CU used only the portion of my material that explained how the consumer should determine the amount of life insurance to buy.

My later research efforts fared better. I had many articles published in academic journals, most notably in *The Journal of Risk and Insurance*. Each year ARIA hands out a few awards for the best articles published in the *Journal*. I was highly honored to receive six awards over the years.

At one point, a major life insurance company asked me to conduct research on a topic in which it was deeply interested, and in which my writings suggested I too would be interested. The company offered to pay a substantial honorarium for me to conduct the research during the upcoming summer break. When I asked about publication of the results, the company said the report was to be confidential, and was to be published only with the company's approval. It then dawned on me that the company wanted to use the report as lobbying material if it turned out as they hoped it would, and suppress the report if it was contrary to their views. I declined their offer, and taught summer classes that year instead. In retrospect, rejecting the company's offer was one of the best decisions I ever made.

My First Book

My first book was *A Report on Life Insurance,* which was the report I submitted to CU after completion of the study CU had funded. The 192-page paper bound book was published in 1963 by the Bureau of Business Research in Indiana University's School of Business.

The first chapter described the fundamentals of life insurance. The second chapter described how to measure one's life insurance needs. The third chapter examined life insurance prices. The fourth chapter discussed other important considerations in buying life insurance, including types of life insurance, how to choose the policy type to buy, important policy provisions, and the role of the agent. A 30-page appendix showed the questionnaire I had circulated to the companies.

Aside from my even-handed treatment of term and cash-value life insurance, CU's two biggest problems were my refusals to (1) rank the recommended companies and (2) identify the companies that were not recommended. My refusals were based on what I perceived as bias in the study. The questionnaire went to 271 companies, but only 80 responded. I sensed that companies with reason to believe they would show up favorably in the study tended to respond, and that companies with reason to believe they would not show up favorably in the study tended not to respond. In other words, if I had ranked the recommended companies, those ranked low probably would have ranked higher had more companies responded. Similarly, if I had identified the companies that were not recommended, some of those companies probably would have been recommended had more companies responded.

My Second Book

I was thrilled when McGill told me the Huebner Foundation was considering publication of my dissertation as part of the foundation's "Studies" series. I agreed to revise, update, and expand the material. When I completed the project and sent McGill the manuscript, he said he needed the names of two individuals who would be willing to read and comment on the manuscript, preferably one who would like it and one who would not like it. I gave him two names: Robert Dineen, former superintendent of the New York Department of Insurance and at the time a senior executive (and later chief executive officer) of Northwestern Mutual Life Insurance Company (Milwaukee, WI); and Henry Rood, chief executive officer of Lincoln National Life Insurance Company (Fort Wayne, IN). I predicted that Dineen would recommend publication, and that Rood would recommend burning the manuscript. McGill thought I was joking.

Dineen submitted a very complimentary review. Rood said that if the foundation published the book, his company would discontinue its annual financial contributions to the foundation and try to persuade other companies to do likewise.

A few weeks later, McGill said five things to me in a memorable telephone conversation. First, he took Rood's threat seriously. Second, he performed calculations and determined that the foundation had enough money on hand to get the current group of foundation fellows through the program. Third, he took the matter to the foundation's board of trustees, which consisted of the chief executive officers of several major insurance companies; they ducked the issue by saying publication decisions should be made by the foundation's administrative board, which consisted of several prominent insurance professors. Fourth, the administrative board decided the foundation should publish the book. Fifth, he personally felt that, if the foundation were to allow contributors to control publication decisions, the foundation would not deserve to exist. I was deeply impressed by everything McGill said, but it was his fifth comment that most vividly illustrated the honesty and integrity of that great man. (After his death at the age of 93, I wrote a memorial tribute to McGill in the May 2013 issue of the *Forum*.)

Thus my second book was *Participating Life Insurance Sold by Stock Companies*. I traced the development of participating (dividend-paying) life insurance, the separation of accounts between the participating policyholders' branch of the company and the shareholders' branch, and the governmental restrictions that had been imposed on the extent to which shareholders were permitted to profit from participating business. A major part of the revision related to life insurance price measurement techniques on which I had worked after completion of the dissertation. The 214-page cloth bound book was published in 1965 by Richard D. Irwin, Inc., which had been publishing the foundation's "Lectures" and "Studies."

I was highly honored for the book. ARIA presented me with its 1966 Elizur Wright Award in recognition of "outstanding contribution to the literature of insurance."

My Third Book

My third book was *The Retail Price Structure in American Life Insurance*. The 300-page cloth bound book was published in 1966 by the Bureau of Business Research in Indiana University's School of Business.

As mentioned earlier, I had developed a system for measuring the price of the protection in cash-value life insurance on a year-by-year basis. Later I worked out a system for averaging those year-by-year prices over a period of years. The book incorporated the expanded system, showed a considerable amount of price information for various types of life insurance, and showed the large price differentials in the market. Indeed, the differentials were so large that they suggested a strong need for a rigorous system of price disclosure for the benefit of insurance consumers.

My Fourth Book

My fourth book was *Life Insurance: A Consumer's Handbook*. The 249-page cloth bound book was published in 1973 by the Indiana University Press. It was also published as a paper bound book.

The 217-page cloth bound second edition of the *Handbook* was published in 1985 by the Indiana University Press. It was also published as a paper bound book. It contains 17 chapters, some of which discuss how to measure life insurance needs, major types of life insurance, the savings component in cash-value life insurance, how to select an appropriate type of life insurance, how to select a company, the price of life insurance, contract provisions, how to select an agent, and how to evaluate an existing life insurance policy.

Despite the age of the book, the principles articulated there for the most part still apply. One major area in which the book is not adequate is the measurement of the financial strength of insurance companies. In the early 1990s I sought to solve the problem by printing each year a special issue of the *Forum* devoted to financial strength ratings. See chapter 22.

The Path to the *Forum*

As mentioned in chapter 1, the path to the *Forum* was strewn with efforts to censor my work. Also, I learned first hand what it means to be associated with a great university. Here I discuss some memorable events.

Alfred Kinsey

When I arrived in Bloomington in July 1962, I began work on the Consumers Union (CU) project. Within a few weeks, I had determined that much of the information I needed was not available in the public domain. Therefore I was at work on a questionnaire to be sent to companies.

Hedges walked into my office one day and said he was headed to a meeting in the office of the Indiana University president. He said they had received a complaint about me from a prominent alumnus in the insurance business. I said I was surprised because I had not yet distributed anything. Hedges said it was widely known I was working on a study for CU. When I expressed concern, he said there was no need to worry. I will never forget his comment: "Joe, you don't understand. Indiana University is where Alfred Kinsey did his research." I was aware of the furor over Kinsey's research on human sexual behavior, and I knew my research could not possibly be as controversial as Kinsey's research.

When Hedges returned from the meeting, he said the university officials had merely requested that I provide for their file a copy of the questionnaire when it was circulated. I did so, and heard nothing further.

The Guest Lecture

A few years later a friend on the faculty at a university in another state invited me to visit his school and present a guest lecture. He said his school might offer me a faculty position. He told me his school would cover my travel expenses. I made the visit, presented the lecture, and met some people there.

Shortly after my return to Bloomington I received a telephone call from my friend informing me the expense check was in the mail. He said he had bad news he felt obligated to share. He said he was embarrassed to inform me there would be no offer of a position. He explained that the chief executive officer of a major insurance company in his school's state had learned of my visit and had told school officials there would be no further contributions by the company to the school if I was appointed to the faculty. My friend said his school decided it could not afford to antagonize a major donor.

My immediate thought was that a financial threat by a donor to influence a faculty hiring decision is not tolerated by a great university, and I was grateful to have avoided a disastrous career move. All I said to my friend was that I understood, and I thanked him for the explanation. That was the first and last time I considered leaving Indiana University.

Allen Steere

Several years later, after I had been granted full rank and awarded tenure, Dean George Pinnell of the School of Business walked into my office one day. He said he had just received a telephone call from Allen Steere, an officer in the government relations department at Lincoln National Life Insurance Company (Fort Wayne, IN). Pinnell said Steere complained about my research and wanted the school to fire me.

Pinnell said to me that he did not try to explain academic freedom and tenure. Instead, he said the school did not want faculty members who are conducting faulty research. He asked Steere to prepare a report about the shortcomings of my research, with the understanding that I would have the opportunity to prepare a response. Pinnell said he offered the full facilities of the school to publish the report and my response. Steere expressed no interest in preparing a report, and ended the conversation.

The Actuarial Club

An actuarial club in Texas invited me to speak at a luncheon meeting. The topic was deceptive sales practices. The club agreed to pay my travel expenses and an honorarium.

I brought with me copies of a one-page, two-sided handout to be distributed after my talk. On one side of the handout was a company advertisement that was a classic example of a type of deceptive practice that I planned to discuss in my talk. On the other side, I asked for a yes or no answer to the question of whether the actuary agreed with me that the advertisement was deceptive, and an explanation of his or her answer. I said the actuary could sign the handout or could remain anonymous by refraining from signing it. I merely wanted to find out how many of the actuaries agreed with me, and for those who did not, why they disagreed.

At the luncheon before my talk, the club president and I sat together at the head table. I told him about the handout. He asked to see it, and I showed it to him. He then called a brief meeting of the club's officers in a corner of the room. When he came back to the table, he said I would not be allowed to distribute the handout.

I briefly considered but decided against walking out and leaving the club without a luncheon speaker. Instead, I asked him to disclose to the club members, when he introduced me, the officers' decision not to allow distribution of the handout. I also said that, if he did not make the disclosure, I would make the disclosure at the beginning of my talk and also would inform the club members that he had declined my request to disclose the officers' decision. That prompted another brief meeting of the officers. They decided to allow distribution of the handout.

The results of the little survey were interesting. Some of the actuaries agreed with me. The explanations given by those who disagreed with me were an embarrassment to the actuarial profession.

The Actuary

The Actuary is a newsletter published by the Society of Actuaries. I wrote a letter to Andrew Webster, the editor. In the letter I asked whether it is the professional responsibility of an actuary to take positive steps to prevent deceptive sales practices, or merely to refrain from endorsing deceptive sales practices. Webster declined to print the letter.

A few years later, Ernest J. "Jack" Moorhead, an eminent actuary, became editor of *The Actuary*. I knew Moorhead would print the letter. He had written to me that he had found my first academic article interesting, we had corresponded about it, and we had become good friends. I resubmitted the letter and he promptly published it. The letter generated several interesting comments from actuaries.

The *Forum*

I wanted to share my views with persons interested in insurance: company executives and employees, agents in the field, regulators, reporters, and consumers. I knew that few of them saw academic journals, and I began considering methods of communicating with them.

My first thought was to start a syndicated newspaper column. When I spoke with the writers of two such columns, they warned me about serious censorship problems. They said newspapers, especially those in small cities, receive so much advertising revenue from the real estate, automobile, and insurance businesses that they would not publish critical columns on those topics. I ruled out the idea of a syndicated column.

My second thought was to have ARIA publish, in addition to its prestigious quarterly academic journal, an informal, quick turnaround newsletter. When I assumed the presidency of ARIA in 1973, I proposed the idea in my presidential address. I said I was planning to ask ARIA's board of directors to approve the plan. I volunteered to edit the newsletter during my year as president, and suggested that a special committee should observe it and decide whether to continue it. To be sure the board understood what I had in mind, I prepared a sample issue, called it *The Insurance Forum*, and included articles with titles such as "How To Pay Premiums for 'A Piece of the Rock' and Have No Insurance Protection" and "What the Equitable of New York Does to Beneficiaries." The board rejected the idea as beneath the dignity of a professional association. They were also concerned about the expense and about libel implications.

My third thought, which was the one that came to fruition, was to publish the *Forum* myself. I formed a corporation— Insurance Forum, Inc.—and capitalized it with $2,000 of personal funds. I lined up a private printing firm in Bloomington and a private mailing service in Indianapolis. I used a one-column layout for several years. Later, to improve readability, I changed to a two-column layout. I retained the four-page length for many years. Eventually I moved to eight-page issues and some longer issues.

I kept the *Forum* separate from my duties at the university. I did not use the school's facilities, and worked on the *Forum* at home. I did not ask anyone for permission to launch the project, but I sent the first issue to the president of the university, the dean of the business school, and a few others I felt needed to know. They thanked me for informing them.

Litigation

I asked an insurance agent to find publishers' liability insurance. He reported that, when he described to insurance companies the nature of the *Forum*, they laughed. The only coverage he found was with a Bermuda company that covered libel judgments but not defense costs. I turned it down because I was not concerned about libel judgments. I was concerned about defense costs of harassment lawsuits.

I retained an attorney who specialized in newspaper liability matters. He reviewed my material in advance and told me when anything concerned him. In all the years of the *Forum* I was never sued for libel. I received a few threats, but shrugged them off. I think no company wanted to give me an opportunity to engage in detailed discovery about their practices.

The only case in which I was a defendant was a copyright infringement lawsuit filed by A. M. Best Company. The case was settled amicably. See chapter 22.

I was the plaintiff in a lawsuit against the North Carolina insurance commissioner; see chapter 5. I was also the plaintiff in many lawsuits over access to public records; see chapters 7, 22, and 30.

Prices and Other Details

I set the price initially at $15 for a one-year subscription. That was very low for a specialized four-page independent monthly periodical that took no advertising, but I wanted to encourage agents, consumers, regulators, professors, students, reporters, and others with limited resources to subscribe. Over the years I increased the price and expanded the content, but the price remained very low for an independent monthly.

Aside from the low price, I persisted in doing things that fly in the face of conventional wisdom. I sent the issue every month by first class mail rather than third class bulk mail. I required payment at the time of enrollment, and, in the case of reprints, I required payment in advance. Many years after the launch I reluctantly began accepting MasterCard and Visa; I say reluctantly because many people use credit cards improperly and get into financial trouble. I always set the prices at round amounts; for example, the first price increase was to $20, not $19 or $19.95.

I never offered special deals for subscribing. I thought it was wrong to offer special deals to non-subscribers without making similar or better offers to faithful subscribers. Marketing consultants with whom I discussed promotional mailings thought I was crazy. They never seemed to grasp that I had no interest in trying to maximize revenue, and that I was interested only in trying to provide the best possible content.

I received many ideas from readers, but very few wanted to write articles. Therefore, I did most of the writing. In a few instances, I published articles written by others under their bylines. In each instance I edited the item and obtained the author's approval of my editing.

Administrative Help

At the outset I retained William Braunlin, a public accountant. His wife Lois helped on a part-time basis managing the mailing list. In 1986 I hired our daughter Ann as business manager. She took over the accounting duties, automated the subscriber list, began managing the list in-house, and handled orders. She also did the spreadsheet work for my tabulations of financial strength ratings, executive compensation, risk-based capital, and surplus notes. In 1992 I hired our son Jeff as circulation manager. He took over the management of the subscriber list and handled orders.

Jeff, Ann, Mike, 1982

Editorial Help

I tried to obtain editorial help, hopefully from someone who could take over as editor when I became unable or unwilling to continue. In 1979 I hired John Dorfman as assistant editor on a part-time basis. He had written about personal finance at *Consumer Reports, Forbes,* and, later, *The Wall Street Journal.* He was an excellent writer and had a good understanding of insurance. Over the next three years, he wrote 24 excellent articles and helped on some I wrote. In 1981 he resigned because of the pressures of other work.

In 1996 I rehired Dorfman as associate editor. Over the next two years he wrote one article and most of our April 1997 large-print special issue for seniors. He again was a great help on articles I wrote. In 1997 he again resigned because of the pressures of other work.

Thereafter I carried on the editorial responsibilities alone. I did not find anyone with the rare combination of seven characteristics I felt were required: (1) a thorough understanding of insurance principles and practices, (2) a strong desire to assist consumers, (3) a thick skin allowing the person to absorb criticism from those seeking to preserve the status quo, (4) the ability to avoid being discouraged by revolving-door regulators who act in their own interest rather than in the public interest, (5) the ability to write well, (6) the willingness to invest enormous amounts of time and energy to the research and writing, and (7) the willingness to invest that time and energy without significant financial compensation.

Without a designated successor, I decided to continue on my own and shut down the newsletter when I was unable or unwilling to continue. I tried hard to maintain a high level of excellence, and I did not want someone to take over and besmirch the name of the *Forum*.

An Aborted Advertisement

Shortly after starting the *Forum*, I encountered yet another instance of censorship. I sought to advertise in insurance trade periodicals to drum up interest among potential subscribers. In a proposed advertisement, I sought to illustrate the nature of the *Forum* by showing the titles of a few articles that appeared in the early issues.

I submitted the advertisement to five trade periodicals. All declined to publish it without changes. For example, one suggested changing the title "How To Pay Premiums for a 'Piece of the Rock' and Have No Insurance Protection" to "How To Pay

Premiums and Have No Insurance Protection." In other words, they wanted to eliminate company names. I gave up on space advertising, because I felt that using actual titles of articles was the only way to describe accurately the nature of the *Forum.*

Cartoons

Shortly after starting the *Forum,* I sought to hire a part-time cartoonist. I approached the cartoonist for our local newspaper. He declined to become involved.

Later I became acquainted with Harry Privette, a talented cartoonist. How I met him is an interesting story. Several years before I started the *Forum,* I prepared a booklet for use by students in the CLU study program on the subject of interest, or the time value of money. In an effort to grab the attention of the students, I showed at the top of the first page a long number that I explained in a footnote.

Privette worked in the advertising department of New England Mutual Life Insurance Company. He was studying for a CLU examination and saw my material. He ran an item about it in his *Mini-Boppers* cartoon strip. One of my subscribers saw the strip and sent it to me. I tracked down Privette and he graciously gave me permission to reprint the cartoon. It ran in the June 1975 issue of the *Forum.*

Over the next 30 years, whenever Privette saw something in the *Forum* that triggered an idea in his mind, he submitted a cartoon. I published many of them. He always refused compensation. Several of his cartoons are shown in this memoir.

Privette died in 2005. He was a gifted, award-winning cartoonist, and was once nominated for a Pulitzer Prize. I regret that I never met him in person. His health in his later years prevented him from traveling and from entertaining guests. Nonetheless he was a dear friend.

A Celebration

On June 9, 2014, three of my closest friends—Professors Travis Pritchett of the University of South Carolina, Joan Schmit of the University of Wisconsin, and Harold Skipper of Georgia State University—threw a celebration to commemorate the 40 years of the *Forum*. The event was held at the Indiana University Foundation in Bloomington. Many friends from Bloomington and from out of town attended. Jack Wentworth, retired dean of the Kelley School of Business, opened the

Marge and Joe, 2009

festivities. The keynoter was David Vladeck, a law professor at Georgetown University, former director of the consumer protection division of the Federal Trade Commission, former director of Public Citizen Litigation Group, and my attorney in the 1981 lawsuit (discussed in chapter 5) against the North Carolina insurance commissioner. Schmit, Pritchett, Skipper, and I spoke. Idalene Kesner, current dean of the Kelley School, closed the festivities. It was a joyous occasion for which I shall always be deeply grateful.

Issues Mentioned in This Chapter

June 1975, April 1997, and May 2013.

4

The Policy Replacement Problem

*R*eplacement, as the word is used in the life insurance business, refers to the discontinuation of an existing life insurance policy and the purchase of a new life insurance policy as a substitute for the previously existing policy. There is nothing inherently wrong or illegal about replacing one policy with another. Some replacements are justified, but many are not justified. I discuss the subject here because it will lead to a better understanding of the events described in chapter 5.

Twisting, as the word is used in the context of replacement, refers to a replacement that is based on a deceptive or incomplete presentation. The word sometimes is used to denote a replacement that is not justified.

Churning is a word used in the securities business, and refers to the rollover of a client's securities portfolio primarily for the purpose of generating commissions for the securities broker. When I use the word in the context of life insurance, I refer to a replacement that not only is twisting but also is motivated primarily by the agent's commission.

The Basic Problem

Replacements often are contrary to the financial interests of not only life insurance policyholders but also life insurance companies. For that reason, and as discussed in this chapter, replacements have been a thorny problem throughout the history of the life insurance business.

The most important cause of the replacement problem is the nature of the compensation system for agents selling life insurance. The first-year commission for the agent who sells a policy usually is more than half the policy's first-year premium, while commissions in subsequent policy years generally are much smaller. A large first-year commission is necessary to compensate the agent for the significant time and effort required to perform four important functions: (1) locating the prospect, (2) persuading the prospect to discuss his or her life insurance needs, (3) convincing the prospect to purchase life insurance, and (4) persuading the prospect to refrain from procrastinating in the purchase of life insurance. I call that fourth step the critically important "anti-procrastination function" performed by life insurance agents.

If a prospect already owns life insurance, the agent has an incentive to replace it because doing so may reduce or eliminate the need to persuade the prospect to come up with additional money to pay for new insurance. However, replacement often is undesirable for the policyholder, who thereby pays the front-end expenses—the agent's commission and the other expenses incurred by the insurance company in issuing the replacement policy—on top of the front-end expenses the policyholder paid when the existing policy was issued.

Furthermore, replacement usually is undesirable for life insurance companies. A company is more profitable when its policies persist (policies persist when they remain in force) rather than when its policies lapse (policies lapse when they are discontinued by the policyholder).

Life insurance companies usually try to discourage agents from engaging in replacement activity. For example, life insurance applications ask whether the insurance being applied for is to replace existing insurance and, if so, the agent is asked to explain the reasons for the replacement. Also, companies reward agents for the persistency of their business, and state insurance regulators sometimes adopt rules requiring notifications and other procedures that discourage replacements.

Justified and Unjustified Replacements

In the February 1976 issue I showed a case that appeared to be a justified replacement. It was a case where the policyholder was considering the replacement of a nonparticipating cash-value policy that had been issued by Travelers Insurance Company with a participating cash-value policy issued by Northwestern Mutual Life Insurance Company. I performed an analysis, the results of which suggested that the Northwestern policy outperformed the Travelers policy after the first year by such a large margin that the replacement seemed justified.

On the other hand, in the January 1978 issue I showed a case that clearly was an unjustified replacement. The four original policies were issued on a standard basis; that is, there was no extra premium because of health problems. The replacement policy, however, was issued on a substandard basis with higher than standard premiums because of the insured's recently developed health problems. The case involved another dimension that made it a tragedy, because the insured committed suicide during the first two years after buying the replacement policy. The result was that, because of the two-year suicide exclusion in the replacement policy, the death benefit was limited to a refund of the premiums. In other words, if the original policies had not been replaced, the full death benefits of the original policies would have been paid. The case is discussed in chapter 12 in a discussion of the suicide clause.

In the July 1984 issue I presented the idea of avoiding attempts to make a complex price comparison between an existing policy and a proposed replacement policy. Instead, I suggested that a person considering a replacement should analyze only the existing policy, and not replace it if the existing policy is reasonably priced. The article made reference to a price measurement system described in the June 1982 issue.

In the December 1984 issue I wrote about a piggybacking scandal involving agents of Prudential Insurance Company of America. Piggybacking occurs when the replacement policy is financed by borrowing against the loan value of an existing policy. The practice is not necessarily wrong, but it raises some troublesome questions.

Another article in the December 1984 issue is about an agent of Provident Mutual Life Insurance Company of Philadelphia. The company terminated the agent's contract, and he used replacements to move business to his new company. In response to the article, I received three major letters about the agent, and I published them in "From the Mailbag" in the March 1985 issue.

A Classic Example of Churning

In the March 2012 and January 2013 issues of the *Forum*, and in blog no. 76 (December 15, 2014), I wrote about the victimization of Mrs. X through life insurance churning. At the time of the replacements, she was aged 81, was the widow of a longtime Ball State University faculty member, lived in Muncie, Indiana, and was wearing an Exelon patch as medication for marked cognitive impairment. She owned two policies issued many years earlier by Northwestern Mutual Life Insurance Company. Both had been issued on a standard basis, which means she had been in good health and had qualified for policies with standard premiums for her age. (When a person has health problems, the insurance company may decline to issue the policy or may issue the policy on a substandard basis, which leads to higher than standard premiums.)

Both policies were cash-value policies, which means they had built up substantial cash values, and those cash values would have continued to grow if the policies had been kept in force. Both policies were participating, which means they were eligible for annual dividends. One policy was premium-paying, meaning that the policyholder was paying premiums, but the large dividends were more than enough to pay the premiums. The other policy was paid-up, meaning no further premiums were required, but Northwestern was continuing to pay substantial dividends on the policy.

Both policies were replaced by a policy issued by Massachusetts Mutual Life Insurance Company. The replacement policy was issued on a substandard basis apparently because of Mrs. X's cognitive impairment. The replacement policy's premium was more than $4,000 per year larger than the standard premium for a woman her age, and in addition she incurred the front-end expenses associated with the replacement policy. In short, the replacement was horribly inappropriate.

Mrs. X also owned annuities issued years earlier by Teachers Insurance and Annuity Association of America (TIAA) and an annuity issued years earlier by Northwestern. TIAA caters mostly to faculty members and senior administrators of colleges and universities. The TIAA and Northwestern annuities were replaced by two annuities issued by Metropolitan Life Insurance Company. The replacements were inappropriate because the new annuities were subject to charges in the event the annuities were surrendered, while the old annuities were not.

The agents who arranged for the replacements were Daniel H. W. Stallings (Muncie) and Bryan Todd Baker (Indianapolis). Mrs. X had met Stallings because she was a customer at the Ball State Federal Credit Union, and Stallings was the credit union's financial "expert" with an office in the credit union.

An interesting aspect of the case was that Mrs. X signed a "Letter of Instruction" to Massachusetts Mutual acknowledging her understanding of the potential impact of replacing her Northwestern policies and her desire to proceed with the application. When Mrs. X's family later asked her about the letter, she said she had no recollection of it.

In my first article about the case, I expressed the hope that the companies would rectify the situation voluntarily by restoring Mrs. X to her original financial position. In my follow-up article, I reported that Northwestern had restored the life insurance policies after making the necessary arrangements with Massachusetts Mutual.

The Indiana Department of Insurance looked into the life insurance aspect of the case, but took no disciplinary action against the agents. I did not learn whether Stallings and Baker had to pay back any of the commissions they received on the sale of the replacement policy.

I did not learn what if any changes were made with regard to the annuities. However, Mrs. X's family filed a complaint with the Financial Industry Regulatory Authority (FINRA) relating to the annuity aspect of the case. FINRA took no disciplinary action, but reported that the complaint was settled, with the family receiving $3,000—$750 from Stallings, $750 from Baker, and $1,500 presumably from a broker-dealer.

The Stallings relationship with the credit union temporarily ended, but later he returned as the credit union's financial "expert." Still later, he was elected president of the East Central Indiana (Muncie) chapter of the National Association of Insurance and Financial Advisors.

Issues and Blog Item Mentioned in This Chapter

February 1976, January 1978, June 1982, July 1984, December 1984, March 1985, March 2012, January 2013, and blog no. 76 (December 15, 2014).

5

The A. L. Williams
Replacement Empire

*D*uring 1980 readers of the *Forum* showered me with unsolicited information about the widespread and indiscriminate replacement of life insurance policies by the A. L. Williams organization (ALW). Because there was enormous interest in ALW activities, I devoted the entire four-page April 1981 issue to an article entitled "The A. L. Williams Replacement Empire." The issue went through many printings to meet the huge demand for reprints, and it was by far the most widely circulated issue in the history of the *Forum*.

The ALW Organization

Arthur Lynch Williams, Jr. was a high school football coach in Georgia before he entered the life insurance business. After several years in the business, he founded ALW in Atlanta in February 1977. ALW was a general agency representing Massachusetts Indemnity and Life Insurance Company (MILICO). By January 1981, ALW was doing business through 40,000 agents in 650 offices in 47 states. In 1980 ALW sold $5 billion face amount of life insurance.

ALW sold term life insurance, which does not build cash values, and which involves lower premiums than cash-value life insurance. The latter builds cash values and acts as a vehicle for the accumulation of savings. Often ALW sold an annuity rider attached to the term life policy to provide for the accumulation of savings.

Although life insurance companies and agents who act in a professional manner usually try to avoid replacement activity, for reasons discussed in chapter 4, most of ALW's business involved replacement of existing cash-value life insurance policies. ALW's sales organization was of the multilevel marketing type—some critics called it a pyramid—with mostly part-time representatives at the lower levels of the organization and mostly full-time representatives at the higher levels.

ALW's Activities

At least seven characteristics of ALW's activities infuriated other life insurance companies and agents. First, ALW engaged in indiscriminate replacement of life insurance policies. All life insurance policies of all life insurance companies were targets of ALW's replacement efforts.

Second, ALW sold term life insurance indiscriminately. In doing so, ALW trained its representatives to denigrate cash-value life insurance by calling it "trash-value life insurance."

Third, ALW recruited huge numbers of part-time representatives and required each recruit to buy a policy on the recruit's own life. Thus there was a blurring of the distinction between the recruitment of representatives and the sale of life insurance. ALW trained its representatives to denigrate the full-time representatives of other life insurance companies. For example, Williams himself made this remark: "To sell life insurance full-time, you might have to be able to read and write."

Fourth, ALW used unfair comparisons. For example, ALW asserted that its term life insurance was "low cost." To support that assertion, ALW compared its term life policies with cash-value policies solely on the basis of premiums. ALW also trained its agents to ignore the dividends often paid on cash-value policies because dividends are not guaranteed.

Fifth, ALW orchestrated the development of positive third-party material and used it as though it was independent. A few examples are described later in this chapter.

Sixth, ALW sought to suppress negative material. A vivid

example of this practice—ALW's 1981 attack on the *Forum* and me—is described later in this chapter.

Seventh, ALW criticized other life insurance companies harshly. For example, at sales meetings it displayed large banners reading "Wet on Met" and "Pee on Pru." Williams himself described other companies' agents as "low life and scum."

The Conclusion in My April 1981 Article

The conclusion in my April 1981 article became important in subsequent developments. Here is the full section:

> There should be no objection to the sale of reasonably priced term insurance when it is appropriate in view of the individual's circumstances and objectives, and there should be no objection to replacement when it is justified. We believe that the sales activities of ALW, however, frequently will result in the sale of inappropriate, high-priced term insurance, and in replacements that are not justified.
>
> The operations of ALW involve the recruiting of large numbers of part-time sales representatives, the use of excessively complex replacement proposals, the obscuring of the high cost of [MILICO's term life] policy through the inclusion of figures for the annuity rider, and an inordinate emphasis on the alleged opportunity for sales representatives to get rich quick. The organization displays some of the characteristics of a chain letter, and like a chain letter will sooner or later run out of prospective recruits and prospective customers. Until the operation runs its course, however, we fear that many people are going to be seriously hurt. Among those to be hurt are persons who replace policies that should not have been replaced, persons who buy high-cost term insurance when they should have purchased low-cost term insurance, and persons who enter the organization with high hopes that are dashed.
>
> The word "churning," as used in the securities industry, refers to the rollover of a portfolio for the purpose of generating commissions. We believe the sales activities of ALW are designed primarily for the purpose of channeling the cash values of existing life insurance policies directly into commissions for members of the ALW organization. For this reason, it

is our opinion that the ALW organization is engaged primarily in the churning of life insurance.

The ALW Attack on the *Forum* and Me

Barry Clause left his position in the North Carolina Department of Insurance and thereafter joined the ALW headquarters staff in Georgia. On June 17, 1981, he wrote a "Dear Ron" letter to Ronald Raxter, a staff attorney and former colleague in the Department. The Clause letter, which I did not learn about until months later, was a complaint against a New York Life Insurance Company agent in North Carolina who, according to Clause, photocopied my April 1981 article.

On July 23 Raxter wrote me that "a number of agents have been using photocopies" of my article "in attempts to conserve their business," and that "We are currently undertaking an investigation of these allegations." He asked for "a list of all persons in North Carolina, if any, to whom you have granted permission to reproduce in whole or in part this article."

On July 31 I responded that I had not granted permission to anyone to reproduce any part of the article, but that many persons had purchased reprints. I asked for the names and addresses of persons circulating photocopies, and said I would write to them demanding that they halt such circulation. Raxter identified two individuals. I wrote to them, and they said they had purchased reprints.

On September 14 Raxter wrote to me asking for "a list of the addresses of the people in North Carolina who have requested reprints" of the April 1981 article. I was astounded by the intrusive nature of his request.

On September 18 I called Raxter. He said he wanted to instruct each person not to circulate my article because the Department disagreed with my opinion about churning. I asked him to put the Department's opinion in writing so I could publish it in my next article about ALW. He declined my request. I suggested he send out a circular letter rather than writing to my customers. He said a circular letter already had been sent out, but said it did not refer specifically to ALW or the *Forum*. I asked him to send me a copy of the circular letter immediately. He said he would do so, but he did not send it to me at that time. I declined his request for a list of my North Carolina customers.

The Amazing Raxter Letter

On October 8, on Department stationery, Raxter wrote an amazing letter (the "Raxter letter") to David den Boer, an ALW executive in Georgia. Here is the full text:

> This is in response to your letter of September 23, 1981 objecting to agent distribution of the <u>Insurance Forum</u> article regarding your company. This Department does not agree with the allegations Professor Belth makes in this article.
>
> We determined some time ago that distribution of this article to prospective consumers is misrepresentation. Our notice to agents of July 28, 1981 specifically mentions newspapers and trade publications as items that could constitute misrepresentation if the contents therein are inaccurate or tend to create an inaccurate impression in the mind of the customer.
>
> We have reprimanded several agents for, among other things, distributing copies of this article to prospective customers. We have also notified Professor Belth that we do not agree with the opinions stated in that article and that we will investigate any allegation that agents are distributing copies of the article to prospective customers.
>
> I hope this information is helpful to you. Please feel free to contact me if you have any questions or comments.

On October 28 I received a copy of the Raxter letter from a Pennsylvania agent of Prudential Insurance Company of America. That was my first knowledge of the letter. It was also my first knowledge that ALW was using the letter as the centerpiece of a national campaign to discredit the *Forum* and me, and to intimidate agents who were trying to protect their policyholders against ALW's replacement activities.

I immediately called Raxter. I asked for several items mentioned in his October 8 letter and for clarification of several points in it. He asked me to put my requests in writing. I asked why he had not sent me the circular letter he had promised to send me. He said he had forgotten, and said he would send it right away. He did not send it to me at that time. I asked if he was aware of ALW's national circulation of his letter. He said he was not aware of such circulation.

On November 4 I wrote to Raxter requesting several items. He responded on November 16. He sent me a copy of the den Boer letter. It said that ALW disagrees strongly with the last paragraph of my article, and that unauthorized distribution of the article by agents in their conservation efforts is an unfair trade practice under North Carolina laws and regulations.

Raxter finally sent me the circular letter. It said in part that "statutes and regulations of this State ... specifically prohibit the sale or conservation of life insurance on the basis of the negative aspects of competing products and companies." I found that statement totally at odds with his cited sections of the law.

Raxter sent me two agent reprimand letters, neither of which mentioned the *Forum*. In response to my request for a list of the "allegations" and "opinions" the Department considers "inaccurate" or that "tend to create an inaccurate impression in the mind of the customer," he said "there exists no Departmental record of that nature," and he referred me to the den Boer letter. In response to my request for the notification to me that the Department does not agree with the opinions expressed in my article, he said "there exists no Departmental record of that nature," mentioned our September 18 telephone conversation, and said his letter was directed solely at the opinion I had expressed about churning. In response to my request for the determination that distribution of my article to prospective consumers is "misrepresentation," he said "there exists no Departmental record of that nature" and "that decision was a result of staff discussion."

After October 28, when I first learned of the Raxter letter, I assembled a large amount of material about ALW's use of the letter. I obtained ALW's cover memorandum to "all regional vice presidents." I saw evidence of attempts by ALW agents to intimidate agents of other companies. I learned that a den Boer letter went to the insurance commissioners of at least 17 states. As far as I know, no department wrote a letter resembling the

Raxter letter. Indeed, I think the campaign was counterproductive to ALW's interests.

My attorney was David Vladeck of Public Citizen Litigation Group, a public interest law firm based in Washington, DC. In late November Vladeck wrote to John Ingram, the North Carolina insurance commissioner, demanding a full public retraction of the Raxter letter. Ingram did not respond to the letter. However, on December 29 Ingram issued a press release that included this intriguing sentence: "Letters by Ronald Raxter should not be misinterpreted or used out of context or otherwise to prohibit any communication."

Our Lawsuit against Ingram

On December 31 Vladeck filed a lawsuit on my behalf against Ingram in the U.S. District Court in Raleigh. We asked the court to do three things: (1) declare that Ingram had acted in violation of the U.S. Constitution in suppressing distribution of the *Forum* article, (2) order Ingram to rescind the Raxter letter, and (3) preliminarily and permanently enjoin Ingram from threatening or taking disciplinary action against insurance companies or insurance agents based upon distribution to consumers of materials discussing negative aspects of competing products and companies so long as the materials are not untrue, deceptive, or misleading.

An assistant attorney general of North Carolina filed a response on behalf of Ingram, and ALW's attorneys filed a motion to intervene. On February 4, 1982, the court heard oral arguments on our motion for a preliminary injunction and on ALW's motion to intervene.

On February 8 the court granted our motion for a preliminary injunction and denied ALW's motion to intervene. The court ordered Ingram to do four things: (1) rescind the Raxter letter publicly, (2) notify ALW it was to cease any further distribution of the Raxter letter, (3) cease all efforts to suppress distribution of the *Forum* article until such time as it was determined to be subject to suppression under applicable North Carolina laws and regulations, and (4) remove from any letters of reprimand placed in the licensing files of any insurance agent or insurance company any reference to actions taken by the Department based on distribution of the *Forum* article.

On April 6, 1983, the court granted our motion for summary judgment. The court ordered Ingram not to suppress distribution of the April 1981 article unless and until it was determined to be subject to suppression under applicable North Carolina laws and regulations. The court decreed that, in the event the article was determined to be subject to suppression, we be afforded at least 20 days' notice and an opportunity to be heard before measures were taken to suppress distribution. The court retained jurisdiction to resolve our claim for attorney fees.

Ingram appealed the decision to the U.S. Court of Appeals for the Fourth Circuit in Richmond, Virginia. On February 27, 1984, at oral argument on the appeal, a three-judge panel unanimously affirmed the district court decision from the bench without requesting oral argument from Vladeck.

On May 8, 1984, the district court awarded us $20,500 in attorney fees and $1,500 in expenses. On June 14, 1984, checks in those amounts were drawn against the Department's account, and the legal battle ended.

I wrote a series of articles as the case progressed—in the January 1982, March 1982, April 1982, and September 1984 issues. One of the more interesting comments I received was from an agent in North Carolina. He said:

> I was not aware of the action taken by the North Carolina insurance department against *The Insurance Forum* until I read an article about it in our local newspaper. I have been a subscriber to your publication, but let my subscription lapse. I have decided now, however, that if our insurance department thinks your publication is not fit to be distributed to the public, I had better be reading it on a regular basis!
>
> Enclosed please find my check for a one-year subscription.

Ingram's Kangaroo Hearing

Two days before we filed our lawsuit, and on the same day Ingram issued the previously mentioned intriguing December 29 press release, he announced a public hearing to be held in

Raleigh on January 21, 1982. The hearing purportedly was to deal with three topics:

- Allegations by Professor Joseph Belth against Jefferson Standard Life Insurance Company in regard to the payment of policyholder dividends. [I had written about Jefferson Standard's dividends in the December 1980 issue, and I later wrote a follow-up article in the July 1982 issue.]
- Allegations by Professor Belth concerning agents' commissions. [This was a veiled reference to the comment about churning in my April 1981 article.]
- Concern by Better Business Bureau of Greater Mecklenburg, Inc. over the "special notice" ad placed in the January 24, 1981 *Charlotte Observer* by the Charlotte Association of Life Underwriters. [This item was not related to the *Forum*.]

I had a conflict on January 21. Vladeck wrote to the Department protesting that the hearing had been scheduled without consulting us on the date. He requested that the hearing be rescheduled for January 29. On January 12 the Department issued a notice that the hearing had been rescheduled for January 29 and expanded to include a fourth topic:

- Preliminary investigation of certain actions by Mutual Benefit Life Insurance Company and its general agent for North Carolina in the termination of agents in the Wilmington, North Carolina area. [This item was not related to the *Forum*.]

The first, third, and fourth items were not discussed at the hearing. Clearly they were on the agenda to divert attention from the purpose of the hearing, which was to conduct an inquisitorial investigation of the *Forum* and me. I wondered about whether to testify at the hearing. I decided to do so because I felt that, if I declined, ALW and the Department would make a big thing out of my absence. Vladeck accompanied me.

Ingram made a short opening statement and turned the hearing over to the Department's hearing officer. Before I took the stand, they served me with an administrative subpoena, despite the fact that I had appeared and agreed to testify voluntarily. I was sworn in and read my prepared statement, which took less than half an hour. For the rest of the day, I was cross-examined, with the bulk of the questions coming from the chief counsel of the Department and, incredibly, from an attorney for ALW.

Prior to the hearing, Vladeck had been assured he would have an opportunity to question other witnesses. However, there were no other witnesses. No one from ALW testified, and neither Raxter nor anyone else from the Department testified. ALW's attorney merely submitted a written statement at the end of the hearing.

The hearing officer invariably overruled Vladeck's objections to questions. An exception occurred when the Department's chief counsel asked about the content of a telephone conversation between Vladeck and me; the hearing officer suggested the question be rephrased.

ALW's attorney asked me a series of questions aimed at getting me to divulge the names of companies and agents in North Carolina who had purchased reprints of my April 1981 article. The hearing officer overruled all Vladeck's objections to the questions. Vladeck instructed me not to answer the questions.

At the end of the hearing, ALW's attorney asked the hearing officer to issue a subpoena *duces tecum* to compel me to produce records showing the names of my customers. Incredibly, instead of rejecting the request out of hand, the hearing officer took the request under advisement. Because Vladeck and I did not know whether an attempt would be made that evening to serve a subpoena, I canceled my Raleigh hotel reservation and Vladeck and I left the state immediately after the hearing. I am not aware of any attempt to serve a subpoena.

The Threat against Northwestern Mutual

The *Forum* and I were not the only targets of the Raxter campaign. He demanded that Northwestern Mutual Life Insurance Company, one of America's oldest, largest, and most respected life insurance companies, stop its North Carolina agents from circulating the April 1981 *Forum* article. David Nelson, an attorney in Northwestern's home office, told Raxter that he (Nelson) saw no reason why a Northwestern agent should be prevented from showing an authorized reprint of the April 1981 *Forum* article to a policyholder, client, or customer. Raxter then said they were going to schedule a hearing on whether Northwestern's license to do business in North Carolina should be

"HE SAYS HE'S FROM A.L. WILLIAMS AND WANTS TO SPEAK WITH YOU PERSONALLY, MR. BELTH."

revoked. Fortunately for Raxter, no such hearing was held. The attack on the *Forum* and me had made Raxter and Ingram a state laughingstock. If they had attacked Northwestern, their certain defeat would have made them a national laughingstock.

Aftermath

Because of the obvious intimacy between ALW and the Department, I wrote to the governor of North Carolina requesting him to determine whether an investigation was warranted. I received no reply, and to my knowledge no investigation was conducted.

Raxter's employment with the Department ended when Ingram's successor took office. Today Raxter is a partner in the Raleigh office of Williams Mullen PC, a law firm and lobbying organization based in Richmond, Virginia.

Other Articles about ALW

Following the excitement generated by my first article about ALW, I received from readers a large and steady stream of information about the activities of ALW. As a result, during the period from April 1981 to November 1990, I wrote 50 articles about ALW in 39 issues of the *Forum*. A few of the articles are discussed briefly here.

The *Saturday Evening Post* Incident

By the time of the events described here, the *Saturday Evening Post* was no longer owned by the Philadelphia firm that had made the magazine into a household name. It was owned by a private company in Indianapolis.

Andrew Tobias was the author of a then recent book entitled *The Invisible Bankers—Everything the Insurance Industry Never Wanted You To Know*. In late 1982 the editor of the *Post* commissioned Tobias to write a cover story about Williams. Tobias and I had been long acquainted, and he was aware of the *Forum*. He contacted me and asked for information about ALW. I sent him all the articles I had written about ALW. Tobias then informed the editor of the *Post* that the story would include some unfavorable comments. The editor terminated the Tobias assignment and assigned the story to Maynard Good Stoddard, an associate editor of the *Post*.

The March 1983 issue of the *Post* carried Stoddard's gushing cover story about Williams entitled "A 'Dad-Gummit' Georgia Football Coach Tackles the Insurance Industry." Sprinkled throughout the story were comments such as these:

> • His environment may have changed, but ex-coach Art Williams is still daring ordinary people to dream the Great American Dream—and telling them how to win.
> • Today, Art Williams directs his inspiring message to the winning people of A. L. Williams Company, the fastest growing insurance sales organization in the country.

Stoddard lived about 20 miles from our house. When the story appeared, I sent him my articles about ALW and made an appointment to see him. During our visit he said that, when he was assigned the story, he had only a few days to turn it in and had no time to conduct research. He readily acknowledged that the story was a rewrite of material furnished by ALW headquarters. ALW distributed hundreds of thousands, if not millions, of reprints of the story to ALW representatives. I wrote about the incident in the April 1983 issue.

The U.S. Congress Incident

In the May 1985 issue I wrote about an ALW booklet entitled *Common Sense*. I said it contained some useful information about financial planning. However, I also said some of its information about life insurance was misleading, some of its recommendations were self-serving, and some of its suggestions represented unsound advice for consumers.

U.S. Senator Paula Hawkins and U.S. Representative Andy Ireland, both of Florida, placed statements in the *Congressional Record* commending ALW on the *Common Sense* booklet. It should be noted that the *Congressional Record* is used routinely by members of Congress to say nice things about their constituents and supporters. ALW used the statements to prepare a four-page promotional brochure. The caption on the brochure's front page was false because Williams was not "honored by United States Congress." The brochure's inside pages showed the Hawkins statement with some comments emphasized. The brochure's back page showed Hawkins handing Williams and his wife a sheet of paper, which the caption called "an official copy of the U.S. Senate resolution praising *Common Sense*." The caption was false because there was no resolution.

The *Congressional Record* statements were prepared by ALW and edited by congressional staffers. It is my understanding that the material was provided to the two members of Florida's congressional delegation by an attorney at Holland & Knight, a prominent Florida law firm.

Hawkins and Ireland were blindsided, because they did not realize how their statements would be used. To their credit, they later tried to undo some of the damage caused by the brochure. I wrote about the incident in the July 1985 issue.

The Southern Illinois University Incident

In October 1987 the College of Business and Administration (College) of Southern Illinois University at Carbondale presented Williams with the "1988 International Entrepreneur of the Year Award." Here is the statement printed in the announcement of the award:

> Arthur L. Williams, 44, is exemplary of the entrepreneurial spirit alive and well in America today. His multi-million dollar term-life insurance company, A. L. Williams, began in 1977 with a sales force of only 92 people. Just a short ten years later, the football-coach-turned-businessman employs 6,000 full-time and over 100,000 part-time people nationwide. His success has been documented by respected publications such as the *Saturday Evening Post* and *Time.* A. L. Williams boasts concepts unique to the insurance industry, such as no advertising and term versus whole life. The company is based in Duluth, Georgia.
>
> The College of Business and Administration is pleased to present this award to A. L. Williams.

The announcement of the award generated a torrent of criticism from College alumni and others in the insurance business. I first learned of the award when I received frantic telephone calls from insurance agents in Carbondale after the announcement. I also received an unsolicited telephone call from the chairman of the finance department of the College. I thereupon requested and received a statement from the dean of the College. He defended the award, and his five-paragraph statement included this paragraph:

> In honoring Art Williams, the College is neither endorsing nor judging the products, methods or practices of A. L. Williams. Rather, in being selected for this award, Williams was judged, as were previous award winners, upon his leadership abilities, diversity in thought, tenacity to succeed and related entrepreneurial characteristics. In the College's opinion, Art Williams is a very worthy addition to the College's past entrepreneurial honorees from many perspectives.

An ALW regional vice president in Carbondale was a central figure in suggesting that the College give the award. The College, like so many other victims of ALW's public relations machine, was blindsided. The furor following the announcement of the award prompted College officials to educate themselves quickly about ALW. It is my understanding that the College asked Williams not to use the name of the College or the University in ALW's promotional activities. I wrote about the incident in the February 1988 issue.

Alan Press

Alan Press is a retired general agent in New York City for Guardian Life Insurance Company of America, a past president of what is now the National Association of Insurance and Financial Advisors, and the recipient of numerous prestigious insurance industry awards. He has long been a close friend of mine. Soon after I began writing about ALW, Press began writing articles and giving speeches about ALW. He felt the activities of ALW were a serious threat not only to life insurance consumers but also to life insurance companies.

Several years after my final article about ALW, Press authored or co-authored with me some articles in the *Forum* about ALW's successor company, which continues to use some but not all of the objectionable practices of its predecessor. By that time, Williams had long since sold his interest and left the organization. He left when he was under investigation for certain allegedly improper business practices, but no charges were ever filed. MILICO became Primerica Life Insurance Company, ALW became Primerica Financial Services, and the organization was acquired by Citigroup. Later it was spun off by Citigroup, and is now Primerica, Inc. (NYSE:PRI). One of Press's articles, in the November 2010 issue of the *Forum*, is entitled "The Primerica Replacement Empire."

Issues Mentioned in This Chapter

December 1980, April 1981, January 1982, March 1982, April 1982, July 1982, April 1983, September 1984, May 1985, July 1985, February 1988, and November 2010.

6

Life Insurance Prices and Rates of Return

$\mathcal{D}$uring my first 12 years at Indiana University, and later during the *Forum* years, a major portion of my research was devoted to measuring the price of the protection component in cash-value life insurance policies. In 1960, while working on my doctoral dissertation at Penn, I had wanted to examine price differences between participating (dividend-paying) life insurance sold by stock companies and participating life insurance sold by mutual companies. However, reliable methods for measuring the price of life insurance protection from the consumer's point of view did not exist at the time. I completed the dissertation without addressing the subject.

Over the next several years, I developed methods for measuring not only the price of the protection component but also the rate of return on the savings component in cash-value policies. Unfortunately, because of the strong opposition of life insurance companies, regulators and legislators have not required the kind of rigorous disclosure that would have provided consumers with the benefits of those methods.

Splitting Protection and Savings

A cash-value policy, which typically has level (unchanging) premiums, provides protection and also provides for the accumulation of savings. At the heart of my work on measuring the price of the protection and the rate of return on the savings is splitting a cash-value policy into its protection and savings components. I used the simple diagram below to show that the protection is the death benefit minus the cash value.

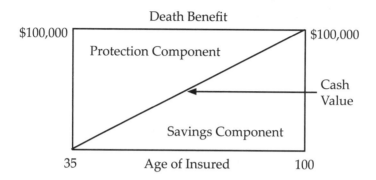

Splitting a cash-value policy into its protection and savings components was anathema to life insurance companies. Here are the reasons. First, when the split is made, it is clear that the protection decreases over time as the cash value increases. Second, when interest (the time value of money) is considered, it is clear that the interest increases over time as the cash value increases. Third, it is clear that the yearly price per $1,000 of protection increases over time in the same way the probability of the insured's death increases over time as the insured's age increases. In other words, the companies wanted people to think the level-premium, cash-value policy provides protection at a level cost, when in fact the policy provides protection at yearly prices per $1,000 of protection that increase with age just as mortality (death) rates increase with age.

There is another serious problem. Once the split is made, and once yearly prices per $1,000 of protection are disclosed, the magnitude of the policy's front-end load is clear. The front-end load consists primarily of the agent's first-year commission and other expenses of issuing a policy. The need for large first-year commissions is discussed in chapter 4.

Kimball's Views on the Split

The late Spencer Kimball was the most prominent legal scholar of his generation on the subject of insurance regulation.

He and Mark Rapaport wrote an article in the *Wisconsin Law Review* in 1972 saying this about the reluctance of life insurance companies to allow the split:

> That the conceptual separation is not only possible, but an appropriate way to look at cash value life insurance, is shown not only by the fact that it is found in major textbooks including those of the insurance saint, S. S. Huebner, but even more persuasively by the industry's own readiness to be recognized as a major savings institution when questions other than price disclosure are under discussion. Thus, the Life Insurance Association of America [now the American Council of Life Insurers], in a scholarly monograph for the Commission on Money and Credit, published in 1962, had no qualms about a chapter entitled "Policyholders' Saving Through Life Insurance." The study talks of industry efforts to push whole-life and endowment as opposed to term, in the hope of "an augmented flow of savings into life insurance." They further expressed hope that the "declining trend in life insurance savings" would be transitory. The readiness of the industry to make the conceptual separation whenever it suits industry purposes makes it impossible for us to take the actuaries' objections to the savings notion seriously enough to argue about it further.

An Anecdote about My Price Formula

Actuary 1, who knew my price formula well, told me about Actuary 2, who had heard complaints about my formula but had never looked at it. I do not remember their names, but my recollection is that they were mid-level actuaries of John Hancock Mutual Life Insurance Company, whose top actuaries were outspoken in their condemnation of my research. See the August 1974 and November 1974 issues of the *Forum*.

Actuary 2 constructed a formula himself. He proudly showed his handiwork to Actuary 1, who told him that the formula was identical to my formula, and that he had better not let anyone else in the company know what he had done. In other words, no actuary who wanted to keep his job could be seen as endorsing my formula.

An Anecdote about Interest

Interest, or the time value of money, has been important in my work because life insurance is a long-term financial instrument and understanding such an instrument is impossible without understanding interest. I learned about interest during my graduate studies at Penn.

The program for those studying for the Chartered Life Underwriter (CLU) professional designation essentially ignored the subject. In the early 1970s, I served on the examination committee for the first part of the five-part study program for the Chartered Life Underwriter (CLU) professional designation. Part I included, among other things, what I call the arithmetic of life insurance, or the calculation of life insurance premiums, reserves, cash values, and dividends. I expressed to my fellow committee members my opinion that the critically important subject of interest should be covered. They agreed, but were concerned about the lack of appropriate study material. I volunteered to write a booklet to be inserted in the study guide, and interest became a full lesson in the 30-lesson Part I. (The booklet brought cartoonist Harry Privette and me together. See chapter 3.)

Three or four questions about interest were included in the 100-question, multiple-choice examination. Then we found that most students answered the questions about interest incorrectly. We never found out whether my booklet was inadequate, whether the students did not work hard enough to master the subject, or whether there was some other explanation. To my disappointment, the committee eliminated the booklet from the study guide and the test questions about interest from the examination. I remember wondering whether study programs for medical professionals eliminate topics that are difficult for medical students.

The Traditional Net Cost Method

When I first began exploring life insurance price calculations, the traditional net cost method was the primary method used in the marketing of life insurance. Usually the calculations were carried out over a 20-year period. The user calculated the simple total of the premiums for the period, subtracted the simple total of the dividends for the period, and subtracted the cash value at the end of the period. The result was the 20-year traditional net cost of the policy.

The traditional net cost method was easy to calculate. However, it dramatically understated the price of life insurance protection. Often it produced a negative result that was heavily emphasized in the marketing process. Here is the kind of language often used in sales presentations:

> You pay premiums for 20 years, and then you get back more than you put in. Thus the life insurance protection you enjoy during the 20 years costs you less than nothing! Isn't that fantastic?

A major problem with the traditional net cost method is that it ignores interest or, if you prefer, implicitly uses an interest rate of 0 percent. Every knowledgeable life insurance person knew the method was deeply flawed, but for a long time no one did anything about it.

Yearly Prices

In 1961 I developed a system for calculating the price of life insurance protection on a year-by-year basis. I took that approach for two reasons. First, life insurance is a long-term financial instrument, and I knew it would be complicated to measure the total or average price over a long period of time. Second, I knew that there were major price differences from year to year, and that the only way to see those differences was to look at the price for each year.

As mentioned earlier in this chapter, I viewed the protection as the difference between the death benefit and the cash value. I also began thinking about using an "opportunity cost" interest rate from the consumer's point of view. I presented an early version of the formula in my first academic journal article. As mentioned in chapter 2, the article was published late in 1961. Over the years I modified the formula slightly. The final version of the formula is in appendix A.

Average or Total Prices

Later I developed two methods for calculating total or average prices for a period of years. The first method is described in my 1966 book, *The Retail Price Structure in American Life Insurance*. The method involves the averaging of yearly prices and takes into account interest and other factors from the consumer's point of view. I called it the "level price method."

The second method is described in an academic article in the March 1969 issue of *The Journal of Risk and Insurance*. The method involves a total price for a period of years. I calculated the values of four items: premiums, death benefits, dividends, and yearly increases in cash value. In calculating the values, I used several assumptions from the consumer's point of view. I subtracted the values of the death benefits, the dividends, and the yearly increases in cash value from the value of the premiums. Originally I called the resulting figure the "E-value," which stands for the value of the "excess of premiums over benefits" from the consumer's point of view. Later I called the resulting figure the "company retention," which stands for the value of what the company keeps to cover its expenses and profit, from the consumer's point of view.

Rates of Return

Parallel to my efforts to disclose prices of protection were my efforts to disclose rates of return on the savings component in cash-value policies. Extensive early work on rates of return was done by M. Albert Linton, an eminent actuary.

The Linton Method

Beginning in 1937 Linton published studies purporting to show the average rate of return on the savings component in cash-value policies. In his final study, in 1964, he showed a 20-year 4.78 percent average rate of return on the saving component of $10,000 policies issued to men aged 35. That rate of return was a respectable figure relative to the then-prevailing rates on comparable savings vehicles.

In 1962 I met Linton for the only time by accident at a luncheon meeting in Philadelphia. He expressed keen interest in my first academic article, which had been published late in 1961. He recognized the close relationship between his work and mine. He calculated rates of return on the savings component based on assumed prices of the protection component, and I calculated prices of the protection component based on assumed rates of return on the savings component.

In his studies Linton did not show rates of return on specific policies. His purpose instead was to show that cash-value life insurance in general provided a respectable rate of return on the savings component.

Three points should be noted about Linton's work. First, he used composite data for ten companies that offered favorably priced life insurance protection and consequently offered favorable rates of return. Second, he showed average rates of return for 20 years, and not for shorter periods that would have shown smaller and often negative rates of return. Third, he assumed as prices of the protection component fairly high term life insurance rates that produced higher rates of return than would have been produced by assuming low term life insurance rates.

I first wrote about calculating rates of return on the savings component in cash-value policies, and about Linton's method, in an article in the December 1968 issue of *The Journal of Risk and Insurance*. In the September 1975 issue of the *Forum*, I showed an analysis of cash-value life insurance policies issued by 20 major companies. Based on the Linton method, the 20-year average rates of return among the companies ranged from 5.03 percent to 2.97 percent. I also showed averages over shorter durations. The 10-year average rates of return among the companies ranged from 4.25 percent to minus 2.36 percent. The 5-year average rates of return among the companies were all negative, ranging from minus 0.08 percent to minus 15.89 percent.

Yearly Rates of Return

As mentioned in chapter 2, my first article about yearly prices was published in the December 1961 issue of what is now *The Journal of Risk and Insurance*. Several years later I developed a method for calculating yearly rates of return on the savings component of cash-value policies. Constructing the formula involved rearranging the formula for yearly prices into a formula for yearly rates of return. In calculating yearly rates of return, it is necessary to assume yearly prices per $1,000 of protection and solve for yearly rates of return. The formula is in appendix A.

Law Review Articles

In 1972 I described my life insurance price disclosure proposals in an article in the *Wisconsin Law Review*. In 1975 I revised and expanded my proposals in an article in the *Drake*

Law Review. I recommended, among other things, that yearly prices per $1,000 of the protection component and yearly rates of return on the savings component in cash-value policies be disclosed to the consumer at the point of sale and annually after the sale. I also recommended that the annual percentage rates associated with fractional (modal) premiums be disclosed; that subject is discussed in chapter 8.

The Interest Adjusted Method

As described in chapter 11, U.S. Senator Philip Hart became keenly interested in the subject of life insurance price disclosure because of some serious problems faced by veterans of military service. In October 1968, in a memorable speech to insurance executives, he warned them to expect truth-in-life-insurance legislation unless they began to provide reliable price information to consumers.

In response to Hart's warning, the life insurance companies—under the leadership of what is now the American Council of Life Insurers (ACLI)—appointed a committee to examine the issue. The committee was chaired by Moorhead, the eminent actuary mentioned in chapter 3. In May 1970, after a long and arduous effort, the committee recommended the interest adjusted method. It was exactly the same as the traditional net cost method, except that an assumed interest rate was factored into the calculation. Initially the assumed interest rate was 4 percent, and later the rate was changed to 5 percent.

The interest adjusted method was a major improvement over the net cost method in that the 20-year results were invariably positive rather than negative. Nonetheless the interest adjusted method was seriously flawed in at least three ways. First, it did not take into account the probabilities (the probability that the insured would survive and the probability that the insured would maintain the policy) associated with dollar amounts payable at different times. Second, it failed to disclose the front-end expenses incurred by the consumer in the first one or two years of a policy. Third, it was susceptible to manipulation to make a policy look better than it deserved to look from a price standpoint.

The Hart Hearing

In February 1973 Hart conducted a four-day hearing on life insurance price disclosure. The hearing was devoted to the problems of life insurance consumers generally rather than being limited to the problems faced by military veterans.

On the first day of the hearing, the leadoff witness was Ralph Nader, the consumer advocate. I was the second witness. The third witness was Moorhead, the previously mentioned actuary who had chaired the life insurance industry committee that developed the interest adjusted method.

On the other three days of the hearing, among the witnesses were Herbert Denenberg, the Pennsylvania insurance commissioner; Mark Dorfman, an insurance professor at Miami University (Ohio); John Durkin, the New Hampshire insurance commissioner; Stanley DuRose, the Wisconsin insurance commissioner; Spencer Kimball, the legal scholar mentioned earlier in this chapter who at the time was a law professor at the University of Chicago; Virginia Knauer, President Nixon's special assistant for consumer affairs; and J. Edwin Matz, senior executive vice president of John Hancock Mutual Life Insurance Company.

After the hearing Hart's staff conducted a major investigation of life insurance prices. The results were made public at a one-day hearing held in July 1974. Also, in November 1975, I testified at a hearing before the Subcommittee on Housing and Insurance of the Senate Committee on Veterans' Affairs. See the June 1976 issue of the *Forum*.

Hart later introduced truth-in-life-insurance legislation. The life insurance industry succeeded in blocking the bill.

The NAIC's Model Regulation

In 1975 the National Association of Insurance Commissioners (NAIC) adopted a model regulation based on the interest adjusted method. Some states adopted the model, and some companies began requiring their agents to disclose interest adjusted cost figures in sales presentations. The regulation was part of what I called the "anti-disclosure strategy" of the life insurance industry. See the August 1977 issue of the *Forum*.

The FTC Report

In the late 1970s the staff of the Federal Trade Commission (FTC) conducted a major study of life insurance from the consumer's point of view. I served as one of several consultants to the FTC staff.

In July 1979 the 440-page report—entitled *Life Insurance Cost Disclosure*—was made public at a hearing before the U.S. Senate Committee on Commerce. The primary focus of the report was on the need for disclosure to consumers of the rate of return on the savings component in cash-value life insurance. The report recommended use of the Linton method, which is discussed earlier in this chapter.

I discussed the report in the September 1979 issue of the *Forum*, and referred to the proposed point-of-sale disclosure of rate-of-return information as an atomic bomb. At the same time, I said the major shortcoming of the report was its failure to recommend yearly disclosure after the sale, and referred to post-sale disclosure as a hydrogen bomb. I mentioned as a "sleeper" in an appendix to the report, but not in the text of the report, the idea that policyholders might be empowered to obtain (for a nominal charge) a report showing rate-of-return information after the sale.

The report estimated that the industry-wide average rate of return on the savings component of existing cash-value policies in 1977 was between 1.2 and 1.85 percent, with a best estimate of 1.3 percent. The report characterized that as "extraordinarily low, even considering that it is essentially tax-free." The authors of the report pointed out that they "are not recommending the wholesale replacement of cash-value policies," because many existing policies provide reasonable rates of return, and replacement of such policies might be inappropriate. They also pointed out that many existing policies, especially nonparticipating cash-value policies issued many years ago, were currently providing very low rates of return.

The ACLI was incensed by the FTC staff report. In its press release after the hearing, the ACLI used the phrases "simplistic statements" and "inaccurate analysis" to characterize the report. The ACLI also said:

We simply do not understand how the FTC arrived at an average rate of return of 1.3 percent for all whole life policies. Their calculation is not a measure of what is currently being credited to policyholders. Typically, companies today are basing their dividends and premium rates on interest rates of 5 to 6 percent.

There were two major problems with the ACLI's response. First, the methodology was spelled out in the report and fully understandable. Second, the "5 to 6 percent" rates mentioned by the ACLI failed to reflect expense charges and therefore had no relationship to the rates in the report. In other words, the ACLI was referring to gross rates of return, while the report was referring to net rates of return.

The life insurance industry's anger over the report and the political power of the industry were on full display following release of the report. The industry not only accomplished a permanent shelving of the report but also mounted a successful effort to enact federal legislation barring the FTC from studying insurance without a formal request from a congressional committee. Here is the current language of the law:

> The Commission may exercise such authority [to conduct studies and prepare reports relating to the business of insurance] only upon receiving a request which is agreed to by a majority of the members of the Committee on Commerce, Science, and Transportation of the Senate or the Committee on Energy and Commerce of the House of Representatives. The authority to conduct any such study shall expire at the end of the Congress during which the request for such study was made. [15 U.S. Code, Section 46—Additional powers of Commission.]

The NAIC Proposal

In November 1980 a life insurance disclosure task force of the NAIC proposed a new model life insurance disclosure regulation. It was an extraordinary proposal. It recommended point-of-sale disclosure of yearly price information, point-of-sale disclosure of yearly information beyond the traditional period of 20 years, disclosure of rate-of-return information, and post-sale disclosure of vital information. The task force strongly rejected the then-current model regulation, which was based on the interest adjusted method. Here is an excerpt from the report of the task force:

> As the task force began its work, few if any members contemplated that it would arrive at the recommendations contained in this report. Its initial work seemed to be aimed at refining and polishing the 1976 model regulation. But as the hearings unfolded and the deliberations proceeded, there was a growing realization that the current system is seriously flawed. Despite its reluctance to depart dramatically from the general approach of the 1976 model, the task force has arrived at the conclusion that life insurance disclosure is too fundamental, too important to consumers, industry, and regulators to continue to rest on a significantly defective base. The task force did not undertake this assignment with preconceived notions. Its opinions have, however, undergone substantial metamorphosis. It has reached these conclusions after long and intense deliberation. The task force firmly believes that its conclusions are soundly conceived and that their implementation will benefit the industry as well as the insurance buying public.

About three weeks later the task force held a hearing on the proposal. Most of the life insurance company representatives attacked the proposal and offered no constructive comments. Several academicians and a few company representatives praised the proposal and offered suggestions on how it might be improved. I discussed the task force report in the January 1981 issue of the *Forum*.

To say the life insurance industry was incensed by the report of the task force is a gross understatement. One coauthor, Jon Hanson, who headed the central office of the NAIC, was fired. The other coauthor, Carolyn Cobb, was hired away from the NAIC by the ACLI. H. Peter ("Pete") Hudson, who was the Indiana insurance commissioner and a past president of the NAIC, chaired the task force. He was fired by Indiana Governor Robert

Orr. The splendid proposal by the task force was shelved, and not a word has been heard about life insurance price or rate-of-return disclosure from any insurance regulators since that time. The interest adjusted method remains to this day the only type of price information given to consumers.

Lack of Success

I did not succeed in my efforts to persuade legislators or regulators to require rigorous disclosure of prices of the protection component and rates of return on the savings component of cash-value policies. The life insurance companies are adamantly opposed to such disclosure, and they have the political power to prevent the adoption of rigorous disclosure requirements. During the past three decades, with the exception of my efforts related to fractional (modal) premium charges, as discussed in chapter 8, I did not again try to advance my disclosure proposals.

Issues Mentioned in This Chapter

August 1974, November 1974, September 1975, June 1976, August 1977, September 1979, and January 1981.

7

The Collapse of Executive Life

$\mathcal{I}$n 1986 California-based First Executive Corporation (FEC) was the publicly owned parent of California-based Executive Life Insurance Company (ELIC), which in turn was the parent of New York-based Executive Life Insurance Company of New York (ELNY). The companies were growing rapidly, investing heavily in junk bonds (also called high-yield bonds or below-investment-grade bonds), engaging in replacement activities without underwriting the replacement policies, and using suspicious arrangements with reinsurance companies based in Bermuda.

My 1986-1987 Articles

After receiving many comments from readers, I published my first article about the FEC companies in the November 1986 issue. The article was entitled "Executive Life's Bermuda Reinsurance." I described the aura of secrecy surrounding not only the identity of the owners of the Bermuda reinsurance companies but also the letters of credit associated with the reinsurance agreements.

An article in the March 1987 issue included references to the reinsurance activities of ELNY and some further detail on letters of credit. An article in the April 1987 issue described the veiled threat I received from an ELIC attorney when I asked him to comment on my November 1986 article.

In March 1987 major media outlets reported that strong action had been taken by what was then the New York Department of Insurance regarding ELNY's reinsurance arrangements. I obtained the Department's examination report, and described it in detail in an article entitled "The Reinsurance Disaster at Executive Life" in the May 1987 issue. I included three lengthy excerpts from the report.

According to the examination report, ELNY had taken credit in a sworn financial statement for reinsurance that did not exist on the "as of" date of the statement. Some reinsurance agreements had been executed after the "as of" date, some had been canceled before the "as of" date, some provided for less reserve credit than was taken in the statement, and some simply never existed. There were also problems with the letters of credit associated with the reinsurance agreements.

The Department fined ELNY $250,000 and required it to infuse $151.5 million of cash into its surplus. The money came from the issuance of intercorporate surplus notes to its parent, ELIC, which in turn obtained the money by issuing intercorporate surplus notes to its parent, FEC, which later borrowed money by issuing promissory notes that eventually played a role in the 1991 collapse of the FEC companies. See chapter 25 for a discussion of surplus notes.

About ten days after release of the Department's report, FEC filed its 10-K annual report with the Securities and Exchange Commission (SEC). The bad news about ELNY's reinsurance was buried deep in the 10-K and did not disclose the situation adequately. I said in the May 1987 issue that the filing "makes a mockery of the disclosure principles on which U.S. securities laws and regulations are based."

Immediately after FEC executives saw my article, they submitted to the SEC an amendment to the 10-K report. In the process, FEC disclosed the surprising terms of the agreement between ELNY and the Department. I described some of the terms in the June 1987 issue. Those terms are discussed later in this chapter.

In the September 1987 issue I reported on a letter to the Department from Fred Carr, ELIC's chief executive officer, and

Ronald Kehrli, ELNY's chief executive officer, agreeing to the settlement. I also reported on the following unsolicited letter I received from Agnar Oppedal, deputy managing director of Storebrand Reinsurance Company (Norway):

> Our Chief Agent in Canada, Mr. Ross Morton, has drawn our attention to an article in your May [1987] issue regarding the predicament of Executive Life in which our company is mentioned as one of Executive Life's reinsurers.
>
> There has never been a reinsurance arrangement between our Company and Executive Life. As a matter of fact we were approached on several occasions with offers of reinsurance treaties from them—and we declined each time. Executive Life must have used our name by mistake and without any foundation in any contract—and certainly absolutely without our knowledge.

My 1988 Articles

In the June 1988 issue I discussed the subject of backdated and postdated documents. For example, ELIC had issued a $170 million intercorporate surplus note to its parent company. The $170 million figure was shown as part of the assets and surplus in ELIC's financial statement as of December 31, 1987, but the note was not executed until March 7, 1988. I wrote to ELIC and asked for an explanation. In response, ELIC's general counsel said the

> subject transactions were given effect for accounting purposes at year end 1987. They were given such effect because under the circumstances present, applicable statutory accounting principles so permit.

That explanation is nonsense. The company officers who sign an annual financial statement swear, among other things, that the statement is

> a full and true statement of all the assets and liabilities and of the condition and affairs of the said insurer as of the thirty-first day of December last.

In the August 1988 issue I discussed, among other things, the fact that the California Department of Insurance had disallowed $180 million of reinsurance credit ELIC had taken in its 1986 annual statement. It was a combination of that disallowance and the backdating of certain transactions that caused me to suggest that ELIC at one point may have been insolvent.

NEWS ITEM: "ANONYMOUS CULPRITS 'ATTACK' THE INSURANCE FORUM."

The Testimony

Three top officers of ELNY were William Adams, general counsel; Allan Chapman, chief actuary; and Merle Horst, chief financial officer. Also, Albert Jacob was a consulting actuary to ELNY. The four individuals held similar positions at ELIC and FEC. The New York Department's examination report said the Department had taken sworn testimony from the four individuals. Pursuant to the New York Freedom of Information Law (FOIL), I submitted to the Department a formal request for the transcript of the testimony. The Department denied my request based on the "trade secrets or confidential financial information" exception in FOIL. At the time I did not file an administrative appeal of the denial because I was not yet aware of the full significance of the testimony.

When I saw FEC's amended filing with the SEC, I learned about the terms of the settlement agreement between ELNY and the New York Department. There was a provision under which Adams, Chapman, and Horst were not permitted to sign a sworn ELNY financial statement that was to be filed shortly with state insurance regulators. There was also a provision under which the individuals were required to resign from their officer positions at ELNY. The individuals were not required to resign from their officer positions at ELIC and FEC.

I was astounded by those provisions, and immediately realized the great significance of the sworn testimony the New York Department had taken from the individuals during the investigation of ELNY's reinsurance. Consequently I submitted to the Department another FOIL request for the transcript of the testimony. The request was denied based on the "trade secrets" exception in FOIL.

My attorney was David Vladeck, who was my attorney in the 1981 lawsuit against the North Carolina insurance commissioner, as discussed in chapter 5. Vladeck filed an administrative appeal, which is in the form of a letter to the New York Department. Alan Rachlin, an attorney in the Department, discussed the matter with Vladeck and with attorneys for the FEC companies.

A few months later Rachlin sent me the transcript with a substantial amount of material blacked out. The transcript consisted of about 5,200 lines. About 2,200 lines (42 percent) were blacked out, for the most part based on the "trade secrets" exception in FOIL. I sensed that too much had been blacked out. Vladeck spoke with Rachlin, who said the blacking out had been done by the FEC attorneys. Rachlin agreed to review the material personally. A few months later he told us he had prepared a second transcript with less material blacked out.

In accordance with FOIL procedures, Rachlin gave the FEC attorneys an opportunity to seek a court order blocking the Department from releasing the transcript. When the FEC attorneys chose not to seek a court order, Rachlin sent me the second transcript. This time about 1,000 lines (19 percent) were blacked out, for the most part based on the "unwarranted invasion of personal privacy" exception in FOIL. (Several years later I had an opportunity to see the transcript with nothing blacked out.

I compared it carefully with Rachlin's second transcript and concluded that Rachlin's blacking out of about 1,000 lines was reasonable.)

I learned from the transcript that Adams, Chapman, Horst, and Jacob testified on March 21, 1986. The first three were represented by Cecilia Kempler and Jeff Stuart Liebmann of the firm of LeBoeuf, Lamb, Leiby & MacRae. Jacob was represented by Sheldon Camhy of the firm of Shea & Gould. The Department was represented by Meyer Baruch, Salvatore Castiglione, Gerard Connelly, John Fernez, Michael Imbriano, Terrence Lennon, Charles Pallas, and Rachlin.

I published the entire transcript in the 48-page October 1988 issue, our largest-ever single issue. I used our normal type size. I printed in regular type the material in the first transcript. I printed in bold type the material that was blacked out in the first transcript but not blacked out in the second transcript. Thus it is easy for readers to see the material that the FEC attorneys had blacked out and that Rachlin had decided should not be blacked out. I used brackets to indicate lines blacked out in the second transcript. I published the entire transcript for three reasons: (1) I saw no way to capture the full flavor of the testimony with excerpts, (2) the testimony provided rare insight into the investigatory style of the New York Department, and (3) the testimony provided rare insight into the obscure world of reinsurance.

The testimony touched on some matters that defied belief. Here are a few matters I describe in plain language as follows:

> An insurance company takes credit in a sworn financial statement for reinsurance that did not exist on the statement date, but was "committed."
>
> An insurance company takes credit in a sworn financial statement for unauthorized reinsurance supported by a letter of credit that did not exist on the statement date, but was "committed."
>
> An insurance company takes credit in a sworn financial statement for unauthorized reinsurance supported by a letter of credit issued because the insurance company pledged assets to the bank issuing the letter of credit.

An insurance company includes pledged assets among its assets in a sworn financial statement but does not disclose in the statement that the assets are pledged.

A consulting actuary acting on behalf of an insurance company arranges a reinsurance agreement between the insurance company and a reinsurance company owned by the consulting actuary.

The transcript took up about 40 pages of the 48-page October 1988 issue. The remainder of the issue was devoted to three other major articles about the FEC companies.

ELIC's Ratings

The November 1988 issue contained an article about ELIC's financial strength ratings. The article turned out to be significant in the history of the *Forum*.

Despite everything that had been published about financial problems at ELIC, A. M. Best Company and Standard & Poor's (S&P) continued to show top ratings for ELIC almost until the end. Whenever ELIC officials and defenders responded to inquiries, they invariably sought to minimize the problems and belittle the critics by citing ELIC's A+ (superior) rating by Best and AAA (extremely strong) rating by S&P. However, nowhere in their responses or in their advertising did they mention the ratings assigned by the two other major rating firms—Moody's Investors Service and Duff & Phelps (later Fitch Ratings). Both of the latter rating firms had assigned significantly lower ratings to ELIC. See also chapter 22.

ELIC's practice of selectively disclosing its financial ratings prompted me to start publishing a special ratings issue of the *Forum* each year. In those issues I listed all the ratings assigned to all the life insurance companies by the four major rating firms. Later I began to include all the ratings assigned by the four major rating firms to large property insurance companies. The special ratings issues became popular; many people who did not subscribe to the *Forum* nonetheless purchased the special ratings issues. Ratings and the ratings issues are discussed in chapter 22.

The Spoof

In 1988 someone at ELIC began circulating a spoof called *The Insurance Bore 'Em,* the editor of which was J. M. Wealth. One cartoon, for example, showed the editor wearing a crown, toga, and sandals, and fiddling while Hartford, Connecticut burned in the background. Such tactics do not bother me, but I did resent the manner in which the creator of the spoof belittled my father, who had died 36 years earlier. I offered a $100 reward for information leading to identification of the anonymous culprit. I did not learn his identity at the time.

My 1989-1991 Articles

During the next three years I wrote several more articles about the financial problems at the FEC companies. For example, the January 1990 issue included an article about how ELIC manipulated some of its junk bond investments to improve their apparent quality and thereby improve the apparent financial strength of the company. There is no way I would have discovered the manipulation on my own. I learned of it through a tip from a "Deep Throat" informer.

Late in 1989 I received an anonymous telephone call from a man who said he had seen my writings about ELIC and had information for me. I asked for his name, but he declined to identify himself. He explained the manipulation and told me where to find the information deep in the company's publicly filed financial statement. I said I would look for the information but asked how I could reach him with any questions. He said he would call me again in exactly one week. I found the information, he called me again, and I said I had what I needed. My article created something of a stir, including an article in *The Wall Street Journal.*

The Collapse

In April 1991 FEC filed for bankruptcy protection, the California Department of Insurance took over ELIC, the New York Department of Insurance took over ELNY, and the Nebraska Department of Insurance took over three other FEC companies. It was the largest failure in the history of the life insurance business. I wrote about it in the June 1991 and July 1991 issues, and expressed the opinion that the collapse meant the life insurance business was entering a new and dangerous era. I wrote about some of the smaller companies that failed soon thereafter, and they were followed by the collapse of some major life insurance companies.

The Schulte Book

Late in 1991 a book entitled *The Fall of Executive Life* was published. The author is Gary Schulte, former senior vice president and chief marketing officer of ELIC. One chapter of the book is entitled "The Irrepressible Professor Belth."

Schulte's theory is that I wrote about the FEC companies for the money. He calls Fred Carr, chairman of FEC, the "protagonist" of the story, and he calls me the "antagonist." Schulte says he dreamed up the spoof and wrote two issues of it. He says he thinks I will not send him the $100 reward; he is correct on that point. I wrote about the book in the December 1991 issue.

Recently I reviewed the website of Coastal Financial Partners Group. Schulte is identified as a co-founder of the group and, according to the website, has been a consultant to such clients as Pacific Life, New York Life, Prudential, Massachusetts Mutual, American International Group, Merrill Lynch, National Financial Partners, and M Financial.

Issues Mentioned in This Chapter

November 1986, March 1987, April 1987, May 1987, June 1987, September 1987, June 1988, August 1988, October 1988, November 1988, January 1990, June 1991, July 1991, and December 1991.

8

Fractional (Modal) Premium Charges

$\mathcal{F}$ractional premium charges, often called "modal" premium charges, are the additional charges an insurance company imposes on policyholders who pay premiums twice a year (semiannually), four times a year (quarterly), or 12 times a year (monthly) instead of once a year (annually). For more than 40 years I have been engaged in a largely unsuccessful effort to require life insurance companies to disclose to their policyholders and prospective policyholders the magnitude of fractional premium charges in the form of an annual percentage rate (APR) or, alternatively, in the form of an annual interest rate (AIR).

My First Encounter

In the early 1950s, as a life insurance agent in Syracuse, I first encountered fractional premium charges. To calculate fractional premiums, my company, Continental American, multiplied the annual premium by "modal factors." For example, the factor for semiannual premiums was .52. When the annual premium was $1,000, each of the two semiannual premiums in one year was $520, and the fractional premium charges in the year were $40 ($520 × 2 = $1,040, and then $1,040 − $1,000 = $40).

I knew interest was the price paid for the use of money, but I did not become knowledgeable about interest rates until my graduate studies at Penn in the late 1950s. Also, the federal

Truth in Lending Act did not become law until the late 1960s; consequently the expression "annual percentage rate" did not yet exist. Nonetheless I sensed that the $40 of fractional premium charges in the above illustration amounted to a high interest rate. Here is how I reached that conclusion.

My company's cash-value policies carried an annual loan interest rate of 5 percent. Suppose, at the beginning of a policy year, when the $1,000 annual premium is due to be paid, the policyholder pays the annual premium by writing a check for $520 and taking a policy loan of $480 from the insurance company. Then suppose, at the end of six months, the policyholder repays the loan in full by sending the company a check for $492, consisting of $480 of loan principal and $12 of interest for six months. (The interest rate of 5 percent applied to the $480 loan for a full year would be $24, or $480 × .05, and the interest for half a year would be $12.) Note that the policyholder saves $28 ($520 − $492) in only one year by paying annually in part with a loan rather than by paying two semiannual premiums.

In short, the interest rate the company was imposing by fractional premium charges was much higher than 5 percent. Years later I learned the APR in this illustration is 16.7 percent and the AIR is 17.4 percent.

The Truth in Lending Act

During the 1960s there was intensive debate in Congress about the need for a Truth in Lending Act. A major reason why legislation was urgently needed was a widely recognized and serious form of deception that lenders were perpetrating on borrowers. The deception stemmed from the widespread practice of quoting the infamous "add-on rate."

Consider a $1,000 loan to be repaid in 12 monthly installments of $90 each. The sum of the 12 installments is $1,080, or $80 more than the $1,000 loan principal. Because $80 is 8 percent of $1,000, the interest rate on the loan was often called an add-on rate of 8 percent. Sometimes lenders did not bother to mention the add-on rate terminology. Instead they simply said the interest rate was 8 percent.

The add-on rate is an outright lie. The AIR on the loan

described in the preceding paragraph is 14.5 percent rather than 8 percent. The reason for the difference is that the borrower pays interest each month during the year on a steadily declining loan principal. In other words, if the borrower keeps the full $1,000 for the entire year, and pays off the loan with $1,080 at the end of the year, the AIR would be 8 percent.

The Truth in Lending Act finally became law in 1969. It requires the lender to disclose to the borrower the interest rate on the loan expressed as an APR. The law also requires the lender to disclose the loan's dollar interest cost, which is called the finance charge.

The APR

The AIR has been around since antiquity, and has been widely used by persons knowledgeable in financial matters. The APR, on the other hand, is an approximation of the AIR and had not yet been invented.

Proponents of the Truth in Lending Act said the lender should disclose the AIR. However, computers were in their infancy, and opponents of disclosure said calculating the AIR was too difficult. To facilitate administration of and compliance with the law, the drafters invented the APR, which remains in widespread use today even though advances in computer technology have made calculating the AIR a simple matter. The APR is slightly lower than the AIR at low interest rates, and the differential is greater at high interest rates.

To understand the difference between the AIR and the APR, consider the previously mentioned example of an annual premium of $1,000 and a semiannual premium of $520. When the first $520 semiannual premium is paid, the policyholder thereby gains the use of $480 ($1,000 – $520) for six months. To the nearest hundredth of a percentage point, the fractional premium charge of $40, which is paid as part of the second semiannual premium at the end of six months, is 8.33 percent of $480 ($40 ÷ $480). Thus the semiannual interest rate is 8.33 percent, which may be converted to an AIR as follows:

$$(1 + .0833)^2 - 1 = .174 = 17.4\%$$

The APR, by contrast, is calculated by simply multiplying the 8.33 percent semiannual interest rate by 2. To the nearest tenth of a percentage point, the APR is 16.7 percent, compared to the AIR of 17.4 percent.

My Credit Union Speech

In the early 1970s, shortly after passage of the federal Truth in Lending Act, I was invited to speak at the annual meeting of the Indiana University Employees Federal Credit Union. The title I selected for my speech was "What Borrowers Should Know about Interest Rates."

In preparation for the speech I called several local lenders. I had a prepared script. I identified myself, said I was preparing a talk for the credit union annual meeting, asked the person to assume I was borrowing $1,000 to be repaid in 12 equal monthly installments, and asked what each monthly payment would be. If, for example, the person said the monthly payment would be $90, I would ask: "What interest rate is that?" The answer invariably was "8 percent add-on" or "8 percent." Then I would ask: "8 percent?" The person would then say: "Oh, if you mean the APR, it is 14.5 percent." Then I would ask, "Do you realize that what you said is a violation of the federal Truth in Lending Act?" The invariable answer would be: "That is the way we always answered such questions."

In the speech I explained the APR. As a result of my little survey of local lenders, I said whenever a borrower wants to know the interest rate on a loan, the borrower must ask specifically: "What is the APR?"

My Disclosure Proposal

In August 1978, in testimony before a congressional subcommittee, I recommended that fractional premium charges be disclosed to consumers as APRs. My testimony included a table showing APRs for fractional premium charges imposed by 15 major life insurance companies. The APRs in the table ranged from 4.9 percent to 29.3 percent.

The December 1978 issue of *The Journal of Risk and Insurance* included my article entitled "A Note on the Cost of Fractional

Premiums." I showed a family of formulas I had developed to approximate the APRs for semiannual, quarterly, and monthly premiums. I derived them from mathematical formulas for approximating APRs on installment loans. The family of formulas is in the first section of appendix B.

The lead article in the December 1978 issue of the *Forum* was entitled "A Forgotten Aspect of Life Insurance Disclosure." I showed the table from my congressional testimony, showed the family of formulas for approximating APRs, and recommended that fractional premium charges be disclosed to consumers as APRs.

My Special Issue

The December 1998 issue was a 12-page special issue on fractional premiums. In an introductory note I said fractional premium charges were still forgotten on the 20th anniversary of the article in the December 1978 issue.

The special issue included discussions of the need for APR or AIR disclosure of fractional premium charges, how APRs and AIRs are calculated, the deception that arises in the absence of disclosure, how the corresponding deception in connection with installment loans was a major reason for passage of the Truth in Lending Act, the inane arguments against APR or AIR disclosure, and why those arguments are not valid. The issue presented AIRs—not APRs—for 104 companies. The AIRs shown in the issue ranged from 0.0 percent to 69.8 percent. The issue also included four appendixes providing background information.

Arguments for Disclosure

There are at least four reasons why fractional premium charges should be disclosed as APRs (or AIRs). First, consumers need the information to judge the desirability of paying premiums annually. For example, if the APR for monthly premiums greatly exceeds the APR for a one-year loan, the policyholder would save a substantial amount by borrowing to pay the annual premium and repaying the loan in monthly installments during the year. Suppose the annual premium is $3,000 and the monthly premium is $285. The APR would be 29.7 percent. Suppose further the policyholder could borrow at an APR of 10 percent. Borrowing to pay the annual premium and repaying the loan at the rate of $285 per month would generate in one year savings of $294, or more than one monthly premium.

Second, wide variations exist among companies. Among the 104 companies surveyed for my December 1998 issue, 77 companies had one or more AIRs in excess of 15 percent, and 33 of those had one or more AIRs in excess of 20 percent. Furthermore the companies included in that survey were those on which I was able to obtain the information necessary to calculate the AIRs. I am certain there are many companies that do not make public the information needed to calculate AIRs or APRs.

Third, wide variations exist within companies. A few years after the 1998 survey, I learned that Lincoln National Life Insurance Company, on certain term life insurance policies, had an APR of 9.5 percent for monthly premiums and an APR of a whopping 49.2 percent for quarterly premiums. I tried to get an explanation from the company, but eventually I received a message that "Lincoln will not be responding."

Fourth, the APR calculation is difficult, and the consumer may be deceived. Dividing the fractional premium charges in a year by the annual premium—a calculation similar to the calculation of the infamous add-on rate—is wrong and greatly understates the APR. The calculation is wrong since the policyholder does not have the use of the entire annual premium for the entire year. At the beginning of the year, the policyholder pays the first fractional premium instead of the annual premium. Thereafter, as additional fractional premiums are paid during the year, the policyholder has the use of a smaller and smaller amount. As for the magnitude of the understatement, APRs for semiannual premiums are more than four times the wrong percentages, for quarterly premiums are almost three times the wrong percentages, and for monthly premiums are more than two times the wrong percentages.

For example, consider the previously mentioned $1,000 annual premium and $520 semiannual premium. If a person divides the year's fractional premium charges of $40 by the annual premium of $1,000, the person would be deceived into thinking the APR is 4 percent. The APR in this instance, as mentioned earlier, is 16.7 percent, and the AIR is 17.4 percent. Both are more than four times the wrong figure of 4 percent.

Arguments against Disclosure

Over the years life insurance companies have made various inane arguments against disclosure of fractional premium charges as AIRs or APRs. One frequently used argument is that fractional premiums do not involve loans and therefore it is inappropriate to express fractional premium charges as AIRs or APRs. The argument is nonsense because the accepted definition of interest is the price paid for the use of money. By paying fractional premiums rather than an annual premium, the policyholder has the use of a portion of the annual premium for a portion of the year.

Another argument by the companies is that consumers have not been demanding the information. That argument also is nonsense. Without the information, consumers do not realize they should be demanding the information because they are not aware of its importance. Catch 22!

Yet another argument by the companies is that it is a simple matter for the consumer to calculate the dollar amount of fractional premium charges if he or she wants the information. As discussed earlier, the consumer will be deceived by looking only at the dollar amount of the charges, because the consumer is likely to take the next seemingly logical step and divide the dollar amount of the charges by the annual premium. In deposition testimony in the New Mexico litigation discussed on the next page, insurance regulators, insurance executives, and others knowledgeable in financial matters divided the dollar amount of the charges by the annual premium, thus demonstrating that they did not know how to calculate APRs, and that they too would be deceived. In one instance, even an actuary admitted he did not know how to perform the calculation, but he did know that dividing the dollar amount of the charges by the annual premium understated the APR.

I wrote about the anti-disclosure campaigns waged by the

life insurance companies through the American Council of Life Insurers, their trade association. See the December 2001 and July 2003 issues.

How to Make the Calculations

Over the years I have developed three simple methods for calculating APRs. First, as previously mentioned, I developed a family of formulas for approximating APRs. The formulas are in the first section of appendix B.

Second, I constructed a simple table with which to approximate the APRs. The policyholder merely calculates the ratio of the fractional premium to the annual premium, looks up the ratio in the table, and reads the APR that appears to the right of the ratio. The table is in the second section of appendix B.

Third, I posted an easy-to-use APR calculator on the website of the *Forum* (www.theinsuranceforum.com). The user merely keys in the annual premium and one or more fractional premiums, and hits the calculate button. The APRs shown are accurate to the nearest tenth of a percentage point. The calculator also shows the dollar amount of the fractional premium charges. See the illustration in the third section of appendix B.

The New Mexico Litigation

Shortly after publication of the December 1998 issue, two attorneys from New Mexico visited me in Bloomington. They were planning to file class action lawsuits against several life insurance companies for failing to disclose fractional premium charges as APRs. They asked me to be an expert witness.

Initially I declined. I had done expert witness work on a few other matters during the early part of my academic career, but I had not done such work—except for one small case in Bloomington—since starting the *Forum*. I felt that expert witness work conflicted with my work as a journalist. I also was certain that any lawsuits filed concerning fractional premium charges would be settled, and that the settlements would not require disclosure of APRs to consumers. The attorneys promised me there would be no settlements without requiring APR disclosure to consumers.

Despite my misgivings, I eventually agreed to help them in the lawsuits. To address the conflict, I disclosed my role and the amount of my compensation in the *Forum*. The attorneys filed several lawsuits in New Mexico state courts. I prepared reports in several of them, and I gave deposition testimony in a few of them. As I had feared, and despite the attorneys' promises, all but one of the lawsuits were settled without requiring APR disclosure to consumers.

The Massachusetts Mutual Settlement

The exception was the settlement of the lawsuit against Massachusetts Mutual Life Insurance Company. The company agreed to begin showing APRs in its policies when the company next revised its policy forms. It was several years later, but the company honored the agreement and began showing APRs prominently in its policies. I wrote in the February 2001 issue about the initial settlement of the case, in the May 2002 issue about the final settlement, and in the April 2012 issue about the nature of the company's disclosure in its policies.

Primerica's "Line in the Sand"

For many insurance companies, fractional premium charges are a revenue source that would be destroyed by disclosure of the charges as AIRs or APRs. The A. L. Williams organization (ALW), discussed in chapter 5, imposed—and its successor company (mentioned later) still imposes—charges equivalent to an APR of 29.7 percent on policyholders who pay monthly premiums. Moreover, its policyholders pay monthly premiums through preauthorized checks rather than by mail in response to a premium notice. Companies that offer a choice between preauthorized checks and monthly premium notices invariably impose smaller charges for preauthorized checks because they are less expensive for the companies. Thus ALW's 29.7 percent APR is particularly egregious. ALW trained its agents to persuade policyholders to pay monthly premiums through preauthorized checks. Also, by way of comparison, ALW's APRs on semiannual and quarterly premiums were—and its successor's APRs still are—16.7 and 16.1 percent, respectively.

Primerica Life Insurance Company, the successor to ALW, was the defendant in one of the New Mexico cases. It still charged an APR of 29.7 percent on monthly premiums, and still pushed policyholders to pay monthly premiums through preauthorized checks. I estimated that Primerica's profit from fractional premium charges was $110 million per year, or more than 20 percent of the company's net operating gain.

In July 2000 the attorneys in the Primerica lawsuit met in settlement negotiations. One of the plaintiffs' attorneys later submitted an affidavit describing what happened. The affidavit included this sentence:

> Primerica drew a line in the sand, and after extensive discussions told us that the matter had been discussed at the highest level and there was simply no way an interest disclosure would be made.

The settlement in the Primerica case imposed no disclosure requirements. I wrote about the case in the February 2001 and March 2001 issues. Today Primerica's monthly premium charges are still equivalent to an APR of 29.7 percent, and policyholders are still pushed into paying the premiums through preauthorized checks.

Website Calculators

In a few of the lawsuits, the companies were required as a part of the settlements to post APR calculators on their websites. Also, a few companies not involved in litigation voluntarily posted APR calculators on their websites. The plaintiffs' attorney in the Massachusetts Mutual case (not one of the attorneys who visited me in Bloomington) threatened another major company with a lawsuit, and the company staved off the lawsuit by agreeing to post an APR calculator on its website.

Unfortunately, the posted APR calculators do not accomplish disclosure because the companies are not required to inform their policyholders that the calculators exist or why the APRs are important information. Also, as one might expect, those companies' APRs are low relative to the APRs of many other companies. I wrote about some of the website calculators in the November 2004 issue.

The Regulators

In all the years I have been dealing with the need for AIR or APR disclosure of fractional premium charges, I have not found a single state insurance regulator who favors disclosure. I think the main reason is that they know what would happen if they attempted to impose disclosure requirements. The attempt would be met with such furious opposition that it would overwhelm the resources of the regulators. Also, the famous revolving door suggests that any regulator with the temerity to favor disclosure would not be able to get a job with a life insurance company after his or her term as a regulator ends. They got a taste of the problem from the fate of the November 1980 disclosure proposal by the National Association of Insurance Commissioners (NAIC), as discussed in chapter 6. In the New Mexico cases, the NAIC joined with the insurance companies to oppose APR disclosure. I wrote about the anti-disclosure campaigns waged by the insurance commissioners through the NAIC. See the December 2001, May 2002, and May/June 2004 issues of the *Forum*.

Indeed, in two jurisdictions—the District of Columbia and Utah—the insurance regulators issued rules prohibiting companies from disclosing APRs. Their inane argument was that APR disclosure would be deceptive because the consumer would be led to believe that a fractional premium arrangement involves a loan. It should come as no surprise who influenced those regulators. In the District of Columbia, it was Phillip Stano, an attorney representing insurance companies strongly opposed to APR disclosure. In Utah, it was Robert Wilcox, a former Utah insurance commissioner, who was being paid as a consultant by insurance companies strongly opposed to APR disclosure, and who had considerable influence in his capacity as a former insurance commissioner.

A Note on Terminology

In the first sentence of this chapter, I said fractional premium charges are often called "modal" premium charges. An explanation is warranted.

The frequency with which insurance premiums are paid usually is referred to by the insurance industry as the premium payment "mode." In other words, when monthly premiums are paid, the policyholder is said to be using the monthly "mode" of premium payment. Thus the industry refers to semiannual, quarterly, and monthly premiums as "modal premiums," and refers to the extra charges imposed for paying premiums more often than once a year as "modal premium charges."

The terminology is insider language that a consumer cannot comprehend. It is so arcane that dictionary definitions of "modal" and "mode" are of no help. Therefore I refused to use that terminology. Early in my research on the subject I began using the expression "fractional premiums" in an effort to make the subject understandable to consumers.

A Personal Observation

I learned a great deal that I would never have learned without immersion in the New Mexico lawsuits. However, I am disappointed that so little tangible progress on disclosure was accomplished. Since then I have refrained from engaging in any expert witness or consulting work.

Issues Mentioned in This Chapter

December 1978, December 1998, February 2001, March 2001, December 2001, May 2002, July 2003, May/June 2004, November 2004, and April 2012.

9

The Secondary Market for Life Insurance

$\mathcal{W}$hen a person or entity buys a life insurance policy from an insurance company, either through a life insurance agent or directly from the company, the transaction is said to be in the "primary market for life insurance." When the person or entity that bought the policy in the primary market sells (transfers the ownership rights in) the policy to another person or entity, the transaction is said to be in the "secondary market for life insurance." After that transaction, the person on whose life the policy was originally issued remains the person whose life is insured. When the party that bought the policy in the secondary market sells the policy yet again, that resale and all subsequent resales of the policy also may be said to be in the secondary market. (Resales of a policy subsequent to the initial sale in the secondary market may be said to be in the "tertiary market for life insurance," but I prefer to avoid that expression.)

Emergence of the Secondary Market

The secondary market for life insurance in the U.S. emerged from the shadows in 1989. Prior to that time, there were rumors about the existence of an underground secondary market for life insurance where an insured could sell the policy to a speculator in exchange for cash. The speculator would become the owner of the policy and take over the payment of subsequent premiums. The speculator would become the beneficiary of the policy and receive the death benefit upon the insured's death. The new owner/beneficiary would be eager for the insured to die as soon as possible, so that the premium payments would stop and the death benefit would be paid. During the years I was teaching, in discussions of life insurance principles and practices, I mentioned rumors of an underground market.

Components of the Secondary Market

The secondary market for life insurance may be divided into two components: (1) "viatical settlements" involving insureds who are terminally ill, and (2) "life settlements" involving insureds who are not terminally ill. Life settlements may be sub-divided into two components: (a) those involving policies origi-nally bought for genuine life insurance purposes, such as family protection, business protection, or estate planning, and where the insureds, because of changed circumstances, decide to sell the policies in the secondary market; and (b) those involving policies originally bought for the purpose of selling them in the secondary market after the expiration of two years. (The reason for the delay is the two-year incontestability clause, which is discussed in chapter 12.) The (b) component of life settlements is what life insurance companies call "stranger-originated life insurance" (STOLI) and what I call "speculator-initiated life insurance" (spinlife). In summary, the components of the sec-ondary market for life insurance are:

1. Viatical settlements
2. Life settlements
   a. Genuine life settlements
   b. STOLI or spinlife

The First Company

Early in 1989 the *National Underwriter*, a weekly insurance newspaper, ran a small story about Living Benefits, Inc. (Albu-querque, NM), a newly formed private company. The story said the company had raised $102 million of capital and was planning to pay cash for policies on the lives of insured persons who were terminally ill. Robert T. Worley, Jr., a life insurance

THE SECONDARY MARKET FOR LIFE INSURANCE

agent, was president of the company. A promotional brochure included this description of the program:

> LIVING BENEFITS is a company that provides a service for the terminally ill. We purchase life insurance policies with cash so one may have more living benefits at their discretion now: such as money for distribution to family members, to friends, to churches, to ministries, to schools, to hospitals, to other charities, to take a memorable trip, to retire an indebtedness, and for any other desire one might have while still living.

The brochure said: "[A]s a general rule, we are able to pay from 60% to 75% of the face value." The policy had to be "individually owned (not a group policy)," had to be in force for at least two years, and had to have a face value of at least $50,000 and not more than $250,000. The brochure also said: "All medical records will be held in the strictest of confidence by our medical staff."

I spoke with Worley before the company bought its first policy. He answered some but not all my questions. He said he expected most of the policies the company acquired would involve insureds who were terminally ill with cancer. I later learned it did not work out that way. When the company began operations, most of its business involved insureds who were terminally ill with AIDS.

Worley said his "medical staff" consisted of five physicians in Albuquerque, but he declined to identify them. I later spoke with the director of the University of New Mexico Cancer Center in Albuquerque. He had not heard of the program. It troubled him, and he said he was not aware of any member of his staff being involved.

Because an insured might want to know who stands to profit from his or her death, and because of the company's proximity to Las Vegas, I asked Worley about his sources of capital. He said there were one or two large investors and some small investors, but he declined to identify them. I asked about the investors because I wondered whether money from Las Vegas was involved in the speculation on human life.

When I asked about his actuary, Worley said he did not need an actuary. When I asked how the company would calculate the purchase price of a policy, he said he and his father, a retired bakery executive who had never been in the insurance business, had constructed a spreadsheet. Worley said all he needed to know was the face amount of the policy and the life expectancy of the insured. He said he did not need information about type of policy, premiums, cash values, dividends, age of the insured, or gender of the insured.

I asked Worley what he would pay for a policy with a face amount of $100,000 on an insured person who had a life expectancy of one year. I heard a few clicks of his keyboard, and he said his company would buy the policy for $66,025.

I asked Worley whether he intended to compensate individuals who referred cases to his company. He said it would be inappropriate to pay compensation, and he did not plan to do so. His answer was interesting in light of the huge compensation that later was paid to intermediaries in the secondary market for life insurance, and that became the main engine for the growth of the market.

My First Article

The four-page March 1989 issue was devoted in its entirety to my first article about the secondary market for life insurance. In the article, entitled "A System for the Exploitation of the Terminally Ill," I discussed the Living Benefits program and expressed this opinion about it:

> In my opinion, the program offered by Living Benefits is a system for the exploitation of the terminally ill. I believe that any insurance company receiving a request for the transfer of a policy to Living Benefits should do what it can to discourage the transfer.

The negative views I expressed in that article about Living Benefits were based on my general distaste for speculation in human life. Today, 26 years later, I still hold negative views about the secondary market.

An Amazing Letter

Ten years elapsed before I wrote another article about the secondary market for life insurance. By that time, the market had grown to include many companies—the one with the most interesting name was Grim Reaper International—and two trade associations. By then some secondary market companies were buying policies from insureds who were not terminally ill.

I had been contemplating a follow-up article for several years, but what finally triggered it was an incident involving a 79-year-old widow in Pennsylvania. She received what

I viewed at the time as an amazing letter from Paul F. Schneider, a certified public accountant in Florida. She showed the letter to a person who by coincidence was one of my subscribers, and he shared it with me. Here is the full text of the letter ("Steve" was an attorney, and the letter included the expression "viatical settlement" because the expression was used at the time even in situations where the insured was not terminally ill):

> As you may know, I am Steve's partner. He has asked that I write to you to explain the process of obtaining an insurance policy and then selling the policy to an investor for a portion of the face value.
>
> The concept is called a "Viatical Settlement." A person such as yourself applies for a policy with a face value of at least $1,000,000. Upon the issuance of the policy, an investor offers to buy the policy from you for approximately 5% of the face value or $50,000. There is no money out of your pocket. The investor makes all premium payments. You would receive the amount directly into your bank account from the investor.
>
> We are then paid our fee directly from you. Our fee is 20% of the funds which you receive. As an example, if you receive $50,000 for the sale of the policy, we would be paid $10,000 from you. The net amount of $40,000 would be taxable to you.
>
> I hope the above will answer any question which you may have. If you have any further questions, please do not hesitate to contact me.

Schneider's letter was my first knowledge of what later became known as STOLI or spinlife, which are mentioned earlier in this chapter. I called Schneider. He said the market is limited to insureds aged 78 and older. In answer to my question about the names of the "investors," he said he did not know who they were, but said he worked with four companies engaged in that type of business. I said I wanted to contact those companies, but he declined to identify them. However, he did say they were investment companies licensed to sell securities. If he had given me their names, I would have asked them what disclosures they made to the investors (speculators in human life), who actually put up the money.

In answer to my question about the names of the insurance companies that issue such policies, Schneider said there were "various" companies, and he mentioned "CNA" and "Hartford." In answer to my question about what would happen if the insured died during the two-year contestability period and the company denied payment of the death claim because of false information in the application for the policy, Schneider said it is a risk borne by the investors. I did not ask about suicide during the usual two-year suicide exclusion period, but I assume he would have said that too is a risk borne by the investors.

I later contacted some viatical companies; they denied buying newly issued policies. They said they were aware of the practice, but were unable or unwilling to identify companies in that business. They also said they were concerned about the practice, and an official in a secondary market trade association said a committee was looking into the matter.

My Second Article

The 12-page March 1999 issue was devoted in its entirety to my second article about the secondary market for life insurance. In the article, entitled "Viatical Transactions and the Growth of the Frightening Secondary Market for Life Insurance Policies," I showed Schneider's letter and described my telephone conversation with him. I also discussed numerous secondary market developments that had occurred during the decade following my first article on the subject, and examined the ways in which the secondary market violates insurance principles. Here is the concluding paragraph of the article:

Life insurance companies have the resources needed to control the excesses of the frightening secondary market for their policies; thus far only the will to use the resources is lacking. Those interested in the welfare of life insurance policyowners and the life insurance industry, and those interested in the public interest generally, should want to see the curbing of an industry in which the basic transaction creates a large financial interest in the early death of an insured person. If viatical contracts are developed to provide adequate protection to insureds who sell their policies and to persons who buy the policies, the sheer complexity of the transactions may discourage some of the activity in the secondary market for life insurance. Further, if rigorous disclosure requirements are adopted, so that insureds who consider selling policies and persons who consider investing in policies understand the risks and implications of the transactions, the secondary market for life insurance will be sharply curtailed. On the other hand, if the current chaotic secondary market continues to grow unchecked, homicides attributable directly to that market will occur, and the reputation of the life insurance industry will be severely damaged.

Further Articles

During the years after the March 1999 article, I wrote more than 100 articles about the secondary market for life insurance. Many of them are about STOLI or spinlife transactions, which display these characteristics:

- The insured is induced to apply for a large life insurance policy, usually with a face amount of at least $1 million.
- The insured usually is at least 70 years old.
- The insured is lured into believing that the arrangement is without cost; the first two years' premiums usually are paid through a nonrecourse loan, where the insured pledges only the policy as collateral for the loan, but sometimes the insured is also required to provide a personal guarantee for all or part of the loan.
- The insured is bribed to apply for the policy with such inducements as an upfront cash payment, "free insurance" for the first two policy years, and a promise of a substantial cash payment when the policy is sold in the secondary market after two years.
- The plan from the outset is to sell the policy—after the two-year contestability period—in the secondary market.
- The insured is not informed about the legal, tax, and financial implications of involvement in the transaction.
- The insured is not informed that the policy can be resold many times, and that the insured probably will not know who has a strong financial interest in his or her death.

• The application for insurance often contains outright lies exaggerating the insured's net worth and income, misstating the purpose of the insurance, and understating the amount of life insurance that already exists on the insured's life.

• The intermediaries conceal from the insurance company the purpose of the arrangement, and invariably use one or more trusts to assist in the concealment.

• The insurance agent collects a large commission on the issuance of the policy.

• The premium finance company and other secondary market intermediaries receive large amounts of compensation in connection with their involvement in the transaction.

Size of the Secondary Market

Based on my experience, it is impossible to assemble reliable national data on the size of the secondary market for life insurance, for at least four reasons. First, state insurance regulators have not promulgated uniform financial statements to be filed by secondary market companies. Second, the financial statements developed by many states contain little or no information about the number or size of secondary market transactions. Third, many states require information only about transactions consummated in those states. Fourth, many states claim that the financial statements are exempt from disclosure under state public records laws.

Nonetheless some consulting firms have published data purporting to show the size of the secondary market for life insurance. They obtain the information through unsworn anecdotal comments by participants in the secondary market who themselves have limited access to reliable data.

I believe that the viatical settlements component and the genuine life settlements subcomponent of the secondary market are small, and that the STOLI (spinlife) subcomponent dominates the market. Also, the heyday of STOLI was from 2004 through 2007, and the market has since dried up, in the sense that secondary market participants who own policies are finding it increasingly difficult to resell them. In other words, investors, who are speculators in human life, are stuck with the policies and face the difficult decision of whether to keep paying premiums or allow the policies to lapse and thereby lose everything they invested in the policies.

Civil Litigation

Since the heyday of STOLI ended in 2007, there has been a huge amount of civil litigation. Some of it stemmed from efforts of life insurance companies to rescind STOLI policies on the grounds that the companies had been hoodwinked into issuing the policies by false information in insurance applications—most commonly lies about the net worth and income of the insured, the purpose of the insurance, and plans for selling the insurance in the secondary market after the expiration of the two-year contestability period.

The cases have produced varied results. In some instances, the insurance companies succeeded in persuading the courts that the insurance companies had been deceived into issuing the policies. In those cases, the companies were able to get the policies rescinded. In some instances, the insurance companies were allowed to keep the premiums that had been paid on the policies, but in other instances the insurance companies were required to refund some or all of the premiums that had been paid on the policies. In other cases the insurance companies were not able to persuade the courts that the companies were deceived into issuing the policies, and in those cases the insurance companies were not able to rescind the policies. Some articles about the civil litigation are in the December 1999, July/August 2004, January/February 2007, January 2008, February 2008, December 2009, and October 2012 issues.

Criminal Litigation

In addition to the huge amount of civil litigation, there has also been some criminal litigation. One of the first criminal cases occurred in 1999, when indictments were filed in a Texas state court against 32 individuals allegedly engaging in fraud in the viatical settlement market. Insureds suffering from AIDS were bribed to lie about their medical condition in nonmedical applications for small policies where no medical examinations were required, obtain the policies, and then sell the policies to viatical companies. One of the ringleaders in the case was a promoter named Walter Alfred Waldhauser, Jr., also known as Michael Lee Davis. He learned about viatical settlements while he was serving prison time for murder, and he entered the viatical business after he was paroled. The case is discussed in the October 1999 and August 2000 issues.

Another criminal case involving alleged life settlement fraud led to a non-prosecution agreement between the U.S. Department of Justice and Imperial Holdings, Inc. (Boca Raton, FL). The existence of the investigation came to light when federal agents raided Imperial's headquarters in 2011. The case is discussed in the May 2012 and October 2013 issues.

There have been many other criminal cases relating to the secondary market for life insurance, usually involving STOLI activities. I wrote about some cases in the June 2000, July 2000, August 2000, April 2011, and March 2013 issues. Relevant blog posts are no. 5 (October 30, 2013), no. 19 (January 9, 2014), and no. 60 (August 8, 2014).

Life Partners

Life Partners Holdings, Inc. (LPHI) and Life Partners, Inc. (LPI), an operating subsidiary, are based in Waco, Texas. The companies were participants in the secondary market for life insurance, and LPI's main business in recent years was the sale of fractional interests in life settlements.

LPHI's top officers were Brian D. Pardo, chief executive officer, and R. Scott Peden, general counsel. Pardo beneficially owns slightly more than half the shares of LPHI. I first mentioned the organization in the March 1999 issue, and later wrote many articles and posted many blog items about it.

In January 2012 the Securities and Exchange Commission (SEC) filed a civil complaint alleging that LPHI and its top officers violated federal securities laws. I wrote about the SEC complaint in the April 2012 issue. In February 2014 the jury ruled in favor of the defendants on some charges, and against the defendants on other charges. My first blog post about the jury verdict is no. 29 (February 10, 2014).

In December 2014 the federal district court judge ordered

LPHI to disgorge ill-gotten gains and pay a civil penalty; the sum of those two penalties was more than twice LPHI's total assets. Consequently I called the order a death sentence. The judge also imposed large civil penalties on Pardo and Peden. My first blog post about the court order is no. 75 (December 10, 2014). The defendants began the process of appeal.

In January 2015 LPHI filed for bankruptcy protection under Chapter 11 of the federal bankruptcy law. In April 2015 the bankruptcy court judge approved the appointment of H. Thomas Moran, II as the Chapter 11 Trustee to operate the company in bankruptcy. The matter is very complicated and as of June 2015 appears headed for lengthy proceedings. Pardo and Peden have not paid their civil penalties; some assets have been seized and some liens have been imposed. My most recent blog post about the situation is no. 102 (May 26, 2015).

Issues and Blog Items Mentioned in This Chapter
March 1989, March 1999, October 1999, December 1999, June 2000, July 2000, August 2000, July/August 2004, January/February 2007, January 2008, February 2008, December 2009, April 2011, April 2012, May 2012, October 2012, March 2013, and October 2013, and blog nos. 5 (October 30, 2013), 19 (January 9, 2014), 29 (February 10, 2014), 60 (August 8, 2014), 75 (December 10, 2014), and 102 (May 26, 2015).

10

Universal Life Insurance

*A*s mentioned in chapter 6 and elsewhere in this memoir, I have tried to achieve, for the benefit of life insurance consumers, rigorous disclosure of prices of life insurance protection and rates of return on the savings component in cash-value policies. In that effort, I divided the life insurance policy into its protection and savings components. That division incurred the wrath of the life insurance industry. When universal life burst on the scene in 1979, an official of one of the companies that pioneered universal life wrote me and said, "Joe, I hope you're satisfied!" The reason for his comment was that one of the claimed advantages of universal life was so-called transparency; that is, the separation of the protection and savings components. Unfortunately, while transparency sounds good, it did not lead to adequate disclosure of prices and rates of return. Instead, it failed to disclose prices and rates of return, and it created a new family of deceptive sales practices.

The Nature of Universal Life

For the purposes of this section, which admittedly is an incomplete description of universal life, I assume that premiums are paid annually. To understand universal life, it is necessary to be familiar with the "cost of insurance" for a year, or COI, which is calculated by multiplying the amount of protection in thousands of dollars by the annual mortality charge per $1,000.

The amount of protection is the death benefit minus the savings component. The mortality charges per $1,000, which increase with age, have maximums guaranteed in the policy, but insurance companies usually assess mortality charges smaller than the maximums.

The person who buys a universal life policy chooses the death benefit and, within limits, the "planned annual premium." As the years go by, the premium payer, within limits, may increase or decrease the premium. The policyholder also may increase or decrease the death benefit, although an increase may require the insured to provide satisfactory evidence of insurability.

A portion of each annual premium covers that year's COI and other expenses, and the remainder of the premium is added to the savings component. At the end of each year, the savings component is credited with one year's interest. The policy contains a minimum guaranteed interest rate, but companies usually credit interest rates higher than the minimum. To keep the policy going—and prevent it from lapsing—the premium payer must pay at least enough to cover the year's COI and other expenses, or the policy must have a savings component large enough to cover the year's COI and other expenses.

The First Articles

I first wrote about universal life in the November 1981 and December 1981 issues. I explained the new product, illustrated its operation with a hypothetical policy, mentioned what the promoters referred to as transparency, discussed the premium and death benefit flexibility, described the new forms of deception, explored income tax issues, examined agent compensation issues, and commented on the critical question of whether and in what way companies would seek to replace existing cash-value policies with universal life policies.

The Golden Rule Advertisement

In the May 1984 issue I showed a vivid example of the new type of deception introduced by universal life. The January 29, 1984 issue of *The Indianapolis Star* carried an astounding advertisement run by Golden Rule Insurance Company (headquartered in Indianapolis) with this large bold heading: "Life Insurance Paying 12% Interest? Unbelievable!" Farther down was the "12%" figure in even larger bold type, and still farther down was this language in regular type: "Smart buyers want the protection of life insurance, but they are no longer content to earn only 2%-4% interest on the accumulated cash value. That's outmoded." This language followed: "If you have outmoded life insurance you can probably replace it with Universal Life for the same premium you now pay."

Golden Rule's advertisement was a classic example of the use of gross interest rates rather than interest rates net of expense charges. I had warned about that type of deception in the November 1981 issue. Prior to writing about the advertisement, I corresponded with Golden Rule, and included in my article a company official's views on the matter. In the years that followed, the emphasis on gross interest rates in universal life advertising and sales illustrations became a plague that even infected traditional cash-value policies. In the June 1984 issue I showed how to evaluate universal life and other new types of life insurance.

The Life of Georgia Advertisement

In the October 1985 issue I wrote about a deceptive advertisement that resembled the Golden Rule advertisement in some respects. The advertisement was run by Life Insurance Company of Georgia in the July 13, 1985 issue of the *Enquirer*, a newspaper in Columbus, Georgia. The advertisement showed what purported to be two death claim checks payable to the same widow. One was a check for $83,000 from Life of Georgia and the other was a check for $48,000 from an imaginary company named "Whole Life Indemnity." Here is part of the explanation in the text of the advertisement:

> Quite simply, it's the interest rate. Your whole life policy pays only 4% or 5%. While our Incentive Life and Responsive Life policies pay up to 11%. So ours earn higher cash values, pay substantially bigger benefits. And can actually cost less per month than yours.

In the January 1986 issue I wrote about the Life of Georgia advertisement again after it appeared in the October 16, 1985 issue of the *Times-Picayune* in New Orleans. I had sent my October 1985 article to the Georgia Office of the Insurance Commissioner. The Office found the advertisement unacceptable, but only because it had failed to include a footnote showing the minimum guaranteed interest rate. Thus the Office apparently had no problem with the advertising of gross interest rates.

Two Important Articles

The lead article in the October 1985 issue was entitled "The Coming Era of Disillusionment," and the lead article in the January 1987 issue was entitled "Are Life Insurance Sales Illustrations Out of Control?" In retrospect, they were important articles. In the first article, I offered this tongue-in-cheek definition of universal life and other "interest sensitive" products in an effort to distinguish them from the interest sensitive nature of traditional, participating cash-value policies:

> Interest sensitive life insurance products are those designed to be sold with heavy emphasis on high gross interest rates at a time when consumers are sensitive to interest rates.

The final paragraph of the October 1985 article contained what turned out to be an accurate forecast of things to come. The paragraph read:

> When consumers begin to experience much smaller cash-value accumulations than anticipated, sharp premium increases, the reappearance of so-called vanishing premiums, sharp reductions in death benefits, or some combination of these items, there will be a backlash against the life insurance industry. During and after the inevitable era of disillusionment for consumers, it will be difficult to rebuild public confidence in the industry. Thus the result of the current marketing emphasis on high gross interest rates may be a permanent reduction in the importance of life insurance companies as financial institutions.

The Crown Life Episode

In the July 1995 issue I said the "era of disillusionment" had arrived and was engulfing life insurance companies in a public relations disaster of unprecedented proportions. The fundamental problem was the aggressive promotion of universal life and other new products through the use of sales illustrations based on high gross interest rates that were not guaranteed and not sustainable. Many major life insurance companies were defendants in lawsuits brought by disgruntled policyholders who alleged that they had been misled. In one case I wrote about, the defendant was Crown Life Insurance Company, a Canadian company with substantial U.S. operations.

The plaintiff was a Mississippi resident who bought a $525,000 policy from Crown in 1987. Part of the money to buy the policy came from a policy issued a year earlier by another company. The sales illustration, which was based on a gross, nonguaranteed interest rate of 13 percent, naturally showed future values that were "too good to be true."

When Crown began lowering interest rates, the plaintiff saw those future values decline sharply. In 1993 he filed a lawsuit against the company alleging intentional or negligent misrepresentation, fraudulent inducement, fraudulent concealment, and tortious interference with contract rights. Some observers estimated that about 30 other lawsuits had been filed against Crown in the U.S. In the article, I concluded that irreparable damage had been done to the reputation of life insurance companies by the use of aggressive sales illustrations in the 1980s.

The New York Life Settlement

In the January 1996 issue I wrote about a proposed settlement by New York Life Insurance Company to end several lawsuits alleging deceptive sales practices through the use of aggressive sales illustrations. In the article I wrote about what I perceived as serious shortcomings of the settlement from the viewpoint of the policyholders.

The Charitable Incident

In the July 2001 issue I wrote about a troubling situation.

The insured bought a $250,000 universal life policy from Valley Forge Life Insurance Company in 1985 and donated the policy to a 501(c)(3) charitable organization in 1999. The illustrated interest rate at the time of the initial sale was 11 percent. When the company sharply reduced the interest rate later, the charity was not able to obtain from the company an indication of the premium needed to keep the policy in effect for the remainder of the insured's life. The company said the premium would have been so large that it would disqualify the policy as life insurance under provisions of the Internal Revenue Code. Those provisions had been enacted to address tax issues that had arisen because of universal life. The charity said it was not concerned about the tax treatment of the policy because, as a charitable organization, it did not pay taxes. Yet the company not only refused to perform the calculation but also would not accept an adequate premium, presumably because the company's system was designed to refuse premiums that would disqualify the policy as life insurance under the Code. Thus the charity was not able to maintain the policy even if it had wanted to do so.

The Conseco Assault

Massachusetts General Life Insurance Company and Philadelphia Life Insurance Company sold many universal life policies in the 1980s based on sales illustrations that were "too good to be true." The policies were headed for serious trouble. In the 1990s, Conseco Life Insurance Company acquired both companies. I do not know whether Conseco at the time was fully aware of the problems it was acquiring.

In 2003 Conseco altered the policies' internal calculations in such a way as to increase drastically the COI charges that policyholders had to pay to keep the policies in force. I devoted the entire 16-page December 2003 issue to what I called "Conseco's Assault on Universal Life Policyholders." Several class action lawsuits ensued, which eventually resulted in substantial settlements for policyholders.

The Controversy over Reserve Liabilities

The February 2012 issue of the *Forum* contains a major article about the controversy over the reserve liabilities that companies should establish for universal life policies with so-called secondary guarantees. For example, one such guarantee (a "no lapse guarantee") says the policy will never lapse (expire) provided premiums are paid at a certain level.

The controversy came to public attention when an actuary in the New York Department of Financial Services sent a strongly worded memorandum to a task force of the National Association of Insurance Commissioners. The actuary said some companies were establishing reserve liabilities that did not meet certain actuarial guidelines. The memorandum created a furor, with some going so far as to suggest that actuaries responsible for the design of such policies should be investigated for possible violations of the actuarial Code of Professional Conduct. Long and difficult discussions followed, eventually leading to a compromise that probably will turn out to be an inadequate solution to the problem.

In my early writings on universal life, I did not anticipate the huge controversy that would arise over the methods used to calculate reserve liabilities for universal life and other new life insurance policies. The life insurance market is now flooded with universal life and other new policies with what may be inadequate reserve liabilities, and what may be devastating potential consequences for life insurance companies and life insurance consumers over the long term.

Nor did I anticipate that the introduction of universal life would lead to the push in recent years for so-called principles-based reserves (PBR). Under PBR, the determination of a company's reserve liabilities would rest with the judgment of the company's actuaries, rather than being prescribed by laws and regulations. Thus the time-tested methods for determining the reserve liabilities associated with traditional cash-value life insurance policies are disappearing from the life insurance landscape. In my view, the move to PBR has the potential to undermine the financial strength of life insurance companies.

Nor did I anticipate the emergence of the secondary market for life insurance, especially stranger-originated life insurance, which is discussed in chapter 9. In my experience, with the exception of viatical transactions involving insured persons who are terminally ill, I have never seen a secondary market transaction involving a traditional cash-value life insurance policy. All of the secondary market transactions that I have seen involve universal life policies with little or no cash value, or term policies with no cash value.

The reason why secondary market investors (speculators in human life) do not buy traditional cash-value policies is that such policies have large cash values (along with large reserve liabilities). The speculators have to offer more than the cash value to the policyholder, because otherwise the policyholder who wishes to dispose of a policy would simply surrender it to the insurance company for the cash value. In other words, secondary market speculators prefer to buy policies that have little or no cash value.

The Phoenix COI Dispute

PHL Variable Insurance Company and Phoenix Life Insurance Company (collectively referred to in this discussion as "Phoenix") are operating subsidiaries of Phoenix Companies, Inc. (NYSE:PNX). In the October 2012 and December 2012 issues of the *Forum*, I wrote about a lawsuit against Phoenix relating to substantial COI increases on 197 universal life policies with death benefits totaling $1.15 billion, an average of $5.8 million per policy. The policies were stranger-originated life insurance, which is discussed in chapter 9. The plaintiff was an investor (speculator) in the secondary market for life insurance, and paid premiums such that the policies built no cash values.

In 2010 Phoenix sharply increased the COI charges on the policies. The policies singled out for the COI increases were those with little or no cash value. The question that arose in the case and in other lawsuits against Phoenix was whether the company had the legal right to single out for COI increases the policies with little or no cash value.

An important aspect of the cases is that the New York Department of Financial Services, after a complaint had been filed with the Department, investigated the "2010 COI increases" and found them to be improper. The Department ordered Phoenix to rescind the increases and refund to policyholders—with interest—the increased COI charges that had been collected, and Phoenix agreed to do so. However, the Department's order applied only to policies issued in New York State.

In 2011 Phoenix imposed another round of COI increases on the New York policyholders. The Department allowed the "2011 COI increases," but it has not been made clear why. Meanwhile, the lawsuits over the "2011 COI increases" in New York are still in progress, but as of June 2015 two of them seem headed for a net settlement of about $27 million.

A complaint was also filed in Wisconsin, where only a few such policies had been issued. The Wisconsin Office of the Commissioner of Insurance found the "2010 COI increases" improper and ordered them rescinded. However, Phoenix refused to rescind those increases on the few Wisconsin policies. An administrative law judge later found in favor of the Office. Phoenix appealed in court, and as of June 2015 the dispute has not been resolved.

Issues Mentioned in This Chapter

November 1981, December 1981, May 1984, June 1984, October 1985, January 1986, January 1987, July 1995, January 1996, July 2001, December 2003, February 2012, October 2012, and December 2012.

11

The Military-Insurance Interlock

*L*ife insurance companies over the years have been reluctant to assume the risk of covering unpredictable numbers of combat deaths. For that reason the U.S. government has long offered life insurance to members of the military. There were differing programs during World War I, World War II, the Korean War, and the Vietnam War.

A Problem for Veterans

In a March 1968 speech I described a problem for some veterans. A group life insurance program had been established by a consortium of life insurance companies led by Prudential Insurance Company of America. Each person on active duty was provided with term life insurance at a low cost. Within 120 days after discharge, the veteran had the right to convert the coverage to cash-value life insurance with no evidence of insurability—in other words, with no questions asked. To exercise the right, the veteran had to buy the new policy from one of many companies licensed to operate in the veteran's state. In Indiana, for example, there were 278 companies. The veteran was provided with a list of the companies and some information, but no guidance on how to choose a favorably priced policy. I suggested the need for price information to help the veteran avoid paying a high price for the converted coverage.

I sent a copy of the speech to Senator Philip Hart (D-MI), who chaired the Subcommittee on Antitrust and Monopoly of the Committee on the Judiciary. My contact was Dean Sharp, a member of Hart's staff. I suggested that Hart ask the Veterans Administration (VA) to compile price information and distribute it to the veterans. Hart made the request, but the VA brushed it off. The incident kindled Hart's interest in life insurance price disclosure. I later described the situation in some detail in the March 1978 issue of the *Forum*.

As mentioned in chapter 6, Hart held a four-day hearing in February 1973 on "The Life Insurance Industry." Ralph Nader was the leadoff witness. In his testimony Nader said:

> Vietnam veterans and other servicemen and women are being victimized by an ongoing military-insurance interlock at the Veterans Administration and the Department of Defense.

Nader undoubtedly had in mind the farewell address—later known as the "military-industrial complex speech"—delivered by President Dwight Eisenhower on January 17, 1961, three days before he left office. Here is the key sentence of his famous warning, which followed a description of the need for a strong military establishment:

> In the councils of government, we must guard against the acquisition of unwarranted influence, whether sought or unsought, by the military-industrial complex.

Ike's expression is in the 11th (2012) edition of *Merriam-Webster's Collegiate Dictionary*. "Military-industrial complex" is defined there as

> an informal alliance of the military and related government departments with defense industries that is held to influence government policy.

The *Army Times* Articles
The July 17, July 31, and August 14, 1974 issues of *Family*,

the biweekly magazine supplement to the *Army Times* and other military newspapers, carried a series of scathing articles entitled "The Brotherhood Built on Insurance." The articles were written by Richard C. Barnard, an associate editor of *Family*. In September 1975 Barnard received for the articles the $1,000 first-place award for excellence in consumer reporting in nationwide competition sponsored by the National Press Club and the Montgomery Ward Foundation.

The *Army Times* articles focused on the Non Commissioned Officers Association of the United States of America (NCOA) and Ammest Group, Inc., a company with ties to NCOA. At the time, policies were being sold to NCOA members by Academy Life Insurance Company, American Defender Life Insurance Company, American Fidelity Life Insurance Company, and Transamerica Life Insurance and Annuity Company. Those policies were reinsured by Ammest Life Insurance Company, which was a subsidiary of Ammest Group.

NCOA, according to the *Army Times* articles, existed "primarily for the purpose of selling high priced life insurance to unsuspecting servicemen." NCOA filed a libel lawsuit against the *Army Times*. In its complaint NCOA denied the allegation that its policies were high priced. The *Army Times* retained me to study the price issue. I did so, and submitted an affidavit in which I concluded that the policy issued by American Defender Life was "high priced relative to similar policies issued by many other companies."

NCOA retained Albert Jacob, a consulting actuary. He disagreed with the conclusion I had drawn, but he offered no analysis in support of his opinion. A decade later, Jacob turned up as a consulting actuary who was heavily involved in the reinsurance scandal at Executive Life, as discussed in chapter 7.

There was another interesting development involving an actuary. In the discovery process in connection with the libel case, the *Army Times* attorneys found a letter that had been written to the president of Ammest Group by William H. Lewis, Jr., a consulting actuary. The letter was dated August 14, 1974, at the very time the *Army Times* articles were being published. The letter showed a price comparison between a policy sold to

NCOA members and similar policies issued by John Hancock Mutual Life Insurance Company, Metropolitan Life Insurance Company, New York Life Insurance Company, and Prudential Insurance Company of America. The Lewis comparison made it appear that the NCOA policy had a lower price than the policies of the other four companies. His methodology, however, was deeply flawed. When I corrected the flaws in his methodology, it was clear that the NCOA policy had a higher price than the policies of the other four companies.

The NCOA's libel lawsuit against the *Army Times* was eventually settled. The terms of the settlement were confidential.

Later I filed a complaint against Lewis with the Society of Actuaries. I alleged that the flawed comparison in his letter to the president of Ammest Group was a violation of the Society's Code of Professional Conduct. The Society never told me the result of my complaint.

I first wrote about the *Army Times* articles in the September 1974 issue of the *Forum*. I described the details of the Lewis comparison in the October 1978 issue.

ALW and the Military

The A. L. Williams organization (ALW) is discussed in chapter 5. ALW at one time was heavily involved in sales activities at military installations. In August 1986 Derek J. Vander Schaaf, deputy inspector general in the Department of Defense (DOD), wrote a memorandum to the secretaries of the Army, Navy, and Air Force asking them to review ALW's sales practices in future inspections. The memorandum referred to ALW's "aggressive sales program." It also mentioned violations of DOD directives, unauthorized solicitation on DOD installations, coercion by senior military personnel in selling insurance to junior personnel, use of personnel files to gain information for insurance sales, failure to comply with state insurance regulatory requirements, and improper advertising.

In November 1986 Barry Clause, ALW's director of compliance, sent a memorandum to all ALW offices with "important new compliance requirements for military selling/recruiting." The strongly worded memorandum amounted to a complete withdrawal of ALW from sales and recruiting activities at military installations and housing near the installations. I was not aware of any government order banning ALW from military installations, but it was difficult to believe that ALW would have withdrawn from the military market in the absence of an order or a pending order. Excerpts from the DOD memorandum and the full text of the Clause memorandum are in the March 1987 issue.

The Banning of Academy Life

In the years following the *Army Times* articles, many problems were identified at military installations relating to the sale of life insurance to members of the military. In 1991, for example, NCOA endorsed the life insurance policies offered by Academy Life Insurance Company. The alliance of NCOA and Academy sold more insurance than any of the other associations and insurance companies that solicited at military bases.

Early in September 1998, following an investigation by the DOD's Office of the Inspector General, the DOD banned Academy for three years from selling life insurance at U.S. military installations throughout the world. On September 27, 1998, CBS's "60 Minutes" ran a segment about the practices of NCOA and Academy. See the March 2003 issue.

The Cuthbert Report

Among the problems at military installations were deceptive sales practices, and even more seriously, pressure exerted by senior noncommissioned personnel on junior enlisted personnel to buy life insurance. DOD contracted with Science Applications International Corporation (SAIC), a research and engineering firm.

SAIC retained Thomas Cuthbert, a retired U.S. Army brigadier general, to conduct a study. In his report, which was dated May 15, 2000, the key recommendation was to "eliminate on base insurance solicitation." Cuthbert said DOD did not have the personnel and other resources needed to protect members of the military from violations of the regulations that had been promulgated by DOD.

U.S. Senators Tim Hutchinson, James Inhofe, and Rick San-
torum, each of whom chaired a subcommittee of the Armed Services Committee, wrote a joint letter to Bernard Rostker, a DOD
undersecretary, urging that problems be handled on a case-
by-case basis rather than by imposing a ban. Rostker agreed,
and the Cuthbert report was shelved without a congressional
hearing. What is now the National Association of Insurance
and Financial Advisors, an insurance agents' association, took
credit for derailing Cuthbert's recommendations. See the June
2001 issue.

The DOJ Lawsuit against Academy Life

In December 2002 the U.S. Department of Justice (DOJ) filed
a civil complaint against Academy, and simultaneously settled
the case. The lawsuit grew out of an investigation by DOD's
Criminal Investigation Service and the Federal Bureau of Investigation into Academy's sales practices directed at military personnel. The company denied the allegations but agreed to pay
a total of $16 million in penalties, costs, and restitution, agreed
never to reapply for permission to sell life insurance at military installations, and agreed it would never sell life insurance
again. The case is discussed in the March 2003 issue.

The *Times* Articles

In July 2004, in the face of mounting problems in Iraq, *The
New York Times* ran a series of scathing articles by financial
investigative reporter Diana B. Henriques about abusive life
insurance sales practices directed at military personnel. The
first article in the series ran above the fold on the front page
of the newspaper. Henriques received three major journalism
awards for the articles.

The *Times* articles generated intense pressure for reform.
First, the DOJ filed a criminal complaint against American-
Amicable Life Insurance Company alleging violations of mail
fraud and wire fraud statutes. The complaint was settled
through a consent order containing the company's denial of the
allegations and alluding to a complaint by the Securities and
Exchange Commission (SEC) and a multistate settlement with

insurance regulators. The order provided for "compensation relief" for affected military personnel, injunctive relief limiting insurance agents' access to military personnel, and compliance procedures.

Second, the SEC filed a civil complaint against American-Amicable alleging violations of federal securities laws. The complaint was settled, and the SEC became part of the multistate settlement with insurance regulators.

Third, at least 39 state insurance regulators entered into a multistate settlement. An estimated 57,000 current and former service members received cash refunds and modifications to existing policies, and another 13,000 service members and 22,000 civilians received increased cash surrender benefits. The cost of the settlement was estimated at $70 million, and the company was banned from military bases for five years.

Fourth, in September 2006, Congress enacted the Military Personnel Financial Services Protection Act. The purpose of the law was "To protect members of the Armed Forces from unscrupulous practices regarding sales of insurance, financial, and investment products."

I wrote about the *Times* articles and the various developments that grew out of those articles. See the November/December 2006 issue of the *Forum*.

Issues Mentioned in This Chapter

September 1974, March 1978, October 1978, March 1987, June 2001, March 2003, and November/December 2006.

12

Distortion of Important Policy Provisions

Over the course of my academic career, including the *Forum* years, I studied some important provisions of life insurance policies. In several instances, I found situations where provisions that were intended to protect policyholders and beneficiaries instead operated against the interests of those individuals. In this chapter I discuss a few of those situations.

Grace and Reinstatement

The lead article in the February 1974 (second) issue of the *Forum* was entitled "How to Pay Premiums for 'A Piece of the Rock' and Have No Insurance Protection." The Prudential Insurance Company of America has long used the Rock of Gibraltar as the company's logo, and in advertising campaigns has long urged people to "own a piece of the Rock." The provocative title of the article created something of a stir, and caused some people to think I had started a scandal sheet. The subject of the article may be described in general terms as the interplay between the payment of monthly premiums and the operation of two important policy clauses relating to the grace period and reinstatement.

The grace period clause says the policy remains in force for 31 days following the due date of the premium. The clause has long been required by state insurance laws, and is intended to protect the policyholder and the beneficiary in the event of an inadvertent delay in the payment of a premium. Suppose, for example, the policyholder fails to pay a premium by the due date, and the insured dies during the grace period. The policy would remain in full force, and the company would pay the full death benefit minus the amount of the unpaid premium.

A related clause is the reinstatement clause, which allows a policyholder to reinstate a discontinued policy by paying the premiums that had not been paid and providing "satisfactory evidence of insurability." That phrase refers to evidence that the insured's health and other characteristics have not deteriorated. Some companies by practice allow the policyholder to reinstate without evidence of insurability—in other words, with no questions asked—for 31 days following the end of the grace period, provided the overdue premium is paid at the time of reinstatement. However, if the policy has not yet developed any cash value that could be used to extend the insurance protection, the policy would not be in force during the 31 days beyond the grace period.

Therefore, if the policyholder consistently pays each monthly premium 62 days after the due date, there would be no insurance protection because when each premium is paid the policy again would be at the end of the grace period. In other words, if the insured person dies during the 31 days after the end of the grace period, the policy would not be in force and the death benefit would not be paid.

My interest in the subject grew out of a $10,000 cash-value life insurance policy (with a $10,000 additional accidental death benefit) that Prudential issued on March 18, 1967 on the life of David. He was a 19-year-old Kansas resident who died in an automobile accident on December 26, 1968. His parents were the beneficiaries of the policy.

The article in the February 1974 issue was a brief discussion of the case. Six years later I devoted the entire four-page April 1980 issue to the case. The latter issue was dedicated to the memory of Lloyd Hall, the Kansas attorney who represented David's family and persisted in the case for almost seven years until he obtained an acceptable settlement.

The premiums for the policy were $13.80 per month. David

paid the first monthly premium with the application. The premiums for the next 13 months were paid at, shortly before, or shortly after the expiration of the grace period. The premiums for the next three months were paid late, and the policy was reinstated. The premiums for the next three months were also paid late (in November 1968), and the policy was again reinstated. The premium due November 18, 1968, was never paid. David died seven days after the expiration of the grace period for that premium.

The family's banker informed Prudential of David's death the day after the accident. On the day of the funeral, a company representative informed David's parents by telephone that the insurance was not in force. A month later David's parents received a letter from the company confirming that the insurance was not in force.

David's parents filed a complaint with the Kansas Insurance Department. After considerable correspondence, and with Prudential continuing to argue that the policy was not in force at the time of David's death, the Department said there was nothing more it could do.

In December 1970 David's parents filed a lawsuit against Prudential. Initially they sought the $20,000 death benefit (including the accidental death benefit) and attorney fees. Later they learned through the discovery process that, if the company had followed certain procedures it already had in place, the policy would have been in force when David died. For example, the company had a procedure by which David could have reinstated the policy by redating—that is, by advancing the policy date so that the premiums paid in November 1968 would have kept the policy in force well beyond the date of death—but David was never informed of that procedure. David's parents thereupon amended the lawsuit to seek $10,000 of damages for mental anguish and $20 million of punitive damages.

Eventually the case was settled on confidential terms. From public documents I learned that Prudential paid the $20,000 death benefit, and that the Kansas law firm retained by the company to defend the case received about $300,000 from the company during the time the case was active. I assume that the company, in the settlement, paid Hall's attorney fees and also paid David's parents a substantial amount in view of the extraordinary difficulties to which they had been subjected.

The Insuring Agreement

The February 1974 issue of the *Forum* also contained an article provocatively titled "What Equitable of New York Does to Beneficiaries." The article related to the insuring agreement, which is a central clause in any policy. Here is the typical language of the insuring agreement in a life insurance policy:

> The XYZ Life Insurance Company promises to pay the face amount to the beneficiary upon receipt at our home office of due proof of death of the insured, subject to the terms and conditions of this policy. All benefits will be payable subject to the policy provisions.

The language above leaves open the question of whether the company will pay interest on the death benefit from the date of the insured's death to the date of the check. That question was the subject of my article, which compared the differing practices of Equitable Life Assurance Society of the United States and Northwestern Mutual Life Insurance Company.

In the 1950s Equitable and Northwestern each issued a $100,000 policy on George's life. George died on September 1, 1973. Each company received the death claim, with the death certificate, on October 1. It is my understanding that there was a delay in obtaining the death certificate because an autopsy was needed.

Each company issued its check on October 22, but the amounts differed despite the fact that the policies had the same death benefit. George's beneficiary sought an explanation, and learned that Equitable added interest for six days while Northwestern added interest for the entire 51 days from the date of death to the date of the check.

Equitable, in response to the beneficiary's request for further explanation, said the policy provided for payment of the death benefit "upon receipt at our home office of due proof of death of the insured." That policy language accounted for the company's failure to pay interest for the 30 days between the date of death and the date of the company's receipt of proof of death. Equitable's explanation prompted me to include in the article this comment, which some readers found offensive:

> If Equitable's agent does the job properly, the agent would be at the insured's bedside to complete the papers the instant the physician pulls the sheet over the insured's face. An alternative would be for the agent to tell the beneficiary not to be concerned because it only costs a trivial $14 (at 5 percent annual interest on the $100,000 death benefit) for each day of delay.

However, Equitable did not stop there. The company went on to explain its belief that, after receipt of proof of death, the company was entitled to a reasonable period of 15 days within which to process the payment. In other words, the company relied on the precise language of the insuring agreement to avoid paying interest for 30 days, and then deviated from the precise language of the insuring agreement to avoid paying interest for another 15 days.

I disagreed with both parts of Equitable's reasoning. I believed (and it was obvious Northwestern agreed with me) that George's death should have been viewed as the triggering event, and that the company should have been obligated to pay the death benefit immediately. In other words, from the date of death the death benefit should be viewed as the beneficiary's property, and any delay in payment should entitle the beneficiary to interest from the date of death to the date of the check.

About two months after my article was published, I received a telephone call from an Equitable agent who was a subscriber to the *Forum*. He said the company had announced to its field force that the company had changed its practice and had begun to pay interest from the date of death to the date of the check.

About 18 months after my first article on the subject, I conducted a survey in an effort to learn about the practices of other life insurance companies regarding the payment of interest after the insured's death. As mentioned in the August 1975 issue, I wrote to 129 companies and received responses from 63. Only 28 respondents said they pay interest from the date of death to the date of the check. Eight of the 35 other respondents said they were considering a change in their procedures.

Several years after my first article on the subject, I received a memorable telephone call out of the blue from a man in Equitable's claims department. He made five points: (1) the claims department had long wanted to change the company's practice with regard to the payment of interest after the insured's death, (2) the department had not been able to get its proposed change on the agenda of the company's board of directors, (3) my article had gotten the proposal on the agenda, (4) the proposal had been adopted, and (5) the members of the department were grateful for my article. I never learned what prompted him to call me. However, I think he was about to retire and wanted to set the record straight about the views of the members of the company's claims department.

Some states today have laws or regulations requiring payment of interest from the date of death. I think most reputable companies now pay interest from the date of death.

The Incontestability Clause

The incontestability clause says that, after a policy has been in force for two years (one year in some policies), the insurance company is barred from challenging the validity of a policy on the basis of false statements made in the application for the policy. State laws requiring the incontestability clause were enacted many years ago because some disreputable companies refused to pay the death benefit many years after a policy was issued by claiming there was a false statement in the application for the policy. Thus policyholders never knew whether their life insurance would serve its purpose because they could never be certain the insurance company would honor a death claim. Reputable companies had trouble convincing people the companies could be trusted, and they urged state legislators to enact incontestability laws. Here is typical language of the incontestability clause:

> This policy shall be incontestable after it has been in force
> during the lifetime of the insured for two years from its effec-
> tive date except for nonpayment of premiums and except as
> to any provision for disability or accidental death benefits.

The September 1985 issue of the *Forum* contained an article entitled "What the Word 'Incontestable' Really Means."
I explained that the incontestability clause is very strong, but
I pointed out that courts in some states had made exceptions in
cases where misstatements made in applications were viewed
as particularly egregious.

As examples I mentioned three extraordinary cases in Pennsylvania. In one case, a woman impersonated her sister in taking
the medical examination for a life insurance policy. In another
case, a man impersonated his father. In yet another case, a truly
astounding one, an applicant who was a physician impersonated his own attending physician by arranging to intercept
the insurance company's request for an attending physician's
statement and forging his attending physician's signature on
a statement containing false information about the applicant's
health. In all three cases, the deaths occurred after the end of the
contestability period, but the courts allowed the companies to
rescind the policies and merely refund the premiums that had
been paid.

In the secondary market for life insurance (discussed in
chapter 9), there have been many cases where false information
was provided in life insurance applications, especially regarding the income or wealth of the proposed insured. In some
cases, courts ruled in favor of the companies and allowed them
to rescind the policies, but in other cases ruled in favor of the
policyholders by saying the incontestability clause barred the
companies from challenging statements made in applications.

With reference to the stranger-originated life insurance
component of the secondary market for life insurance, a special situation exists with respect to "insurable interest." An
applicant (other than the proposed insured) for a life insurance policy is said to have an insurable interest in the life of the
proposed insured when the applicant has either a close family

relationship or a close business relationship to the proposed insured. In many cases, courts have allowed companies to rescind policies—even after the expiration of the contestability period—when the party behind the application did not have an insurable interest in the life of the proposed insured.

The Suicide Clause

The January 1978 issue contained an article entitled "A Life Insurance Tragedy." The incident involved the interplay between the replacement problem (discussed in chapter 4) and the suicide clause in life insurance policies.

Life insurance companies usually include a suicide clause in their policies. Under that clause, the full death benefit is paid even though the insured person commits suicide, provided the suicide occurs more than two years (one year in some policies) after the policy is issued. However, when suicide occurs within two years (one year in some policies), the premiums that had been paid by the policyholder are refunded to the beneficiary and the death benefit is not paid.

Peter owned four life insurance policies issued by Bankers Life Company (Des Moines, IA), which is now Principal Life Insurance Company. The policies were issued from 1955 to 1962. Their combined death benefit was $52,000. All were issued on a standard basis; that is, the premiums were not increased because of health or other problems.

By October 1972 Peter had financial, health, and marital problems. After consulting with his Bankers Life agent, Peter purchased a new $15,000 policy with a rider that provided an additional $45,760 of decreasing-term life insurance. The new policy was issued on a substandard basis; that is, it involved a higher-than-standard premium presumably because of Peter's health problems. The old policies and the new policy all contained the usual two-year suicide clause.

To pay the first annual premium on the new policy, Peter surrendered three of the four old policies. In October 1973, to pay the second annual premium on the new policy, Peter surrendered the fourth and last of the old policies. The replacement was inappropriate and unjustified for several reasons, such as the substandard rating of the new policy, the front-end expenses associated with the new policy, and the fact that Peter could·have maintai؈d the old policies by paying premiums through the use of policy loans.

In April 1974, at age 44, Peter committed suicide. Bankers paid the beneficiary $1,842, which was the sum of the two annual premiums that Peter had paid on the new policy. The company explained that the suicide clause limited the company to returning the premiums.

Peter's estate went to court. Four years later, just before trial, the case was settled for $23,000. It was not clear from court papers how much the estate netted from the settlement after the payment of attorney fees.

There is no perfect solution to the problem of suicide in connection with life insurance. If suicide were fully covered throughout the duration of a policy, the sale of a new policy might be considered as encouraging suicide and thereby contrary to the public interest. On the other hand, if suicide were excluded throughout the duration of a policy, the policy might not serve its function of protecting the family of the insured person because the company would deny the death claim many years after the policy was issued if the insured person committed suicide. Thus the clause excluding suicide for two years and covering suicide during the remaining years of a policy is a compromise between two imperfect solutions to the problem.

The Age Clause

In the April 1974 issue of the *Forum* I mentioned a campaign waged by the late Professor Oscar Goodman of Roosevelt University in Chicago. He called attention to abuses related to the age clause (often called the "misstatement-of-age" clause) that is required by state laws. Here is the language of the typical age clause:

> If the age of the Insured has been misstated, any amount payable under any of the provisions of this policy will be the amount that the premiums paid would have purchased at the correct age.

Here is how the age clause works. If the age of the insured is misstated in the policy, the death benefit would be adjusted upward or downward to the death benefit that the premiums paid would have purchased at the insured's correct age.

Consider a simplified example. The annual premium for a $100,000 policy on the life of a person aged 35 was $2,400, or $24 per $1,000. The policy, which was issued based on information in the application for the policy, said the insured was aged 35. The insured died exactly 30 years later. The death certificate filed with the company as proof of death said the insured was aged 70 at the time of death. If the policy had said the insured was aged 40 when it was issued, the $2,400 annual premium would have purchased an $80,000 policy, because the annual premium for age 40 was $30 per $1,000. The insurance company therefore reduced the death benefit from $100,000 to $80,000.

In other words, if the age of the insured is understated in the policy, the death benefit would be reduced. If the age of the insured is overstated in the policy, the death benefit would be increased. Until I saw Goodman's criticism of the age clause, I thought the provision was eminently logical, and I had never considered its potential for the abuse of beneficiaries.

In the December 1968 issue of *The Journal of Risk and Insurance*, Goodman wrote a blistering article about the age clause. Here are a few of the abuses or potential abuses he identified:

• To simplify the sale of a policy, the company does not demand proof of age when a policy is applied for.

• To simplify the underwriting of a policy, the company does not verify the age stated in the application.

• To simplify the payment of a death claim, the company does not verify the age stated in the death certificate.

• When the death benefit is reduced because of an age discrepancy that favors the company, the beneficiary may face a daunting task in obtaining proof that the age stated in the death certificate is incorrect, especially in the case of an insured who was born in a foreign country.

• The company may reduce the death benefit when an age discrepancy favors the company and not increase the death benefit when the discrepancy favors the beneficiary.

One of Goodman's recommendations was that state legislatures eliminate the age clause as a required provision in life insurance policies. I think that would not solve the problem, because companies could include an age clause in their policies as an optional clause. In other words, to eliminate the clause, it would be necessary to enact legislation prohibiting it. Also, in the absence of an age clause, I do not know how companies should deal with age discrepancies.

Another of Goodman's recommendations was to extend the protection afforded by the incontestability clause to cover age discrepancies. That is an interesting idea that might be worthy of exploration, but I think the idea has not been considered.

One of Goodman's harshest criticisms was that some companies use the age clause when the adjustment favors the company and ignore the age clause when the adjustment favors the beneficiary. However, he did not cite specific examples of such a practice. When I learned of an example, I wrote an article in the September 1976 issue of the *Forum*. On page 213 in the examination report on Mutual Life Insurance Company of New York as of December 31, 1972, the examiner said:

> When the death benefit is reduced, the reduced check and explanation are given to the beneficiary. When the proof of death shows a younger age, payment is made on the basis of the birth date in the application. It appears that these practices were discussed with the Company at the time of the previous examination, but that no change was made in such procedures. It is the opinion of the examiner that the Company's policy on age discrepancies should be consistent. The Company has indicated that the procedures will be revised.

Goodman presented a statement to the appropriate committee at the 1969 annual meeting of the National Association of Insurance Commissioners. However, his statement was ignored, and was not even included in the published proceedings of the meeting. Therefore, Goodman submitted the statement to *The Journal of Risk and Insurance*, which published the statement in the March 1971 issue of the *Journal*.

I consider this matter a subject worthy of attention for many reasons, of which the following are a few. First, as Goodman said, companies do not demand proof of age when policies are issued, thus making policies easier to sell. Second, the age shown on the death certificate may be determined simply by someone asking a bereaved family member: "How old was he?" Third, placing on the beneficiary the burden of disproving the age on the death certificate is regrettable, because it is often impossible to obtain reliable proof of age. To my knowledge, nothing has been done by life insurance companies or regulators to address Goodman's concerns.

Beneficiaries and Settlement Options
    The owner of a life insurance policy designates the beneficiary who is to receive the death benefit, and may designate or allow the beneficiary to designate whether the death benefit is to be paid in one sum or through settlement options, which are installment payments over a period of time. Because a life insurance policy may be in force for a long time, and because family circumstances may change significantly, it is important to make sure beneficiary designations and settlement options are changed as necessary to prevent them from becoming out of date.

    The May 1979 issue of the *Forum* contained an article entitled "The Case of the Outdated Settlement Agreement." In 1929 Stewart purchased a $5,000 policy from New York Life Insurance Company and named his wife Susan the beneficiary. In 1941 he selected a settlement option under which Susan was to receive the death benefit in monthly installments for the rest of her life. When he died in 1977, Susan was aged 91, and the payments were about $29 per month. Susan and her family asked the company to pay the proceeds to her in one sum, but the company felt (and I also felt) that it had no choice but to honor the ancient settlement agreement. The agreement possibly was appropriate under conditions in 1941 when Susan was 55, but it was certainly inappropriate under conditions in 1977 when Susan was 91. The case illustrated the drawbacks of rigid settlement agreements that are not frequently reviewed.

The October 2013 issue of the *Forum* contained an article entitled "Minnesota Life's 'New' and 'Unique' Irrevocable Settlement Option." In February 2013, Minnesota Life Insurance Company issued a press release announcing a new policy that included a provision called an income protection agreement (IPA). The IPA provides

> an irrevocable settlement option that pays part or all of the policy's death benefit as a guaranteed monthly or annual benefit over a specified installment period. The schedule of payments is determined at issue and may not be altered while the policy is in force.

When the policy is applied for, the applicant decides what portion of the death benefit (not less than 50 percent) is to be paid under the IPA, the period over which the installments are to be paid (at least ten years), and the frequency of the installments (monthly or annually). I asked the company several questions about the IPA, but received no reply.

I was appalled by the rigidity of the settlement arrangements because of the virtual certainty that the arrangements would become inappropriate with the passage of time. The IPA was widely approved by state insurance regulators. I asked the Indiana and Nebraska Departments of Insurance to reconsider the matter. Indiana withdrew its approval. Nebraska also reconsidered but took no action.

Issues Mentioned in This Chapter

February 1974, April 1974, August 1975, September 1976, January 1978, May 1979, April 1980, September 1985, and October 2013.

13

Deceptive Sales Practices

$\mathcal{D}$uring my academic career I became interested in the subject of deceptive sales practices in the life insurance business. The subject is closely related to my work on measuring prices of the protection component and rates of return on the savings component of cash-value policies. When reliable information about prices and rates of return is not available in the market, the void is filled by deceptive information.

The Nature of Deception

It is important to make clear the meaning of the word deceptive and how it differs from the word fraudulent. Here is how I have drawn the distinction in my work:

> A presentation is deceptive when it tends to give the recipient an erroneous impression of important relationships. The emphasis is on the recipient. When I describe a presentation as deceptive, I do not intend to suggest that the deception is necessarily deliberate on the part of the presenter. On the other hand, when the presenter understands the presentation and deliberately gives the recipient an erroneous impression of important relationships, the presentation is fraudulent.

Categories of Deception

As discussed in chapter 6, U.S. Senator Philip Hart conducted four days of hearings in February 1973 on life insurance.

In my testimony there, I discussed not only the need for rigorous disclosure of prices and rates of return, but also the subject of deceptive sales practices. Later I wrote a major article in the June 1974 issue of *The Journal of Risk and Insurance* about deceptive sales practices. In my testimony and in the article, I divided deceptive sales practices into three categories, which for convenience I labeled class A, class B, and class C deception.

Class A Deception

Class A deception involves the misallocation of interest. I illustrate the concept with a savings account analogy. A person puts $1,000 into a savings account at the beginning of each year for ten years and makes no withdrawals. The account earns 5 percent interest compounded annually. With reference to the first two years and the last two years of the ten-year period, here is the amount of interest credited to the account at the end of the year and the balance in the account at the end of the year:

Year	Interest	Balance
1	$ 50	$ 1,050
2	103	2,153
—	—	—
9	551	11,578
10	629	13,207

The interest credited at the end of the tenth year is $629. Suppose someone says: "This wonderful account pays 62.9 percent interest ($629 divided by $1,000)! Isn't that fantastic?" In other words, in the tenth year the depositor puts in $1,000 at the beginning of the year and earns $629 of interest at the end of the year. The presentation is deceptive because all the interest earned in the tenth year is allocated to the tenth-year payment. In fact only $50 of the interest credited at the end of the tenth year should be allocated to the tenth-year payment, and the remaining $579 should be allocated to prior years' payments. As stated at the outset, the account earns 5 percent interest each year. Over the years I have seen many examples of interest misallocation. Three of them are described here.

The Harris Article

Richard Harris, a Texas agent of American General Life Insurance Company, wrote an article that appeared in the February 1970 issue of *Life Insurance Selling* magazine. In the article, Harris presented an exciting sales idea that he said he had been presenting at many luncheon meetings of agents. The idea was designed to persuade people to buy cash-value life insurance rather than term life insurance, or to convert term life insurance to cash-value life insurance.

The heart of the idea was a table showing, among other figures, that $989 was the difference between the tenth-year premium for a $100,000 cash-value life insurance policy and the tenth-year premium for a $100,000 decreasing term life insurance policy. The cash value of the cash-value policy increased in the tenth year by $1,427.

Harris said the policyholder earned a spectacular 44.3 percent tenth-year rate of return on the premium difference ($1,427 divided by $989, minus 1, with the result expressed as a percentage). The problem was that he allocated the entire tenth-year increase in the cash value to the premium difference in the tenth year. If he had used a proper formula (see the formula for the yearly rate of return discussed in chapter 6 and shown in appendix A) to allocate the increase, the rate of return on the savings component in the tenth year of the cash-value policy would have been 3.8 percent, based on a reasonable assumption about the yearly price per $1,000 of the protection component in the tenth year. Thus the relationship between 44.3 percent and 3.8 percent is comparable to the relationship between 62.9 percent and 5 percent in the savings account analogy.

I was personally acquainted with an actuary at American General Life. I sent him my Senate testimony, in which I had included the Harris idea. The actuary agreed with me. He was so appalled that he presented Harris's sales idea at a meeting of the company's board of directors. He told me he regretted doing that because an elderly director turned so red when he saw the sales technique that the actuary feared the director might suffer a stroke. The company invited Harris to the home office to discuss the matter. The actuary told me Harris was a successful salesman but could not be made to understand the problem with his sales idea. However, the company extracted a promise from him to refrain from using the technique in sales presentations, articles, or speeches to agents.

The Provident Advertisement

Provident Life and Accident Insurance Company ran an advertisement in the April 1970 issue of *Life Insurance Selling* magazine. The company showed some figures for a $100,000 cash-value policy. The annual premium each year was $1,689, and the cash value increased in the third year by $1,700. In the advertisement, the company emphasized the "extraordinary" third-year "net cost" of minus $11 ($1,689 – $1,700).

The problem is that the company allocated the entire third-year increase in the cash value to the premium paid in the third year. If the company had used a proper formula (see the formula for the yearly price per $1,000 of protection discussed in chapter 6) to allocate the increase, the third-year price would have been $1.69 per $1,000 of protection (assuming an interest rate of 5 percent on the savings component).

This is the advertisement that led to the actuarial club incident described in chapter 3. As mentioned there, some of the actuaries disagreed with me when I said the advertisement was deceptive, and their explanations were inane.

The Northwestern Mutual Advertisements

Northwestern Mutual Life Insurance Company (Milwaukee, WI) was a television sponsor of the 1976 Summer Olympics. The company ran an advertisement based on what I later called the "dividend exceeds the premium" theme. The advertisement incorporated interest misallocation, and my first article about the advertisement was in the February 1977 issue of the *Forum*. Here is the full text of the advertisement:

> LEAD-IN: Northwestern Mutual Life works hard to earn your trust ... as experience shows ...
> MAN: The other day I was going through some of my bills. And when I got to my life insurance bills, I found that

the dividend on one of my older Northwestern policies was actually more than the annual premium. Well, I figured it was a mistake. So I checked with my agent. He told me the same thing happened on 290,000 Northwestern policies last year alone! You know, I had some other insurance when I bought my first Northwestern policy. Since then I've noticed that the Northwestern has been a real leader. It's in the way the dividends they've paid exceeded the ones they showed me when I first bought my policies. And, the longer I've had Northwestern policies, the more I've appreciated that.

TAG: Northwestern Mutual Life ... The Quiet Company. Putting minds at ease for over a century.

The problem is that the advertisement allocated all the interest to the current year, but much of the interest should have been allocated to prior years. (See the savings account analogy earlier in this chapter.) I asked a company spokesman what significance should be attached to the fact that the dividend exceeds the premium. Instead of answering the question, he dodged it by saying the advertisement showed "valid insight into the treatment of old policyholders." That comment prompted me to write a follow-up article in the July 1977 issue showing how a company could demonstrate its favorable treatment of old policyholders without using interest misallocation.

Northwestern continued to use the "dividend exceeds the premium" theme in its advertising, and I complained to the Wisconsin insurance commissioner. He said the advertisement was not deceptive, but expressed concern to the company over the absence of a statement that a year's dividend is not related to the year's premium. See the June 1978 issue.

Northwestern did not include the statement and continued to run the advertisements. I continued to criticize them and annoy the commissioner, without results. Eventually I gave up.

Several years later an interesting development occurred. I did not mention it in the *Forum* because I considered it old news, but I will mention it here. I received a call from a woman at J. Walter Thompson, the advertising agency handling the Northwestern account. She said that they were working on a new advertising campaign, and that Northwestern asked her to call me. She said she did not know the reason for the request. I knew the reason, and suggested she buy reprints of certain issues of the *Forum*. She did so. She never called back, but I never again saw a Northwestern advertisement based on the "dividend exceeds the premium" theme.

Class B Deception

Class B deception involves comparisons of dollar amounts payable at different times without considering the time value of money. For example, comparisons are often made between the simple total of a series of payments spread over a period of years and a lump sum payable either at the beginning of the period or at the end of the period. (See the discussion of the traditional net cost method in chapter 6.)

I illustrate the concept with a work contract analogy. Jones retained Smith to do a particular job. It was understood that, upon satisfactory completion of the job, Smith would receive $1,000 per year for forty years, a simple total of $40,000. After satisfactorily completing the job, Smith asked Jones to begin the payments. At that point, Jones said:

> Smith, you have done such a great job that I am going to pay you 10 percent more than we originally agreed upon. I am going to pay you $600 per year for thirty years and $2,600 per year for the final ten years. That is a total of $44,000, which is 10 percent more than the $40,000 I originally agreed to pay you. Isn't that generous of me?

Jones failed to consider the time value of money. At an annual interest rate of 5 percent, the present value of the payments under the original agreement was $18,017, and the present value of the payments under the modified agreement was $14,562. Thus what Jones described as an arrangement providing 10 percent more than originally agreed upon provided 19 percent less, assuming 5 percent interest.

The Brinton Speech

Dilworth Brinton, an Arizona agent of the New York Life

Insurance Company, gave a speech at the 1970 annual meeting of what is now the National Association of Insurance and Financial Advisors. His speech dealt with certain purported advantages of cash-value insurance over term insurance. He sought to illustrate the price superiority of cash-value insurance compared to term insurance. He said the "net return over cost" (the price generated by the traditional net cost method) of the cash-value policy for the first 40 years was minus $30,923, and the cost of the term policy (the simple total of the premiums) for the first 40 years was $34,579. He then concluded that, for the 40-year period, the "total difference" in favor of the cash-value policy was $65,502 ($30,923 + $34,579). I discussed Brinton's technique in the February 1981 issue.

The problem was Brinton's failure to recognize the time value of money. When an annual interest rate of 5 percent was used, the "total difference" in favor of the cash-value policy was $570 rather than $65,502. At 6 percent, the comparison slightly favored the term policy. Thus the prices of the two policies were similar, and the choice should have been based on the circumstances of the client rather than relative prices.

A Further Exaggeration

With reference to a participating (dividend-paying) life insurance policy, the policyholder has several options concerning how the dividend each year should be used. The common options are: (1) apply the dividend toward the premium that is currently due, (2) have the company send a check in payment of the dividend, (3) use the dividend to buy a small amount of so-called paid-up life insurance, and (4) leave the dividend with the insurance company to accumulate at interest.

One of the steps in class B deception is to calculate the simple total of the dividends payable over a period of years. I recall one presentation that included not the simple total of the dividends, but rather the dividends accumulated with interest under the fourth option mentioned in the previous paragraph. Subtracting the accumulated dividends from the simple total of the premiums generated an even larger negative result than subtracting the simple total of the dividends from the simple total of the premiums. In other words, it exaggerated the already deceptive results of class B deception.

Class C Deception

Class C deception involves presentations that are simply false. Over the years I have seen many examples of this form of deception. A few examples are discussed here.

Frank McIntosh

In the 1970s Frank McIntosh was a harsh critic of cash-value life insurance. He published a booklet purporting to show the price superiority of term life over cash-value life insurance. The formula he used to calculate the price of the cash-value insurance was wrong in several respects. (I called his formula an abomination.) It would serve no useful purpose to show the formula and explain all the problems associated with it. It is sufficient to say the biggest problem with the formula was the failure to recognize that the cash value increases from one year to the next. He said, for example, that the "yearly cost per $1,000" in the tenth year of a hypothetical $100,000 cash-value policy was $173.60, as contrasted with $5.61 for a hypothetical $100,000 term life policy. When I applied the proper formula for the yearly price per $1,000 of protection in the cash-value policy (see chapter 6), I arrived at $8.93, assuming 5 percent interest.

Venita Van Caspel

Venita Van Caspel, a financial planner, wrote several books giving financial advice to consumers. In a 1975 book, her life insurance chapter was entitled "Life Insurance: The Great National Consumer Fraud?" In a 1980 book, it was "Life Insurance: Still the National Insurance Dilemma."

Van Caspel used a formula purporting to show the price superiority of term life insurance over cash-value life insurance. Her formula was wrong in several respects, but the most important problem was the failure to recognize that the cash value increases from one policy year to the next. In other words, the primary problem was precisely the same as the primary problem in the formula used by McIntosh.

Other Examples of Class C Deception

Over the years there have been many other examples of Class C deception. Most of them have been presented by harsh critics of cash-value life insurance, and generally, as in the examples cited above, they fail to recognize that the cash value increases from one policy year to the next.

An early item is a 1936 book by Mort and E. A. Gilbert entitled *Life Insurance: A Legalized Racket.* (The book is mentioned in chapter 2.) Others are a 1963 book by Norman Dacey entitled *What's Wrong with Your Life Insurance,* a 1966 book by Robert Karhoff entitled *This Is Where Your Money Goes,* and a 1968 book by Scott Reynolds entitled *The Mortality Merchants.*

One of the most extreme examples of Class C deception of which I am aware was the practice of the A. L. Williams organization to ignore cash values entirely. The organization claimed that term life insurance is lower in price than cash-value life insurance solely by comparing the premiums. That practice was mentioned briefly in chapter 5.

The LEAP System

In 2001 I received inquiries from many readers about a life insurance marketing system called the Lifetime Economic Acceleration Process, or LEAP. I reviewed LEAP advertisements in the insurance trade press, and I reviewed the LEAP website. I attempted to contact LEAP headquarters, but received no response. I contacted some life insurance companies that had endorsed LEAP. I received some responses but no specific information. Robert Castiglione created LEAP and was the chief executive officer of LEAP SYSTEMS, Inc. He called me, apparently at the request of a company I had contacted.

That call was the beginning of a protracted but unsuccessful effort to obtain detailed information from LEAP. Castiglione offered to meet with me for two days to explain LEAP. I insisted on obtaining detailed information that I could study prior to the meeting. Castiglione refused to send me detailed information in advance so that I could prepare for the meeting. We were never able to resolve the standoff. I obtained detailed information about LEAP elsewhere.

From late 2001 through early 2003, articles about LEAP appeared in ten issues of the *Forum*. Here are a few excerpts from my April 2002 special 12-page LEAP issue:

> LEAP uses fancy phrases such as "personal financial engineering," "velocity of money," and "protection and savings growth" to make the simple proposition that the client's wealth supposedly can be increased by moving money around. Irrespective of the client's present financial situation, LEAP says the situation can be improved substantially by diverting funds into cash-value life insurance.
>
> LEAP says everything other than cash-value life insurance is a "problem." Municipal bonds, money market accounts, 401(k) plans, term life insurance, mortgages with rapidly shrinking balances, dollar cost averaging, and the needs approach to selling life insurance are problems. Castiglione says compound interest is a "wealth-eroding concept" and a "nightmare" rather than a "miracle." LEAP emphasizes that the improvement in the client's financial situation can be accomplished at "no additional out-of-pocket cost." It is my opinion that the latter expression is deceptive.
>
> At its heart, LEAP consists of two steps. First, LEAP exaggerates the costs associated with the client's current financial situation, no matter what the situation is, to make it look bad. Second, LEAP exaggerates the benefits of the "ideal plan," which involves the diversion of funds into cash-value life insurance, to make it look good.

I have not followed LEAP closely since 2003. According to a March 2014 press release from Penn Mutual Life Insurance Company, LEAP became an affiliate of Penn Mutual in September 2012.

Two Troubling Incidents

When I was writing and testifying about deceptive sales practices, I received occasional invitations to address insurance groups on the subject. In addition to the actuarial club incident described in chapter 3, there were two incidents that were troubling and in a sense related to one another.

The first incident grew out of an invitation to address life insurance agents who were members of the local chapter of a national organization. After my talk, an agent came to me with tears in his eyes. He said that he had listened carefully, and that he agreed with me. He said he had sold life insurance to family members, close friends, and other faithful clients using precisely the deceptive techniques I had described. He was obviously distraught. I tried to console him, because I was quite concerned about his state of mind.

The second incident grew out of an invitation I received to address senior executives of small life insurance companies who had been invited to a conference sponsored by a reinsurance company. After my talk, which was about deceptive sales practices, the individual who had invited me to address the group took me aside to tell me he had noticed some executives in the audience taking careful notes of my remarks. He had spoken with some of them and they said they were taking notes so they could teach their agents how to use the techniques I had described to help sell life insurance. My host seemed amused, but I was aghast that executives would train their agents to use deceptive sales practices.

The Consumers' Dilemma

Consumers are trapped. Proponents of cash-value life insurance often understate the price of the protection component or overstate the rate of return on the saving component. Opponents of cash-value life insurance often overstate the price of the protection component or understate the rate of return on the savings component. In short, serious problems exist for life insurance consumers because of the absence of a mandated system of rigorous disclosure of prices of the protection component and rates of return on the savings component of cash-value life insurance policies.

Issues Mentioned in This Chapter

February 1977, July 1977, June 1978, February 1981, and April 2002.

14

Professional Codes of Ethics

*B*efore and during the *Forum* years I had several experiences with the enforcement machinery of the codes of ethics of various professional organizations in the insurance business. In some instances, the codes appeared to be little more than exercises in public relations.

The CLU Code

My first encounter with codes of ethics involved the Chartered Life Underwriter (CLU) code of ethics. Early in 1970, I saw in an insurance trade magazine a short article presenting a life insurance sales idea. The article was written by a now deceased agent who held the CLU designation and represented New York Life Insurance Company. The article purported to explain how a person could buy a $50,000 whole life policy, which had an annual premium of $1,000, for a cost of only $40 per year. The article ended with this rhetorical question:

> Mr. Prospect, that's $50,000 of death protection for $40 per year. Can you really afford to invest in anything else?

I later learned that the article was a condensed version of an article that had appeared previously in New York Life's magazine for its field force. Here is the three-sentence final paragraph of the article in the company's magazine:

> After digesting this sales idea, I would hope that any knowledgeable agent of our company could poke holes in my logic. However, I have found that, for me at least, sophisticated agents of our company historically have been a very poor market. My prospects are just as rich but not as sophisticated.

I agreed with the sentiments expressed in the first sentence, because the sales technique described in the article was deceptive. However, the second and third sentences demonstrated an outrageous disrespect for prospective clients.

In June 1970 I filed a complaint against the agent pursuant to the CLU code of ethics. Because New York Life's magazine was circulated nationally, I sent the complaint to the CLU Society's national Committee on Ethical Guidance. I expressed the opinion that the agent had violated at least two—and perhaps as many as six—provisions of the code of ethics.

Four months later, the committee chairman told me that complaints are handled at the local chapter level, and that the chapter's ethical guidance committee had recommended that no action be taken. He said there were two reasons for the decision: (1) New York Life printed in its agents' magazine a "poor and incomplete summary of a convention speech delivered to a sophisticated group of fellow agents," and (2) the chapter had knowledge of the agent's reputation, character, and ability.

I requested a copy of the convention speech and a copy of the letter to New York Life expressing concern about publication of the "poor and incomplete summary." I never received those items. I concluded that the enforcement machinery of the CLU code of ethics was a public relations gimmick.

A few years later I wrote about the incident. The article was entitled "Observations on the Enforcement Machinery of the CLU Code of Ethics." I raised questions about the relationship between the national and local chapter committees on ethical guidance, the secrecy surrounding ethics cases, and the problem of CLUs who are not members of the CLU Society. I expressed the hope that the enforcement machinery would be improved. In the concluding section, I said in part:

> Along with continuing education, there is nothing more important in a professional organization than a rigorously enforced code of ethics. Stated another way, an organization without a rigorously enforced code of ethics is not a professional organization, and its members are not professionals.

I submitted the article to the *CLU Journal,* which declined to publish it. The rejection was one of the 31 incidents of censorship that eventually led to the launching of the *Forum.*

I later submitted the article to *The Journal of Risk and Insurance,* which published the article in its March 1974 issue. I also published an article about the matter in the March 1974 issue of the *Forum.* The Society later changed the enforcement machinery in what I considered a satisfactory manner. However, I remain concerned that the enforcement machinery may not effectively deter violations of the CLU code of ethics.

The MDRT Code

The Million Dollar Round Table (MDRT) is an organization of top life insurance producers. The back cover of the September 1974 issue of *Round the Table,* MDRT's quarterly publication, displayed the code of ethics the MDRT had just adopted.

I wrote to Roderick L. Geer, executive director of the MDRT, and asked for a description of the enforcement machinery. He responded that there was not yet an enforcement machinery, and that the membership committee would continue to review ethics cases and report its findings and recommendations to the executive committee for formal action.

My March 1975 issue carried an article entitled "Lip Service from the MDRT." I said the MDRT code of ethics was a public relations gimmick. Geer was so upset that he said he would never speak with me again, and he never did.

Almost 40 years later, in its 2013 *Overview,* the MDRT showed its code of ethics. I requested a description of the enforcement machinery, but a spokesperson said it is confidential. I asked a few questions, such as how a person who wants to file a complaint should proceed, what the possible outcomes are, how many complaints were filed in recent years, and the results of those complaints. The spokesperson responded: "As stated, the process is confidential and we will not be sending any additional information." I published an article about the incident in the June 2013 issue of the *Forum*. I still believe that the MDRT code of ethics is a public relations gimmick.

The FIC Code

Knights of Columbus (K of C), whose headquarters is in New Haven, Connecticut, is a large fraternal benefit society that sells insurance. In November 2012 an Indiana agent of K of C sent a prospective customer a two-page promotional letter and a one-page attachment. A *Forum* subscriber brought the promotional material to my attention. I found the material objectionable, and wrote to the agent to ask some questions. I also asked him some questions about his Fraternal Insurance Counselor (FIC) designation.

In response I received a letter from William M. Brown, Jr., the chief compliance officer at K of C headquarters. He said that the agent had violated K of C's "established compliance procedures," that the agent's contract with K of C had been terminated, and that K of C had sent letters of apology to recipients of the material. I commended K of C, but never learned how my letter had gotten to K of C headquarters.

The National Association of Fraternal Insurance Counselors has a code of ethics for FICs, and the Fraternal Field Managers Association grants the designation. However, according to the directory of designations on the website of the Financial Industry Regulatory Authority, there is no established public disciplinary process associated with the FIC designation. I never learned whether K of C notified those organizations of its action. Nor did I ever learn whether K of C notified the Indiana Department of Insurance about the situation. I wrote about the incident in the March 2013 issue of the *Forum*. I believe that the FIC code of ethics is meaningless.

The CFP Code

The Certified Financial Planner Board of Standards (Washington, DC) grants the Certified Financial Planner (CFP) designation, and the CFP Board has a Disciplinary and Ethics Commission (DEC). In November 2012, the CFP Board issued a shocking press release that disclosed the resignations of Alan Goldfarb, who was the chairman of the CFP Board's board of directors, and two members of the DEC. I wrote about the matter in the January 2013 and February 2013 issues of the *Forum*.

The press release said the CFP Board had become aware of allegations that the three individuals may have violated the CFP Board's Standards of Professional Conduct. The CFP Board's board of directors had appointed a special committee to investigate the allegations, the special committee had found sufficient merit in the allegations to refer them for further confidential proceedings under the CFP Board's Disciplinary Rules and Procedures, and the three individuals had decided to resign their positions after they were presented with the findings of the special committee. The press release did not identify the two DEC members, and did not indicate the nature of the allegations.

In April 2013, according to its website, the CFP Board issued a "letter of admonition" to Goldfarb. The DEC determined that he misstated his compensation, first as "fee only," and later as "salary," in an online financial planner database, when in fact he received a small amount of compensation based on other factors. To my knowledge, the CFP Board has not disclosed the identity of the other two persons who resigned (although some commentators claimed they had figured out who the other two persons were), the nature of the charges against those other two persons, or the disposition of those charges. Nonetheless, the manner in which the matter was handled, and the openness of the process relative to the process in some other professional organizations in the insurance business, suggest that the CFP Board is serious about the enforcement of its code of ethics.

The Actuarial Code

The first of my several encounters with ethics enforcement in the actuarial profession occurred in 1978. In chapter 11, in a discussion of the libel lawsuit by the Non Commissioned Officers Association of the United States of America against the *Army Times*, I said I filed a complaint against a consulting actuary. He had written a letter to his client, the president of an insurance company, containing a flawed life insurance price comparison. I filed the complaint with what was then the Committee on Complaints of the Society of Actuaries alleging that the flawed comparison was a violation of the Society's Code of Professional Conduct. I did not receive a formal acknowledgment of the complaint, but a high ranking officer of the Society told me informally that all complaints are investigated. I never learned the result of the complaint. I wrote about the incident in the September 1978 and October 1978 issues of the *Forum*.

In 1992 the actuarial profession created a nine-member Actuarial Board for Counseling and Discipline (ABCD) and changed the complaint handling procedures. The ABCD considers complaints on behalf of the various actuarial organizations in North America and makes disciplinary recommendations to the organizations of which the subject actuaries are members. The ABCD discloses to the complainant the disposition of the complaint, does not disclose the reasoning behind the disposition, and marks the letter "confidential." When I wrote in the *Forum* about my complaints, I did not treat the letters as confidential. I discussed the ABCD's procedures in the December 2008 and January 2012 issues of the *Forum*.

In 2004 I filed a complaint with the ABCD against an actuary who had provided what I considered a false answer to an interrogatory in a sworn financial statement filed by an insurance company. The ABCD conducted an investigation. However, the actuary was required to provide deposition testimony in litigation relevant to the subject matter of the interrogatory, and the ABCD postponed the investigation until the litigation was settled several years later. In 2008 the ABCD informed me it had dismissed the complaint, but it did not disclose the results of the investigation or the reasoning behind the dismissal. I discussed the incident in the July/August 2004 and October 2008 issues of the *Forum*.

In 2005 I filed a complaint with the ABCD against a consulting actuary who had what I considered a conflict of interest. He operated a rating firm and at the same time acted as appointed actuary for some of the companies he rated. The chair and the two vice chairs of the ABCD reviewed the complaint and the actuary's response. They determined that the actuary's actions "did not create a conflict of interest situation" and "had not materially violated" the actuarial Code of Professional Conduct. They dismissed the complaint without an investigation, did not disclose the nature of the actuary's response, and did not disclose its reasoning. I discussed the incident in the May/June 2005 and October 2005 issues of the *Forum*.

In 2006 I filed a complaint with the ABCD against a consulting actuary who had designed for a client insurance company a policy that I felt was seriously underpriced. Virtually all the company's sales for several years involved that policy, and eventually the company failed. The ABCD conducted an investigation of my complaint. The ABCD informed me it had dismissed the complaint, but it did not disclose the results of the investigation or the reasoning behind the dismissal. I discussed the incident in the October 2008 issue of the *Forum*.

My experiences cause me to question the effectiveness of the enforcement machinery for the actuarial Code of Professional Conduct. I believe that the Code is enforced in such a way as to protect actuaries rather than serve the public interest.

The NAIFA Code

The National Association of Insurance and Financial Advisors (NAIFA) has a code of ethics. Complaints about possible violations of the code are handled exclusively by the local chapters of NAIFA and, according to a booklet published by NAIFA, may be filed by "any person."

In chapter 4 I discussed the case of Mrs. X. In 2014, because I considered the life insurance aspect of the case one of the most egregious replacements I had ever seen, I filed a complaint against Daniel Stallings, an agent involved in the replacement. In the complaint I expressed the belief that Stallings engaged in conduct unbecoming a member of NAIFA and in violation of its code of ethics. I sent the complaint to the president-elect of the local chapter because Stallings was the president of the chapter. After two follow-ups seeking acknowledgment that the complaint had been received, I received this one-sentence e-mail from the president-elect: "I have received both your letters and your e-mail and we as a board have no comment." I sent another e-mail asking: "Will you have a comment for me at some future date?" I received no further reply. I doubt that I will ever learn the result of the investigation of the complaint, or even whether an investigation was conducted. I believe that the NAIFA code of ethics is a public relations gimmick.

Issues Mentioned in This Chapter

March 1974, March 1975, September 1978, October 1978, July/August 2004, May/June 2005, October 2005, October 2008, December 2008, January 2012, January 2013, February 2013, March 2013, and June 2013.

15

Credit Life Insurance

*O*stensibly the primary purpose of credit life insurance, which is insurance on the life of someone who has borrowed money, is to pay off the loan upon the borrower's death and relieve the borrower's family from having to pay off the loan. In reality, however, the primary purpose of credit life insurance is to increase the revenue of lenders and merchants.

There are other forms of credit insurance, such as credit disability insurance, credit property insurance, and credit unemployment insurance. The discussion in this chapter is limited to credit life insurance. According to the 2014 *Life Insurers Fact Book,* the face amount of credit life insurance in force in the U.S. at the end of 2013 was about $81 billion, down about 6 percent from the end of 2012.

My First Exposure

My first exposure to credit life insurance was a memorable personal experience. In 1958, when I began my graduate studies at Penn, I obtained a student loan from a bank in my home town of Syracuse. The loan interest rate was 4 percent. The loan was guaranteed by the New York State Higher Education Assistance Corporation (HEAC), which paid the interest while I was in school. When I completed my studies, I was to repay principal and interest in equal monthly installments over six years.

When I completed my studies in 1961, I wrote to the bank and said I wanted to start repaying the loan. The bank sent me a booklet containing 72 monthly payment slips, and said in the cover letter that credit life insurance was included. I checked the market and learned that the cost of the credit life insurance was several times higher than the cost of individual term life insurance that was available on the open market. Because my original loan agreement with the bank said nothing about credit life insurance, I returned the booklet and asked for a new booklet without the premiums for the insurance. The bank sent me a corrected booklet.

Years later, during a trip to Syracuse to see my mother, I visited the bank officer with whom I had corresponded. I was surprised when he said he remembered me vividly. He said that, of the hundreds of students who had taken HEAC loans, I was the only one who turned down the insurance. I said that was hardly surprising because there was no indication that the insurance was optional, and there was no easy way for the borrower to know the insurance was relatively expensive. He said the bank had to prepare the corrected booklet for me manually, because the system was designed to prepare the booklets with the insurance premiums included.

The bank officer candidly explained the situation. He said the bank's credit life insurance was with Prudential Insurance Company of America, and the company paid the bank each year a "dividend" equal to about 80 percent of the credit life insurance premiums paid by the borrowers. He said that the bank could not make an adequate profit on student loans at the 4 percent interest rate required in the HEAC program, and that the dividends increased the bank's profit on its portfolio of student loans. (The compensation received by a lender or merchant from a credit life insurance company is called a "dividend," "commission," "experience rating credit," or, by some critics, a "kickback.") The incident is discussed in the January 2005 issue of the *Forum*.

Reverse Competition

Credit life insurance is a classic example of a phenomenon called "reverse competition." In a competitive market, competition reduces prices to consumers because sellers compete

by reducing prices. In credit life insurance, however, competition increases prices to consumers. The reason is that credit
life insurance companies compete by offering large dividends
to lenders and merchants, and the companies therefore charge
high premiums that make it possible for them to pay large dividends to lenders and merchants. Reverse competition is discussed in the March 1986 issue of the *Forum*.

Regulatory Efforts

State insurance regulators have long been aware of the high
prices borrowers pay for credit life insurance. The regulators
have tried in various ways to keep the price of credit life insurance reasonable, but the efforts have not been successful.

One approach is to limit the amount of compensation paid
to lenders or merchants by credit life insurance companies.
Lenders and merchants quickly circumvented such limitations.
For example, a group of automobile dealers in Indiana joined
forces to create a small Arizona-based reinsurance company.
The dealers sold credit life insurance to automobile buyers who
borrowed to finance their purchases. The dealers obtained the
credit life insurance from a Chicago-based credit life insurance
company, which in turn reinsured most of it with the reinsurance company. The dealers received the profits of the reinsurance company on top of the compensation they received directly
from the credit life insurance company. That and other circum-
vention techniques are discussed in the March 1986 issue.

A Politically Impossible Solution

Typically the borrower pays a single premium at the incep-
tion of a loan to cover the cost of the credit life insurance for the
entire term of the loan. The single premium is added to the loan
principal and paid back over the term of the loan at the annual
percentage rate (APR) applicable to the loan.

Lenders and merchants usually do not make clear to borrowers that credit life insurance is optional. Instead, lenders
and merchants have developed into an art form the technique
of making borrowers think the insurance is mandatory without actually saying so. "We are including credit life insurance,"

which is essentially what the bank said in my personal case, is a favorite line. In actuality, credit life insurance is mandatory only when the lender or merchant automatically includes the insurance in all loans, makes no specific charge for it, and may use "free credit life insurance" as a selling point. In such a situation, the lender or merchant seeks to buy the insurance from a credit life insurance company at the lowest possible price. The result is normal rather than reverse competition. Today mandatory credit life insurance is virtually extinct.

Under federal truth-in-lending regulations, when credit life insurance is mandatory, the cost of the insurance is added to the finance charge but not to the loan principal, and the APR on the loan is increased. On the other hand, when the insurance is optional, the cost of the insurance is added to both the finance charge and the loan principal, and the APR on the loan is not increased.

Many years ago I proposed a solution to the problem of disclosing the cost of credit life insurance. I suggested changing the truth-in-lending regulations to require, even when the insurance is optional, that the cost of the insurance be added to the finance charge but not to the loan principal. Then adding insurance to a loan would increase the APR on the loan even when the insurance is optional.

Here is an example. In buying a car, an individual takes out a 36-month loan at an APR of 11 percent and buys the optional credit life insurance. The APR on the entire loan, including the cost of the credit life insurance, would be 11 percent. However, if the truth-in-lending regulations were changed to require that the cost of credit life insurance be added to the finance charge even when the insurance is optional, the APR might be 13 percent rather than 11 percent. Thus the cost of the insurance would be disclosed to the borrower in a visible way, and the lender would have an incentive to arrange for low-cost insurance to minimize the spread between the APR with insurance and the APR without insurance. For further details, see the March 1986 issue of the *Forum*.

I mentioned the proposal years ago during a private conversation with a senior staff person in the office of a U.S. senator.

The staffer said there was no way such a change could be made in the Truth in Lending Act or regulations. He said the credit life insurance industry is an extremely potent lobbying force, and such a proposal would go nowhere. The staffer was politically knowledgeable, and I have no reason to disagree with him.

Issues Mentioned in This Chapter
March 1986 and January 2005.

16

Disability Insurance

*D*isability income insurance, referred to in this chapter as disability insurance, is one of three major forms of health insurance. The others are medical insurance and long-term care insurance, which are discussed in the next two chapters.

The purpose of disability insurance is to provide the insured person with an income when the insured is unable to work because of an illness or injury. The purpose of the income is to replace some of what the insured loses because of being unable to work. The discussion in this chapter is limited to individual disability insurance policies and does not explore the group disability insurance that is offered to employees by their employers.

Policy Dimensions

A disability insurance policy has three dimensions. One is the benefit amount. It is the amount of each benefit payment during a disability, and is usually a monthly figure. The larger the benefit amount, other things equal, the higher is the premium for the policy.

Another dimension of a disability insurance policy is the maximum benefit period. It is the maximum period over which benefit amounts are paid during a disability, and is usually expressed as a number of years or runs to a specified age. The longer the maximum benefit period, other things equal, the higher is the premium for the policy.

Another dimension is the elimination period, which is often called the waiting period, and which is usually expressed in days or months. It is the period of time between the beginning of the disability and the beginning of benefit payments. For example, a 30-day elimination period means the benefit payments begin after the insured has been disabled for 30 days. The longer the elimination period, other things equal, the lower is the premium for the policy.

The Definition of Disability

A critically important element of a disability insurance policy is its definition of disability. In general, the definition makes reference to the insured's inability to perform occupational duties as the result of an illness or an injury. More specifically, total disability is the insured's inability to perform any occupational duties, while partial disability is the insured's inability to perform some occupational duties.

An "own occupation" definition of disability refers to the insured's inability to perform duties of the insured's own occupation. An "any occupation for which suited" definition of disability refers to the insured's inability to perform duties of the insured's own occupation or any other occupation for which the insured is suited as a result of the insured's education, training, experience, and prior earnings. Many disability insurance policies have an own occupation definition for the first two years of a disability, followed by an any occupation for which suited definition after the first two years.

Some policies have solely an "any occupation" definition of disability, which refers to the insured's inability to perform the duties of the insured's own occupation or any other gainful occupation. This is such a strict definition of disability that a consumer should avoid buying a disability insurance policy with an any occupation definition.

The Continuance Clause

Another critically important element of a disability insurance policy is the continuance clause. It addresses the policyholder's right to maintain the policy and the insurance company's right to increase the premiums. In terms of the continuance clause, there are noncancellable policies and there are guaranteed renewable policies.

A noncancellable disability insurance policy has two characteristics. First, the policyholder has the right to maintain the policy until a specified age. Second, the insurance company does *not* have the right to increase the premiums beyond those specified in the policy.

A guaranteed renewable disability insurance policy has two characteristics. First, the policyholder has the right to maintain the policy until a specified age. Second, the insurance company has the right to increase the premiums for classes of policies (a class usually consists of all the company's policies of a particular type issued in a particular state), although the company does *not* have the right to single out a policy for an increase.

Premiums for a guaranteed renewable policy, other things equal, are lower than the premiums for a noncancellable policy. The reason is that a guaranteed renewable policy allows the insurance company to increase the premiums for classes of policies, while a noncancellable policy does not allow the company to increase the premiums.

The terminology here is perplexing and even contradictory in several ways. First, the word noncancellable used alone suggests correctly that the insurance company is not allowed to cancel the policy. However, the word fails to disclose that the company is not allowed to increase the premiums beyond those specified in the policy.

Second, the expression guaranteed renewable used alone suggests correctly that the policyholder has the right to maintain the policy. However, the expression fails to disclose that the insurance company is allowed to increase the premiums for classes of policies.

Third, a policy may be noncancellable and guaranteed renewable. That expression suggests correctly that the insurance company is not allowed to cancel the policy and that the policyholder has the right to maintain the policy. However, the expression fails to make clear that the company is not allowed to increase the premiums.

A Continuance Clause to Avoid

A renewable at company option disability insurance policy is one in which the policyholder does not have the right to maintain the insurance because the insurance company has the right to terminate the policy at any time. Consumers should avoid disability insurance policies containing this type of continuance clause.

I wrote occasionally in the *Forum* about how insurance companies issuing this type of disability insurance policy pulled the rug out from under insureds who had paid premiums faithfully for many years. For example, the November 1974 issue contains an article about an insured who bought a disability insurance policy from Life Insurance Company of North America (LINA) in May 1963 at age 38. The policy contained a "renewal subject to consent of the company" clause. The insured paid the premiums for 11 years and never filed a claim. In May 1974 he received a letter from the company informing him the policy would terminate in May 1975. The company suggested in the letter that the insured contact his LINA agent "to discuss possible alternative coverages." In the article I expressed doubt that the insured would be on speaking terms with his LINA agent after receiving such a letter.

Susceptibility to Dispute

Disability insurance is a form of insurance in which it is often difficult to determine whether the insured has suffered a loss of the type covered under the policy. In other words, it is a form of insurance highly susceptible to disputes.

I wrote many articles in the *Forum* about claim disputes between insurance companies and policyholders. There were numerous articles about Unum Group, a few articles about Reliance Standard Life Insurance Company, and a few articles about other companies.

Unum Group

What is now Unum Group is the largest provider of disability insurance in the U.S. Among its operating subsidiaries are Colonial Life & Accident Insurance Company, Paul Revere Life

Insurance Company, Provident Life and Accident Insurance Company, and Unum Life Insurance Company of America.

In 1993, when J. Harold Chandler became chairman, president, and chief executive officer of Unum, the company made a major shift from a "claims payment philosophy" to a "claims management philosophy." In plain English, that means the company changed its emphasis from paying claims to denying claims. The techniques the company used to deny, terminate, and settle claims generated hundreds if not thousands of lawsuits alleging unfair claims practices.

In 1999 Victor J. Gianunzio, an attorney in California, wrote a lengthy letter to "60 Minutes" about Unum's practices. In 2002, in a federal district court lawsuit in Maryland, the judge said the company's behavior "bordered on outright fraud." Also in 2002, a federal district court judge in California said:

> There was testimony from experts and others that [Unum] used a biased medical examiner, failed to advise the insured of covered benefits, targeted claims like [the insured's] for termination, failed to settle a claim when liability was clear, and forced its insured to litigate to obtain benefits.

Late in 2002 Unum's disability insurance claims practices were the subject of extensive coverage by such major media outlets as "60 Minutes," "Dateline NBC," the *San Francisco Chronicle,* and *The Wall Street Journal.* My first article about Unum's claims practices, in the February 2003 issue, dealt with the media attention and some developments that led to the attention.

During 2005 and 2006 I wrote several articles in the *Forum* about actions taken by state insurance regulators relating to Unum's disability insurance claims practices. I discussed the terms of a settlement between UNUM and the regulators in several states, the terms of a settlement between Unum and the California Department of Insurance, and the terms of a settlement between Unum and the Georgia Office of the Insurance Commissioner. The settlement in Georgia was noteworthy because it was impossible to find out the scope of the investigation until an attorney in New Jersey succeeded in gaining access to the report of the investigation through protracted litigation under the Georgia public records law. My most important articles were in the February/March 2005, April 2005, January 2006, and February/March 2006 issues.

In the March 2009 issue I wrote about a pair of federal district court decisions handed down late in 2008 that were highly critical of Unum's disability insurance claims practices. The events cited in those cases occurred prior to the settlements with various state insurance regulators, but there has been evidence in recent years suggesting that the company continues to engage in questionable claims practices.

Reliance Standard Life

Reliance Standard Life Insurance Company (Philadelphia, PA), now a member of the Tokio Marine Group, issues disability insurance. Over the years I wrote several articles about Reliance's claims practices.

In the June 2010 issue, for example, I discussed how Reliance entered into "independent contractor agreements" with physicians who act as medical reviewers on disability insurance claims. I discussed some disputes that led to lawsuits against Reliance and involved William S. Hauptman, M.D., who practices gastroenterology and internal medicine in Philadelphia. From 2002 through 2005, Hauptman conducted 446 medical reviews for which Reliance paid him a total of about $400,000, or an average of about $900 per review. Reliance paid him by the hour for such services as medical record reviews, research, deposition testimony, trial preparation, and trial testimony.

Hauptman's name appeared in decisions handed down in at least seven federal district court cases. In one case, the judge provided numerous examples of bias in Hauptman's reports. One example was his use of boldface type and underlining in his reports to emphasize his points supporting denial of the claim. In another case, the judge said:

> Reliance is the only insurance company for which Dr. Hauptman works, and he derives approximately one-third of his income from his work with Reliance. Reliance prohibits

Dr. Hauptman from contacting [an insured's] treating physicians to discuss those physicians' opinions unless he first
receives permission from Reliance.

The Future of Disability Insurance

As mentioned in this chapter, disability insurance is a form
of insurance that is highly susceptible to dispute over whether
an insured person is or is not disabled. For that reason, disability claims often will result in disagreements between insured
persons and insurance companies, and many of those disagreements will generate lawsuits. Yet disability can present serious
financial problems and is a type of exposure that deserves the
attention of members of the public.

Issues Mentioned in This Chapter

November 1974, February 2003, February/March 2005,
April 2005, January 2006, February/March 2006, March 2009,
and June 2010.

17

Medical Insurance

$\mathcal{M}$edical insurance policies cover medical expenses that the insured person incurs as the result of an illness or an injury. The discussion in this chapter is limited to individual medical insurance policies and does not explore group medical insurance offered to employees by their employers.

In medical insurance there is no such thing as a "noncancellable" policy, which, as explained in chapter 16, is a policy where the insurance company does not have the right to increase the premiums. The reason is that the companies consider it impossible to predict, far into the future, the rate of inflation in the cost of medical services and the rate of utilization of medical services. Therefore, medical insurance policies usually are guaranteed renewable, which means the insurance company has the right to increase premiums on classes of policies.

The short lead article in the January 1974 (first) issue of the *Forum* was about an insured who bought a medical insurance policy from Mutual of Omaha Insurance Company in 1967. The annual premium was $164, and the policy was guaranteed renewable. Three years later, the company notified the insured that the annual premium was being more than tripled, to $507. At the same time the company offered the insured an opportunity to exchange the policy, no questions asked, for a policy that provided far less protection for an annual premium of $153. In the article I questioned the apparent effort to force an insured to discontinue a policy with relatively generous benefits.

The Politics of Medical Insurance

Although I did not discuss the politics of medical insurance in the *Forum*, I mentioned it in blog no. 12 (December 4, 2013), and there were reader comments in no. 18 (January 6, 2014) and no. 32 (February 20, 2014). I discuss the subject briefly here. My comments are based in part on an article entitled "Perspectives on Medicare," which was published in the Winter 1995 issue of *Health Affairs*. The author was Robert M. Ball, who served for 30 years at the Social Security Administration and headed the agency during the presidencies of John Kennedy, Lyndon Johnson, and Richard Nixon. Ball died in 2008.

Medical insurance has long been a hot political issue. The idea of the U.S. government providing medical insurance — often called "national health insurance" or "universal health insurance" — dates back at least to 1916. Advocates in the early days were impressed by national health insurance plans that had been established in England, Germany, and other countries. Interestingly, one of the early advocates of national health insurance was the American Medical Association, but within a few years it became a strong opponent of the idea. Also interestingly, one of the early opponents of national health insurance was organized labor, but within a few years it became a strong supporter of the idea.

National health insurance was not among the recommendations that led to the enactment of the Social Security program in 1935. President Franklin Roosevelt was concerned that national health insurance was so controversial that trying to include it might jeopardize enactment of Social Security. Although he seemed favorably disposed toward national health insurance, he did not push the idea.

President Harry Truman advocated national health insurance, but he did not have the political support to enact it. Early in 1952, near the end of his presidency, what is now the Department of Health and Human Services suggested a more modest plan to provide medical insurance for Social Security beneficiaries. That suggestion evolved into the idea of providing medical insurance for the elderly, and what became Medicare. It was considered as a politically possible first step toward national health insurance. A possible second step—called "Kiddicare"—was medical insurance for children.

Medicare was enacted in 1965 as part of President Lyndon Johnson's "Great Society." I view the enactment of Medicare as a political miracle. Robert A. Caro, the acclaimed winner of two Pulitzer Prizes in Biography, is working on the final volume of his massive biography of Lyndon Johnson. I hope the final volume will contain a detailed Caro-style description of how Johnson accomplished the enactment of Medicare.

The Patient Protection and Affordable Care Act adopted early in the administration of President Barack Obama has become a political lightning rod. In my view, it was a compromise between national health insurance and no program at all for the millions of people with no medical insurance or inadequate medical insurance. In other words, 80 years after President Franklin Roosevelt viewed national health insurance as politically too controversial, national health insurance—often referred to as "Medicare for All"—remains politically too controversial. Thus the U.S. remains the only developed nation in the world without national health insurance.

Issue and Blog Items Mentioned in This Chapter

January 1974, and blog nos. 12 (December 4, 2013), 18 (January 6, 2014), and 32 (February 20, 2014).

18

Long-Term Care Insurance

Long-term care insurance, originally referred to as "nursing home insurance," is designed to pay part of the expense when the insured person is admitted to a long-term care facility, and may also pay part of the expense when the insured person requires home care. In terms of the continuance provision, a subject discussed in chapter 16, long-term care insurance policies usually are guaranteed renewable, meaning that the insurance company has the right to increase the premiums for classes of policies. There is no such thing as noncancellable long-term care insurance, under which the company would not have the right to increase the premiums, because the designers of the insurance think it is impossible to predict certain important components in the pricing of the insurance.

In the August 1991 issue of the *Forum* I explained that long-term care is an exposure that is inconsistent with important insurance principles. For that reason I expressed the opinion that the financing of long-term care is a problem that must be handled by money rather than insurance. I said that the three sources of money are savings, charity, and government, and that a national debate was needed on the relative roles of those three sources of money in solving the problem of financing long-term care. I elaborated on the subject in the July 2008 issue.

Over the years most companies in the long-term care insurance business have gotten out of it. Some of those company departures from the business are mentioned in this chapter.

The Union Fidelity Promotional Package

My first article about long-term care insurance was in the February 1988 issue. The article grew out of an unsolicited promotional package I received in the mail in October 1987 from Union Fidelity Life Insurance Company. The package included an endorsement letter from Danny Thomas, the legendary comedian who founded the St. Jude Children's Research Hospital. A careful reading of the package caused me to have serious concerns about the proposed plan.

The package referred to the plan as group insurance. That means the insurance is offered through a "master policy," and each insured person receives a "certificate" describing the provisions of the master policy. I wrote to the company asking for a copy of the master policy and a copy of the certificate. A senior company officer said that the mailing I received was for a "first generation" product, and that the company was no longer offering the product. He expressed the belief that no useful purpose would be served by an article about the product, and he invited my suggestions about the direction of the company's development efforts in long-term care insurance. I declined his invitation because I did not want to serve as a consultant. I obtained a copy of the six-page certificate elsewhere, but was not able to obtain a copy of the master policy.

The certificate said one way for the insurance to end was for the master policy to terminate. It is standard practice in group insurance for the insurance company to have the right to terminate the master policy unilaterally, and I surmised that the master policy in this instance contained such a provision. Yet neither the promotional package nor the certificate disclosed that the company had the right to end the insurance by terminating the master policy.

The certificate contained complex and restrictive definitions of "qualified hospital confinement," "hospital," "qualified nursing facility," "qualified skilled nursing facility," "qualified home health care agency," "home health care visit," "necessary skilled nursing care," and others. It was my opinion that the definitions and other provisions in the certificate imposed limitations beyond those mentioned in the promotional package.

My article took the form of an open letter to Thomas. I expressed the opinion that the plan would not provide the protection he and the company implied it would provide. I also expressed the belief that he would not have endorsed the plan if he had understood its limitations.

The Consumers Union Study

My second article about long-term care insurance was in the August 1991 issue. I described an 18-page study that appeared in the June 1991 issue of *Consumer Reports,* the magazine published by Consumers Union (CU). The study was entitled "An Empty Promise to the Elderly?" The study criticized "gatekeeper provisions" that determine whether an individual will qualify for benefits, described how agents "mislead and confuse" buyers, discussed efforts by state insurance regulators to deal with problems in the design and marketing of long-term care insurance policies, and explained why the company a consumer picks may not be around when the benefits become payable. The study rated 46 policies. None of the policies was rated "excellent" or "very good."

The CU study did not discuss the fundamental reasons why it found no excellent or very good long-term care insurance policies. Therefore, as mentioned briefly at the beginning of this chapter, I explained in my August 1991 issue certain conditions that are essential to the proper functioning of the mechanism of private insurance, and explained how the long-term care exposure violates several important insurance principles. I acknowledged that elderly persons and their families face potentially devastating expenses associated with long-term care, but expressed the belief that excellent or very good long-term care insurance policies will never be found.

The Special Seniors Issue

My third article about long-term care insurance was part of the 28-page April 1997 large-type "Special Seniors Issue" of the *Forum.* The issue was written by John Dorfman, my then associate editor, with my assistance. In the section entitled "Nursing Home Insurance," we concluded in part:

If you are either wealthy or poor, you almost certainly can do without nursing home insurance. Wealthy people can afford to absorb the cost of nursing home care themselves. Poor people can get help from Medicaid....

If you are neither wealthy nor poor, the desirability of purchasing nursing home insurance is unclear, but we would generally advise against it. As noted above, the premiums are very large, and the benefits fall far short of full coverage.

The Genworth Promotional Letter

My fourth article about long-term care insurance was in the May 1997 issue. It described a promotional letter circulated by General Electric Capital Assurance Company, which at the time was part of General Electric and is now part of Genworth Financial, Inc., one of the few remaining major companies in the long-term care insurance business.

The promotional letter offered a guaranteed renewable long-term care insurance policy, and was over the signature of a senior company officer. The letter included this sentence, with the indicated underlining: "<u>Your premiums will never increase</u> because of your age or any changes in your health."

I wrote to the company officer and said that, although the sentence is technically correct, it gives the impression that the premiums will never increase. I suggested that the promotional letter should mention explicitly the company's right to increase the premiums on classes of policies.

In response, the company officer said he understood my concern in view of the fact that some companies have increased premiums significantly for existing policyholders. However, he expressed the view that "we are not misleading the public," and he gave three reasons. First, he said the company "has <u>never</u> raised rates on existing policyholders" (he underlined the word never), and he mentioned the company's "internal commitment to rate stability." Second, he said that the promotional letter was an "invitation to inquire" rather than a "direct sales piece," and that the letter invited persons to respond in order to receive "complete details about the benefits, costs, limitations and exclusions of this valuable plan." Third, he said that "our long-term care specialists are trained to review every part of our sales brochure with clients," and that the brochure includes this paragraph (with the indicated emphasis):

> Premiums will not be raised because of changes in your age or health. *We reserve the right to adjust future premiums* for all insureds in the same class and state, but only after giving prior written notice. However, *we have never increased premiums* for any of our long-term care policyholders.

When I first wrote to the company, I requested and received a sample policy, which said it "is intended only for agent information and is not to be distributed to customers or clients." I wrote again asking about the reasons for the restriction and whether the company would give a sample to a prospective buyer upon request. In response a company official said that the sample policy is "designed for agent training," that it is "not state specific," and that the company has not created sample policies for all states "mainly because of the time and expense involved in preparing samples."

Several months later I saw another Genworth promotional letter. It was virtually identical to the previous letter, with one major exception. The company omitted the sentence that said: "Your premiums will never increase because of your age or any changes in your health."

The 1997 incident described here is ironic in view of the substantial premium increases that Genworth has imposed in recent years on the owners of long-term care insurance policies that have been in effect for many years. Furthermore, it appears likely that still more substantial increases lie ahead for those elderly policyholders.

The TIAA Transfer to Metropolitan Life

In November 2003 Teachers Insurance and Annuity Association of America (TIAA) notified its long-term care insurance policyholders that it was getting out of the long-term care insurance business and was transferring its existing policies to the Metropolitan Life Insurance Company. That transfer, about which I wrote articles in the March/April 2004, December 2005, and June 2007 issues, is discussed in chapter 23.

State Government Promotions

On February 26, 2008, *The Wall Street Journal* ran a front-page story entitled "States Draw Fire for Pitching Citizens on Private Long-Term Care Insurance." The story was triggered by a sales letter on California stationery displaying the state seal and bearing the name of then Governor Arnold Schwarzenegger. The story prompted me to write an article in the July 2008 issue of the *Forum* about the California program, which involved the state's partnership with a few long-term care insurance companies. The sales letter was used to generate leads that were turned over to a private Texas-based lead development company, which sold the leads to insurance agents. In that article I expanded on what I had said in the August 1991 issue about the inability of long-term care insurance to solve the problem of financing long-term care.

I also wrote an article in the January 2012 issue about a similar Indiana program involving a partnership with a few long-term care insurance companies. The Indiana program used a sales letter signed by then Governor Mitchell E. Daniels, Jr. The mailing package included a note on Indiana Department of Insurance stationery signed by Carol Cutter, then Indiana commissioner of insurance. The program used the same Texas lead development firm involved in the California program.

Only a few states have long-term care insurance partnerships with insurance companies. I think it is wrong for governments to be involved in such partnerships, because they give the appearance of endorsing specific companies and policies. The programs prohibit agents from saying the companies and policies are endorsed by the states, but the programs display all the earmarks of government endorsements.

Conseco's Settlements with State Regulators

I wrote two articles about investigations by state insurance regulators into the claims practices of long-term care insurance subsidiaries of Indiana-based Conseco, Inc., which is now CNO

Financial Group, Inc. (NYSE:CNO). In the first article, in the August 2008 issue, I described a settlement agreement between several states and two Conseco subsidiaries. In the second article, in the January 2010 issue, I described a settlement agreement between California and a Conseco subsidiary.

Conseco's Separation from a Subsidiary

In 2008 Conseco announced a "separation" ("divorce" would have been a better word) from Conseco Senior Health Insurance Company (CSHI), a financially troubled long-term care insurance subsidiary domiciled in Pennsylvania for regulatory purposes. Conseco had poured more than $900 million into CSHI over the previous decade. CSHI had stopped selling new policies in 2003, and was operating in "run-off" mode.

Conseco wanted to end its relationship with CSHI, and did so by creating an independent trust to own all the stock of CSHI. Conseco transferred the assets, liabilities, and surplus of CSHI to the trust, along with a final contribution of $175 million to the surplus of CSHI. The trust was based in Pennsylvania, the plan of separation was approved by the Pennsylvania insurance commissioner, and CSHI was renamed Senior Health Insurance Company of Pennsylvania (SHIP).

SHIP is still carrying on. It is unclear what would happen if the funds run out before SHIP completes the run-off of all its policies. On the other hand, if there are funds left over at that time, the funds would be donated to charity. I wrote about the separation in the November 2008, January 2009, and June 2009 issues.

In February 2012 a policyholder, on behalf of himself and others similarly situated, filed a lawsuit in a California state court over SHIP's claims practices. In May 2013, the parties settled the lawsuit. I wrote about the case in the May 2012 and November 2013 issues.

Ability's Claims Practices

Ability Insurance Company (Omaha, NE) handles long-term care insurance policies transferred to it by companies that have gotten out of the long-term care insurance business. Ability was in financial difficulty, the Nebraska director of insurance placed the company under supervision, and the company later was acquired by an investment firm. The company had engaged in highly irregular claims practices that resulted in the filing of numerous lawsuits by disgruntled policyholders. I wrote about one of the lawsuits in the May 2013 issue.

The insured and her husband bought a long-term care insurance policy in the 1980s, and her husband died in 1998. The policy was transferred from company to company, and ended up at Ability. The insured was diagnosed with dementia in 2007. Her condition steadily worsened and she became unable to function on her own. In January 2008, when she was in her late 80s, she qualified for long-term care insurance benefits after entering a "supervised, assisted care facility." In January 2010, the company terminated her benefits on the grounds that she was independent and did not require continual supervision. Her daughter, who held a power of attorney, appealed to the company, which denied the appeal.

In September 2010 the daughter sued Ability in federal court. After a one-week trial, the jury decided the company had no reasonable basis for its actions and awarded the insured substantial benefits, including a whopping $32 million in punitive damages. The judge reduced the punitive damages to $10 million to comply with state law, but in his ruling he made these harsh comments about the company's actions:

> Defendants' wrongful termination of long-term care insurance [benefits] in an effort to save money is highly reprehensible. The evidence at trial demonstrated Defendants were aware that [she] needed daily assistance with meal preparation, medications, maintaining her personal hygiene and generally all of the activities of daily living ...
>
> Prior to the wrongful termination of benefits, Defendants sought no information from her treating physician..., sent him no [attending physician statement] forms, and ordered none of [his] medical records of [her]. This was not an oversight. It was intentional. [An Ability claims examiner] testified she has never contacted a treating physician because that is the way she was taught to do it ...

The astounding evidence in the case included information about "withdrawn claims," a concept with which I previously was not familiar. The company had a regular practice of contacting claimants by telephone to try to persuade them to agree verbally to withdraw their claims. The evidence included transcripts of telephone conversations, many of which revealed that the company's case managers often gave false information about benefit eligibility. Some of the recorded conversations were with a claimant, some were with a holder of a claimant's power of attorney, and some were with a person who did not hold a power of attorney.

Penn Treaty's Battle in Pennsylvania

In January 2009 Penn Treaty Network America Insurance Company (Allentown, PA), a long-term care insurance company, was found to be insolvent. In April 2009 the Pennsylvania insurance commissioner filed in state court a preliminary rehabilitation plan. He said he intended to file a formal plan in October 2009, but instead he petitioned the court to allow him to convert the rehabilitation into a liquidation. The company opposed the petition, and the case went to a bench (non-jury) trial. In May 2012 the judge denied the liquidation petition and ordered the commissioner to develop a rehabilitation plan. I had never before heard of a case where a court denied an insurance commissioner's petition to liquidate an insurance company. I wrote about the case in the August 2012 issue.

Issues Mentioned in This Chapter

February 1988, August 1991, April 1997, May 1997, March/April 2004, December 2005, June 2007, July 2008, August 2008, November 2008, January 2009, June 2009, January 2010, January 2012, May 2012, August 2012, May 2013, and November 2013.

19

The Annuity Business

*D*uring my years as an agent in the 1950s, I sold only one annuity, which I will describe in this chapter. Today annuities are widely sold. According to the 2014 edition of the *Life Insurers Fact Book*, U.S. companies received $103 billion of premiums for individual life insurance in 2013, compared to $180 billion for individual annuities.

Terminology

I think the complex annuities sold today are not fully understood by the buyers or the sellers, in part because terminology in the annuity business is not widely understood and can be confusing. Some expressions associated with annuities are in the glossary beginning on page 335. A more detailed annuity glossary is in the August 2007 issue of the *Forum*.

A Deceptive Sales Idea

The April 1978 issue carried my first article about annuities. It was prompted by a sales idea published in an insurance sales magazine. The author was a top agent in Idaho for National Public Service Insurance Company (Seattle, WA). He presented the idea to overcome the frequent "no money" objection encountered in sales work. In selling a tax-sheltered annuity to a public school teacher through monthly payroll deduction, he said: "It's the take-home pay that counts." He said the teacher could increase from 0 to 2 the number of tax exemptions claimed, and that the reduced tax withholding would roughly pay the monthly premium for the annuity. He falsely referred to the reduced withholding as a "tax saving." I expressed the opinion that his idea was a deceptive sales practice.

I sent my article to the agent and requested his comments. He thanked me for my interest in his article and said in part:

> The questions that you raise are covered very carefully during the interview. The article was well received and seems to have been understood by the salesmen that read it....

I also sent my article to C. W. Hurlbut, the president of the agent's company. I asked for his comments on the sales idea and whether it emanated from the home office. He said:

> National Public Service Insurance Company has as much or more interest than you in seeing that a knowledgeable, fair and honest presentation of our policies is made to a prospect, and we would not permit an agent to engage in any type of deceptive sales practice under any circumstances.

Hurlbut said the idea did not emanate from the home office, and the agent had been asked for an explanation. I asked for a copy of the agent's explanation, but did not receive it.

I also sent my article to the Idaho Department of Insurance. An official said the matter was under investigation. I did not receive any information about the results of the investigation.

MONY's Questionable Brochure

The April 1979 issue carried my second article about annuities. It too related to tax-sheltered annuities. Mutual Life Insurance Company of New York (MONY) prepared a brochure showing a 30-year comparison for a person aged 35 in a 25 percent income tax bracket.

First, the brochure showed the accumulation of $1,000 per year for 30 years in a 5 percent savings account. The brochure said the account (net of income taxes on the interest) after 30 years was $41,863.

Second, the brochure showed a tax-sheltered annuity accumulation of $1,000 per year for 30 years, assuming 5 percent interest minus MONY's expense charges. The amount in the account at the end of 30 years was $66,020. The brochure referred to the amount in the annuity account as 58 percent larger than the amount in the savings account.

I felt the comparison was unfair. Showing only the accumulation period and ignoring the liquidation period is wrong because liquidation of an annuity account is more heavily taxed than liquidation of a savings account. "Accumulation period" and "liquidation period" are defined in my glossary.

A Discussion of Annuities

The April 1997 special large-print seniors issue of the *Forum* included some advice about annuities. The discussion included warnings about various fees that often are not clearly disclosed, substantial surrender charges, and gimmicks that are often surrounded by onerous conditions.

A Troublesome Sales Idea

The November 1997 issue carried an article about a troublesome sales idea published by Western Fraternal Life Association (Cedar Rapids, IA) in a magazine for the field force. The idea was attributed to David Brown, the director of agencies. He said money would double in about 12 years in an annuity, but in about 17.9 years in a certificate of deposit.

I wrote to Brown expressing concern that the comparison unfairly exaggerated the income tax advantages of the annuity by failing to include the liquidation period. Brown acknowledged the problem, said the presentation in the magazine inadvertently omitted his discussion of the tax treatment during the liquidation period, and called attention to the problem by distributing a memorandum to the field force.

A Question for Readers

In the August 1998 issue I asked readers a question that later led to articles about possible drawbacks of life annuities. First, I said life insurance policies and life annuities are in a sense opposites, because a life insurance policy provides protection against dying too soon and a life annuity provides protection against living too long. Second, I said I had developed methods for measuring the price of the protection in a life insurance policy (see chapter 6). Third, I asked this question:

> How should one measure the price of the protection in a life annuity? In other words, how should one measure the price of the protection against living too long?

To assist in answering the question, I described the situation of Adams, a hypothetical individual who was aged 65 and in good health. He had a $1 million retirement accumulation created solely through pre-tax contributions and tax-deferred investment earnings, so that all payments from the accumulation would be taxable. He had significant other assets, so he did not feel an urgent need to buy protection against living too long. For simplicity, I asked readers to assume he had only three options with regard to the accumulation: (1) a pure life annuity, (2) a life annuity with ten years certain, or (3) systematic annual or monthly withdrawals of any amount with the ability to change the amount at any time. I said that, if he chooses the third option, he would have to check each year after age 70½ to make sure the amount withdrawn would meet the required minimum distribution to avoid tax penalties. I also said that, under the third option, his retirement accumulation might be exhausted before he dies.

I said further that, although Adams did not feel the urgent need for protection against living too long because of his other assets, he might select one of the two life annuity options if the price of the protection is reasonable. However, he was reluctant to select a life annuity option without knowing the price of the protection.

Aftermath of the Question for Readers

In the November 1998 issue I reported that several readers responded by discussing factors Adams should consider, but they did not explain how to measure the price of the protection in a life annuity. The respondents were agents and financial planners; no actuaries responded.

I then tried to answer the question myself. I was not comfortable with my methodology, in part because of the sensitivity of the results to the assumptions made. Nonetheless I concluded that the purchase of either of the life annuities was inappropriate, and that Adams should take systematic withdrawals without the protection against living too long.

About 14 years later, in the August 2012 issue, I tackled the problem differently. I said the individual in question was a hypothetical professor named Baker. He retired at the end of 1988 at age 70, and when he retired he had a $1 million retirement account with College Retirement Equities Fund (CREF), an affiliate of Teachers Insurance and Annuity Association of America (TIAA). (CREF and TIAA cater to the academic community.) I also said he took systematic monthly withdrawals that complied with the required minimum distribution rules to avoid income tax penalties.

I obtained the data from TIAA, performed the calculations, and showed the results for the first 25 years following Baker's retirement. During the first year after his retirement, he received taxable withdrawals of $3,200 per month. In 2011, when he was aged 93, he received taxable withdrawals of $14,400 per month, and at that point his account value was slightly above $1.4 million. I concluded that his use of systematic withdrawals tied to required minimum distributions was a satisfactory alternative to a life annuity.

In the November 2012 issue I tackled the problem yet again. This time I compared Baker's situation to that of Corbett, who also retired at the end of 1988 at age 70, but who retired with a $1 million retirement account consisting of shares in Vanguard's 500 Index Fund. The results for Corbett were slightly better than the results for Baker. I said the results provided further support for the conclusion I stated in the August 2012 article.

The Legal Attacks

The March/April 2007 issue included my first article about legal attacks against the marketing of unsuitable annuities to seniors. In January 2007, Lori Swanson, the Minnesota attorney general, filed a civil complaint in state court against Allianz Life Insurance Company of North America (Minneapolis, MN) alleging violations of Minnesota laws. Among the allegations were deceptive advertising and deceptive sales practices.

The August 2007 issue included a major article about the expanding crackdown on the improper marketing of annuities to seniors. I mentioned the following developments: (1) an administrative complaint filed by the Massachusetts Securities Division against a Colorado-based broker; (2) a civil complaint filed in state court by the California attorney general and the California insurance commissioner against several companies and individuals for alleged violations of the state business and professions code and the state insurance code; (3) three civil complaints filed in state court by the Texas attorney general against three developers of lists of seniors; (4) a civil complaint filed in state court by the Pennsylvania attorney general against several companies and individuals for alleged unauthorized practice of law and use of deceptive practices; (5) a civil complaint filed in state court by the North Carolina attorney general against two companies and two individuals, with allegations similar to those in Pennsylvania; (6) two civil complaints filed in state court by the Illinois attorney general against developers of lists of seniors; (7) a civil complaint filed in state court by the Minnesota attorney general against two companies, with allegations similar to those in Pennsylvania and North Carolina; (8) an order issued by the Florida Office of Insurance Regulation against a company and two individuals for unlicensed and unauthorized transactions involving insurance and annuities for Florida consumers; (9) a civil complaint filed in state court by the Minnesota attorney general against Iowa-based American Equity Investment Life Insurance Company, with allegations similar to those against Allianz Life; (10) a class action lawsuit filed in 2006 in federal court in Minnesota against Allianz Life alleging deceptive sales practices; and (11) three other class action lawsuits filed in federal courts against Allianz Life.

The December 2007 issue included an article about the settlement of the civil lawsuit filed by the Minnesota attorney general against Allianz Life. The order provided for Allianz to enhance its suitability standards, pay restitution to policyholders, and pay for the cost of the investigation and the cost of administering the settlement.

The May 2008 issue reported developments relating to legal attacks on the marketing of unsuitable annuities to seniors. The Minnesota attorney general settled her complaint against American Equity Investment Life, and filed a complaint against Iowa-based Aviva USA. The California insurance commissioner settled his complaint against Allianz. The Minnesota commerce commissioner, who regulates insurance, settled allegations of wrongdoing against American Investors Life Insurance Company (Topeka, KS) and two related companies.

The January 2010 issue included an article about the results of the class action lawsuit filed in 2006 in federal court against Allianz Life alleging deceptive sales practices. The class was certified in 2007, and the case went to trial in 2009. The jury ruled that Allianz Life had used deceptive sales practices and had intended that the plaintiffs would rely on those practices. However, the jury also ruled that the plaintiffs had not been harmed as a direct result of the deceptive practices. The company's press release about the jury verdict mentioned the "no harm" portion of the verdict but did not mention the "deception and intent" portion of the verdict. Consequently news stories about the verdict—and the headlines in those stories—differed widely. Some were accurate, suggesting the reporters had done their homework, and some were inaccurate, suggesting the reporters had relied on the company's press release.

The June 2010 issue included an article about two legal actions against Iowa-based American Equity Investment Life. The first action was a consent order issued by the Minnesota Department of Commerce alleging the company had sold 541 unapproved annuities to Minnesota citizens. The order alleged that the Minnesota residents had traveled to Iowa, Wisconsin, and elsewhere to buy the annuities because the annuities had not been approved for sale in Minnesota. The company paid a civil penalty of $275,000 and agreed to a number of remedial actions, including reductions in surrender charges.

The second action was a civil complaint filed by the Securities and Exchange Commission (SEC) against the company's publicly owned parent and two individuals. The SEC complaint alleged that certain transactions benefited the two individuals. The individuals paid civil penalties to the SEC of $900,000 and $130,000, and the parent company agreed to take certain other important steps.

A Personal Experience in the 1950s

Continental American, the company I represented as an agent in the 1950s, specialized in life insurance and sold few annuities. My first and only experience with annuities occurred when a friend asked me to arrange a single-premium, immediate, pure life annuity for his 82-year-old father. What my friend wanted was for his father to pay one premium and receive annuity payments of $1,000 per year beginning one year after the purchase and continuing until his father's death, with no refund upon his father's death. My friend explained that his brother was an eminent physician who had examined their father thoroughly and considered him to be in such good health that the best investment their father could make was the purchase of a pure life annuity.

I checked around and found an annuity issued by Manufacturers Life Insurance Company, a large Canadian company that was active in the annuity business. The single premium, as I recall, was about $4,000. My friend's father wrote a check for the premium, the company issued the annuity, and I received a commission of about $120. Many years later, long after I had left the insurance business, I learned that my friend's father had just died at the age of 100. Thus he received $18,000 on the investment of about $4,000, and the physician son was right about his father's good health. Indeed, I believe that my friend's father survived both his sons.

In retrospect, despite the favorable end result, I should have refused to be involved in the transaction. My friend's father had adequate assets and had no need for the annuity payments. Thus the purchase of the annuity was sheer speculation on the life span of my friend's father.

A Horribly Unsuitable Annuity

In 1999 an unmarried college professor executed a will providing bequests to family members, friends, charities, and for the care of her animals. In 2000 she retired at age 70 after 30 years of service. Almost her entire estate consisted of a $1.3 million retirement accumulation with TIAA, which caters to members of the academic community. When she retired, she exchanged almost her entire account for an immediate, pure life annuity that provided monthly payments as long as she lived and no refund after her death.

At the professor's retirement, she was suffering from advanced emphysema. Her illness caused her death six months later. Her death wiped out almost her entire account and almost her entire estate. The pure life annuity option she selected was horribly unsuitable in view of her life-threatening illness, her bequest objectives as reflected in her will, and her lack of other assets with which to accomplish her objectives.

In 2003 the executrix of the professor's estate filed a civil lawsuit in federal court alleging that TIAA had not done enough to prevent her from selecting an inappropriate annuity option. Among the claims were securities fraud, common law fraud, breach of fiduciary duty, and negligent misrepresentation. In 2006 the district court dismissed the case.

In 2008 a three-judge appellate panel affirmed in part and reversed in part the district court's ruling. The panel affirmed the dismissal of the securities fraud and common law fraud claims, reversed the dismissal of the fiduciary duty and negligence claims, and sent the case back to the district court for further proceedings.

The professor's election of the pure life annuity option was carried out entirely through telephone conversations and correspondence with the TIAA home office. Among the documents in the case were transcripts of recordings of telephone conversations, which suggested at least the possibility that the professor did not understand what she was doing. Also among the documents was a letter from the professor that had the earmarks of a "CYA" letter signed by the professor. I wrote about the case in the January 2010 issue.

The case never went to trial. In November 2014, TIAA and the executrix of the professor's estate finally settled the lawsuit. That was more than 13 years after she died, and more than 11 years after the lawsuit was originally filed. The terms of the settlement are confidential. The law firm that represented TIAA was Traub Lieberman Straus & Shrewsbury LLP. According to documents filed with the New York Department of Financial Services and its predecessor, TIAA paid the firm about $350,000 during the period the lawsuit was pending. There is no way of knowing whether the case discussed here was the only legal matter that the firm handled for TIAA.

When I retired from my position at Indiana University, most of my retirement account was with CREF, an affiliate of TIAA. However, some of it was with TIAA. With regard to the TIAA portion, one of the options, and the one I selected, was an annuity certain providing for 11 annual payments, with the first annual payment at the time of retirement. I think that would have been a highly suitable option for the professor in this case. She would have received the first annual payment at the time of her retirement, and the remaining ten annual payments after her death would have been paid to her estate and would have accomplished the objectives stated in her will.

Issues Mentioned in This Chapter

April 1978, April 1979, April 1997, November 1997, August 1998, November 1998, March/April 2007, August 2007, December 2007, May 2008, January 2010, June 2010, August 2012, and November 2012.

20

The Secondary Markets
for Annuities

$\mathcal{T}$he secondary market for life insurance is discussed in chapter 9. Here I discuss secondary markets for life annuities, retirement annuities, and annuities in structured settlements.

Life Annuities

My first brush with the secondary market for life annuities was an unexpected telephone call from an attorney seeking my views about a case in which he was involved. He gave me a few details, and I made a few comments. After I got off the telephone and thought more about what he said, I kicked myself for not asking more questions and for not writing down his name and telephone number. I stewed about the matter for a long time. Finally I wrote a short article in the June 2009 issue of the *Forum* describing the little I had learned in the telephone call and speculating that the case might involve money laundering.

In the April 2010 issue I wrote a major article about stranger-originated life annuities and discussed two situations. The first was the case I had heard about by telephone; by then I had learned about the relevant lawsuit, which was filed in federal court in Florida by MetLife Investors USA Insurance Company. The second situation involved several civil lawsuits filed in federal court in Rhode Island by Transamerica Life Insurance Company and Western Reserve Life Assurance Company of Ohio against a number of parties: Joseph Caramadre (an attorney and accountant), Raymour Radhakrishnan (a Caramadre employee), and others.

The MetLife Lawsuit

In 2008 a newly created Florida trust that soon moved to New Jersey applied to MetLife for a large variable annuity on the life of Sherry Pratt, an Illinois resident. The trust had no relationship to Pratt; nonetheless, the trust was the beneficiary of the annuity. The premium that accompanied the application was $975,000. The annuity contract contained this sentence: "We will accept amounts up to $1,000,000 without underwriting."

The broker who submitted the application to MetLife was Moshe Marc Cohen (Brooklyn, NY). He also applied for annuities on Pratt to five other companies: Genworth Life and Annuity Insurance Company, Hartford Life and Annuity Insurance Company, ING USA Annuity and Life Insurance Company, New York Life Insurance and Annuity Corporation, and Sun Life Assurance Company of Canada (U.S.). The premiums sent to the six companies totaled about $12 million.

Pratt was age 38 and lived in a Chicago nursing home. She had suffered a severe neck injury caused by a gunshot wound years earlier, and she was a quadriplegic. She was near death when the applications were submitted, and died 12 days after MetLife issued the annuity. She left an estate of less than $100. I was struck by the national scope of the conspiracy—from a trust in Florida and New Jersey, to a broker in New York, to a "finder" and a terminally ill person in Illinois, and to people in California who apparently organized the scheme.

The death benefit of the annuity was the return of the premium or the account value of the annuity, whichever was larger. The trust filed a claim for the death benefit. Six months later, after MetLife completed an investigation, the company informed the attorney for the trust that "we have reason to believe that Ms. Pratt did not actually sign the application." That was a polite way of saying her signature was forged.

A few months later, MetLife rescinded the annuity. In accordance with the annuity contract, a rescission required the company to refund the premium. The company did not know whether to send the funds to the trust or to Pratt's estate. Therefore the company paid the funds into court in connection with an interpleader lawsuit, under which the court is asked to determine where the funds should go. The federal district court awarded the $975,000 to the trust. Pratt's estate appealed, and the appellate court affirmed the district court's ruling.

In the many documents I reviewed in the Pratt case, I found no discussion of the motivation for the scheme. Commissions surely were an incentive, and the broker could have shared commissions with the investors (speculators). However, I question whether commissions alone would have been a sufficient motivation. When I first heard about the case in the original telephone call, my suspicion was that money laundering was the purpose, but I found no discussion of that subject. In the end, here is the opinion I expressed about the case:

> I think the outright lies, fraudulent misrepresentations, deceptive practices, concealment of material information, forgery of documents, bribery of relatives, perjured testimony, identity misappropriation, and other forms of wrongdoing that allegedly occurred in the case warrant investigation into the existence of a criminal conspiracy—sweeping across the country from New York to Illinois to California—to misappropriate the identities of terminally ill individuals.

The SEC Orders

The Pratt case later blossomed into a national enforcement action taken by the Securities and Exchange Commission (SEC), but it was a civil rather than a criminal action. In July 2014 the SEC issued several orders directed at brokers, "finders," and others associated with the national scope of the conspiracy. One order was directed at Michael A. Horowitz, a broker in Los Angeles, who the SEC said was the "architect" of "a fraudulent scheme to profit from the imminent deaths of terminally ill hospice and nursing home patients" through more than $80 million of variable annuities. Horowitz had submitted a settlement offer that the SEC had accepted. Horowitz agreed to admit wrongdoing; pay $850,000 to the SEC in disgorgement of ill-gotten gains, prejudgment interest, and civil penalties; cease and desist from violating federal securities laws; and be barred from the securities industry.

Seven other individuals and a company were subjects of SEC orders. Some, including Cohen, were involved in the Pratt case. Cohen is fighting the order against him; as of June 2015 the appeal is pending. I wrote a blog about the SEC case against Horowitz and the others. See no. 61 (August 8, 2014).

The Civil Lawsuits against Caramadre

In the April 2010 issue I mentioned several lawsuits filed in 2009 against Caramadre and others. They had concocted a scheme under which they ran advertisements offering $2,000 in cash to terminally ill individuals in exchange for allowing the issuance of variable annuities on the lives of those individuals. The advertisements were made to appear to be from a "compassionate organization," and ran in general circulation newspapers and in periodicals for hospice patients and their families.

The annuities contained features creating at least a possible short-term profit for Caramadre and his investors. I prefer to call the investors "speculators in human life." If there was a short-term loss, the speculators would not lose because the death benefit was the return of the premium or the account value of the annuity, whichever was larger. In other words, the investors had the possibility of at least a modest short-term investment profit without a risk of investment loss.

The insurance companies alleged in the lawsuits that Caramadre and his associates took advantage of the companies by selling annuities for short-term investment purposes rather than the long-term investment purposes for which annuities are intended. The lawsuits dragged on for some time, and the companies did not have much success in the courts. However, the cases were soon overshadowed by federal criminal charges.

The Criminal Charges against Caramadre

In November 2011 the U.S. Attorney in Rhode Island filed an indictment against Caramadre and Radhakrishnan. Each was charged with 65 criminal counts of wire fraud, mail fraud, conspiracy, identity theft, aggravated identity theft, and money laundering. Caramadre was also charged with one count of witness tampering.

The charges were based not only on the annuity scheme but also on a bond scheme. The bond scheme involved corporate bonds owned jointly by an investor and a terminally ill person, with the right of survivorship. A bond would be purchased at a price well below its face value. At the death of a co-owner, the surviving co-owner would redeem the bond at its full face value. The victims of the bond scheme were the corporations that issued the bonds. The indictment alleged that Caramadre profited by more than $15 million from the annuity scheme and more than $10 million from the bond scheme. I wrote about the case in the March 2012 issue.

The Caramadre criminal case went to a jury trial in November 2012. The government presented four days of devastating testimony from 14 witnesses. On the fifth day (a Monday), in a stunning development, the defendants pleaded guilty to one count of wire fraud and one count of conspiracy in plea agreements that had been hammered out over the weekend. After questioning the defendants, the judge accepted the guilty pleas and set a date for sentencing. See the February 2013 issue.

In January 2013, in an even more stunning development, a new attorney for Caramadre filed a motion to stay all proceedings to permit the filing of a motion to withdraw the guilty pleas prior to the sentencing date. A few days later, after an in chambers hearing, the judge postponed sentencing. A few months later, after the filing of briefs, the judge denied the defendants' motion to withdraw the guilty pleas and granted the government's request that Caramadre be jailed immediately because of flight risk. See the April 2013 issue.

A few weeks later Caramadre filed a motion for reconsideration of the detention order; the judge denied the motion. Caramadre appealed the denial of the motion; the appellate court affirmed the denial. See the October 2013 issue.

In December 2013 the judge sentenced Caramadre to six years in prison, followed by three years of supervised release. The judge sentenced Radhakrishnan to one year and one day in prison, followed by three years of supervised release. A magistrate judge issued a report for restitution purposes. She found that the total losses from the two schemes were $46.3 million, that the annuity scheme caused losses of $33.9 million to numerous insurance companies, and that the bond scheme caused losses of $12.4 million to numerous bond issuers. See no. 17 (January 2, 2014).

Retirement Annuities

I wrote about the secondary market for retirement annuities in the August and October 2011 issues. For the purposes of discussion, assume the retiree is a man age 75. He has an annuity certain that will pay him $1,000 per month for 240 months, or a simple total of $240,000. He may have qualified for the annuity through his employment in a large business, a small business, a state or local government, or the federal government (including in military service). The annuity payments are designed to provide the retiree with income during his retirement years.

Factoring companies are in the business of paying cash to buy retirement annuities from retirees. Suppose a factoring company approaches the retiree, or the retiree responds to a newspaper or television advertisement. Further suppose the factoring company offers the retiree a lump sum of $55,000 in exchange for the 240 monthly annuity payments of $1,000 each. If the retiree accepts the offer, he would receive a check for $55,000 from the factoring company, and he would sign the necessary papers so that the factoring company would receive the 240 monthly payments totaling $240,000.

Thus the retiree may think he pays $185,000 ($240,000 minus $55,000) to receive the lump sum instead of the 240 monthly payments, but that belief is based on simple arithmetic without consideration of the time value of money. In other words, the factoring company must be compensated for giving up the use of the money and receiving a series of payments instead. Question: How should the retiree assess the price he pays for taking the lump sum instead of the annuity payments?

The question may be answered by understanding that the retiree in essence obtains a $55,000 loan and promises to repay the loan at the rate of $1,000 per month for 240 months. Those figures are tantamount to a very high annual interest rate of 23.8 percent. The concepts of annual interest rate, an approximation called the annual percentage rate (APR), and the differences between them are discussed in chapter 8.

The calculation of the annual interest rate is complex and tricky. However, there is a simple way to get an approximation. Call a friendly banker and ask for the APR on a $55,000 mortgage loan that is to be paid off in 240 equal monthly installments of $1,000 each. Your banker will promptly tell you the APR is 21.5 percent, a figure he will derive from a simple mortgage calculator. He has ready access to a calculator, because he is required by the federal Truth in Lending Act to disclose to a borrower the APR on a mortgage loan or any other loan.

In short, the crucial figure our retiree needs to understand the price paid for the arrangement is the annual interest rate (or the APR as an approximation), and the APR must be disclosed routinely when a person takes out a loan. In the secondary market for retirement annuities, however, there is no such disclosure, for two reasons.

First, factoring companies and others in the secondary market for retirement annuities have the gall to claim that the retiree's receipt of a lump sum in exchange for giving up a series of payments does not constitute a loan. With that ridiculous claim, they have succeeded in fending off disclosure requirements.

Second, with one notable exception, regulators and legislators who are supposed to protect the public in general and retirees in particular, have allowed the factoring companies to avoid the disclosure requirements of the federal Truth in Lending Act. The exception was Eliot Spitzer, the former New York attorney general. Therein lies a story.

The J. G. Wentworth Agreement with Spitzer

J. G. Wentworth (JGW) is a major factoring company that advertises heavily on television and the internet. Its slogan is "Get Cash Now!" In July 1999, after JGW contacted Spitzer seeking comments on JGW's sales practices, and after Spitzer conducted an investigation that found, among other things, inadequate disclosures and high costs, JGW and Spitzer entered into an agreement to address Spitzer's concerns.

JGW agreed to several undertakings, two of which related to the "effective annual discount rate." That expression is the annual interest rate used to calculate the present value of the annuity payments acquired by JGW in exchange for the lump sum, and is precisely the annual interest rate mentioned in the previous section of this chapter as the "crucial figure" the annuitant needs in order to understand the cost of obtaining the lump sum. Under the agreement between JGW and Spitzer, the two undertakings were to (1) disclose the annual interest rate to any New York resident who gives up annuity payments in exchange for a lump sum, and (2) limit the annual interest rate to no more than 25 percent.

A few years later, unfortunately, the New York legislature enacted a law that overrode those important provisions of the agreement. The law did away with the requirement to disclose the annual interest rate, and removed the 25 percent upper limit on the annual interest rate. Today I am not aware of any law or regulation imposing such requirements on factoring companies. In other words, the legislators, undoubtedly at the behest of lobbyists representing the factoring companies, overrode the important provisions of the agreement between JGW and Spitzer. The JGW case is discussed in the October 2011 issue.

Military Retirees

In recent years, several articles have appeared in major news outlets describing horror stories about military retirees who took cash in exchange for their military retirement annuities, or parts of those annuities. It is my understanding that there are some legal prohibitions on such arrangements, but those prohibitions apparently have not been enforced. One article described the case of a U.S. Navy retiree who paid an annual interest rate of more than 30 percent. In addition, because it was a life annuity (an annuity whose payments are contingent upon the annuitant's survival), the retiree was required to buy life insurance to protect the factoring company in the event of the retiree's death before all the payments were made.

Annuities Used in Structured Settlements

In the August 2011 and October 2011 issues I discussed secondary market annuities used in structured settlements. An injured person who settles a claim against a party that caused the injury may elect to receive an annuity rather than a lump sum. In that situation, the liability insurance company representing the party that allegedly caused the injury usually buys an annuity from a life insurance company for the benefit of the injured person. The settlement is "structured" in the sense that the annuity payments may change from time to time. For example, if the injured person is a youngster, the annuity payments might increase during the anticipated college years.

At some point the injured person—the annuitant—may want to sell part or all of the annuity in the secondary market; that is, the annuitant may want to take a lump sum in exchange for transferring some or all of the future annuity payments to the party that provides the lump sum. When the annuitant sells future annuity payments, the sale must be approved in court because the original structured settlement was approved in court. However, it is my understanding that court approvals of such sales are routinely given.

As mentioned in the earlier discussion of retirement annuities, the crucial figure needed by the annuitant to understand the price of obtaining the lump sum is the annual interest rate. Unfortunately, there are no requirements for that rate to be disclosed to the annuitant.

Issues and Blog Items Mentioned in This Chapter

June 2009, April 2010, August 2011, October 2011, March 2012, February 2013, April 2013, and October 2013, and blog nos. 17 (January 2, 2014) and 61 (August 8, 2014).

21

Charitable Gift Annuities

*D*eceptive sales practices relating to annuities are touched on in chapters 19 and 20. I have also written about deceptive practices used by charitable organizations in the promotion of charitable gift annuities (CGAs).

The Nature of a CGA

A CGA is bought by a donor to provide financial support for a charitable organization. CGAs come in many varieties. Here the discussion is limited to one simple, widely used type of CGA. The donor purchases the CGA from the charity by giving the charity a lump sum of cash. The annuity payments by the charity to the donor begin one year later and thereafter are made annually for the rest of the donor's life. When the donor dies, the payments stop and any money left over is kept by the charity. Other things equal, the older the donor at the time the CGA is purchased, the larger are the annuity payments. When the CGA is purchased, part of the purchase price is immediately deductible by the donor as a charitable contribution for income tax purposes. Also, a portion of each annuity payment is a return of principal, and that portion is excluded from the donor's taxable income.

My first articles about CGAs were in the February 1978 and August 1978 issues. There I discussed CGAs offered by the Billy Graham Evangelistic Association. Those articles addressed regulatory rather than promotional issues.

The Central Deception

I did not write about CGAs again until the July 2010 issue. There I explained how charities, in promoting CGAs, often refer to the ratio of the annual annuity payment to the purchase price as a CGA's "yield" or "rate of return." Moreover, some charities compare that yield or rate of return to the yield or rate of return on a certificate of deposit (CD) or other type of investment. For example, suppose a donor aged 75 purchases a CGA for $25,000 in cash, and each annual annuity payment to the donor is $1,575. It is false—and deceptive—to say the CGA's yield or rate of return is 6.3 percent ($1,575 divided by $25,000, with the quotient expressed as a percentage) and thus higher than, say, a 2 percent rate of return on a CD.

The figure of 6.3 percent significantly overstates the rate of return of the CGA. Moreover, the figure of 6.3 percent is not comparable to the rate of return on a CD. The central deception stems from the facts that a CGA exhausts principal and a CD preserves principal. The payments from a CGA are partly interest and partly return of principal, while payments on a CD prior to maturity are entirely interest.

The Mid-America Scandal

Robert Dillie controlled the Mid-America Foundation (Scottsdale, AZ), which sold CGAs from 1996 to 2001 through commissioned "facilitators" such as financial planners and insurance agents. The comments here are from a June 2009 decision of the U.S. Court of Appeals for the Ninth Circuit. The plaintiff was the court-appointed receiver for Mid-America. The defendants were facilitators. Mid-America raised $55 million from the sale of more than 400 CGAs. One promotional brochure, under the heading "Attractive Returns," said:

> To get this same return through the stock market, [the hypothetical investor] would have had to find investments that pay dividends of 19.3%! (Even the most profitable companies rarely pay dividends of more than 5%.) The rate of return on a Mid-America Foundation "Gift Annuity" is hard to beat!

Instead of turning the money over to the charities designated by the donors, Mid-America used the money to pay earlier donors, pay commissions to facilitators, and pay Dillie and others to cover lavish personal expenses, including gambling debts. The arrangement was a classic Ponzi scheme, where money paid by later donors is used to pay what appear to be attractive returns to earlier donors. In 2001 the Securities and Exchange Commission closed down Mid-America through a restraining order issued by a federal court. Dillie was later indicted and pleaded guilty to several counts of wire fraud and money laundering. He was sentenced to 121 months in prison.

The Syracuse University Brochure

In March 2010, as an alumnus of Syracuse University, I received in the mail a brochure offering a CGA. The brochure emphasized "higher yields" and "higher rates of return" on CGAs. Here was one of the statements in the brochure:

> Dollar for dollar, a Syracuse University Charitable Gift Annuity yields a higher rate of return than a traditional CD.

The brochure included a table, three columns of which were "age of annuitant," "annual income," and "rate of return." The table showed figures at every five years of age from 60 to 90 for a $25,000 CGA. Each rate of return was calculated by dividing the annual income by the $25,000 purchase price and expressing the quotient as a percentage. I wrote to the university's office of gift planning and explained my concerns about the brochure. I received this response:

> While we do not regard our CGA promotion as "deceptive," we did forward our current brochure to the attorneys for review. Effective with the next CGA brochure, we will discontinue use of the words "rate of return" in regard to annuity payments. I have been involved in CGA promotions for 20 years and yours is the first complaint. Thank you for your attention to the accuracy of our materials and for your lesson about the annual rate of return on an investment.

I then asked for a copy of the revised brochure when it was ready, but did not receive it. In September 2011 I visited the university's website. It contained this description of a CGA:

> A charitable gift annuity is an especially attractive type of deferred gift. It enables you to receive a fixed annual income for life—typically at rates higher than CDs. Plus, a portion of that income may be tax-free!

I wrote to the university's office of gift planning again, reminded them of my request for the revised brochure, and expressed concern over the website description of a CGA. The office said they would send me the revised brochure when it was ready, but said nothing about the website description. To date I have not seen a revised brochure, and have not received another CGA promotion from the university.

In August 2014 I visited the university's website again. This was one of the listed benefits of a CGA: "In many cases, increase the yield you are currently receiving from stock or CDs."

The American Council on Gift Annuities

The American Council on Gift Annuities (ACGA) "actively promotes responsible philanthropy through actuarially sound gift annuity rate recommendations, quality training opportunities, and the advocacy of appropriate consumer protection." The ACGA website, probably because of the Mid-America scandal, urged charities to avoid selling CGAs through commissioned facilitators. The website also discussed the June 2009 federal appellate court decision in the Mid-America case. An attorney who chaired the state regulations committee of the ACGA wrote the discussion. He said in part:

> It's OK to talk about payments to the annuitant, and to express those payments as a percentage of the amount transferred to the charity. But we should avoid referring to those percentages as "yields" or "returns," or comparing charitable gift annuities to investments like stocks, bonds and certificates of deposit.

The ACGA attorney was correct that it is acceptable to talk about "payments to the annuitant." However, it is deceptive to express each payment as a percentage of the purchase price of the CGA, because doing so implies that the percentage is the rate of return on the CGA. Furthermore, it is deceptive to use the word income because each payment is partly a return of principal.

Similarly, it is deceptive to use the word rate, especially when it is expressed as a percentage, because doing so implies that the percentage is the rate of return on the CGA. The word factor should be used instead of the word rate, and the factor should be expressed as a decimal rather than as a percentage. For example, in the illustration mentioned early in this chapter, the figure of 6.3 percent should be called a factor and should be written as .063. Then it could be stated accurately and non-deceptively that the annual annuity payment of $1,575 is the $25,000 purchase price of the annuity multiplied by the factor of .063 for age 75.

I wrote to the ACGA about the situation. In response, the ACGA president said the "gift annuity best practices" section of the ACGA website was being revised and will discourage the use of rate of return, yield, or comparisons to other financial instruments. Here is the relevant revised paragraph:

> Gift annuities are first and foremost a way of making a gift to your organization. You should exercise caution when comparing gift annuity rates with returns from other financial instruments, and avoid using terms like "product," "purchase," "yield," "rate of return," and "effective rate of return" when describing gift annuities and the percentage payout from a gift annuity. Your marketing materials should clearly explain that the gift annuity agreement is irrevocable, that donors irrevocably part with the assets they use to make their gift, and that part of the annuity payment received will consist of a return of original principal. Do not use the phrase "guaranteed income" because though the annuity's payments are backed by the general assets of your organization, the annuity payment is not "guaranteed" in the legal sense of the term, and a return of principal is not "income."

Other Charities

I have visited the websites of some other charities. In most cases there are no references to rates of return or comparisons with investments. However, I have not obtained proposals or reviewed the promotional material they distribute. Thus I do not know the extent to which the deceptive practices described in this chapter are used by other charities.

Commercial Vendors

Many charities obtain website and other services from commercial vendors. I solicited comments from several vendors about the language that should be used in CGA promotions. I received responses from only two of them; they agreed with most of my concerns.

State Laws

The ACGA website contains detailed information about state laws relating to CGAs. The states do not address the manner in which CGAs are promoted. Some state laws require charities to register and file annual statements; the primary concern is the maintenance of sufficient reserves to assure that CGA obligations will be met. Some state laws require charities to register but not to file annual statements. Some state laws require charities to meet certain criteria but not to register or file annual statements. Some state laws are silent on CGAs.

The Uphill Struggle

There seems to be general agreement in the CGA community about the concerns expressed in this chapter, but only limited progress has been made in addressing the concerns. Much remains to be done to eliminate deceptive practices used by charities in promoting CGAs.

Issues Mentioned in This Chapter

February 1978, August 1978, July 2010, March 2012, and June 2013.

22

Financial Strength Ratings

*F*inancial strength is the most important factor a consumer should consider in selecting a company from which to buy life insurance. In modern times, major life insurance companies almost always have been capable of meeting their financial obligations. Consequently many people fell into the habit of taking the financial strength of life insurance companies for granted.

Everything changed in 1991, when First Executive Corporation filed for bankruptcy protection and its Executive Life subsidiaries in California and New York were taken over by state insurance regulators, as discussed in chapter 7. The public then learned it is possible for a major life insurance company to fail. In the years that followed, several other life insurance companies—some of them major companies, including the venerable Mutual Benefit Life Insurance Company—were taken over by state insurance regulators.

Lack of an FDIC

Most bank depositors are protected by the Federal Deposit Insurance Corporation (FDIC). Speed is a major characteristic of the FDIC. For example, it is not uncommon for a bank in financial trouble to close at the end of a business day and reopen for business the next morning under the supervision of the FDIC.

The arrangements in the case of an insurance company in financial trouble are significantly different. Each state has a guaranty association created by state law to provide limited coverage of the losses incurred by policyholders of failed insurance companies. Under such a law, after an insurance company failure, the guaranty association is authorized to force other insurance companies doing business in the state—through assessments—to help cover the losses of a failed insurance company. The process can take months or even years, during which policyholders may face aggravation, uncertainty, delay, and possible financial losses.

When a state insurance regulator takes over an insurance company, the action must be approved by a state court judge in the state where the company is domiciled for regulatory purposes. The objective of the regulator is to rehabilitate or sell the company. Either of those results is preferable to liquidation, in which the company's assets are converted to cash, the cash is distributed to policyholders, and the policies are canceled.

When a life insurance company is in very poor financial condition, the regulator may ask the court to order contractual changes in the policies previously issued by the company. In one case, for example, the regulator asked and the court ordered interest-bearing liens to be placed on the cash values of the policies. That meant that a policyholder who surrendered a policy would have a certain amount, with interest, deducted from the cash value. In other words, the court unilaterally reduced the company's liabilities at the expense of the policyholders.

To increase the likelihood that the benefits of a life insurance policy will be paid promptly and fully when they come due, consumers should buy life insurance from financially strong companies. The trick is to figure out how to evaluate the financial strength of a company.

Rating Firms

Financial analysis of an insurance company is a complex process requiring specialized knowledge. Even understanding the terminology in a company's financial statement is a challenge. For those reasons, consumers should rely on opinions expressed by rating firms that are in the business of evaluating the financial strength of insurance companies.

A. M. Best Company was the first rating firm to report on life insurance companies. Its first reports were issued in 1906 by its founder, Alfred M. Best. In the early days, adjectives and adverbs were used instead of letter ratings. The stronger the adjectives and adverbs, the stronger were the implied ratings.

Best began using letter ratings in 1930. It stopped doing so in 1935, probably under pressure from insurance companies. Then it started using recommendations with adjectives and adverbs. Again, the stronger the adjectives and adverbs, the stronger were the implied ratings. In the first (January 1974) issue of the *Forum*, in an article entitled "Attention: Regulatory Officials," I listed some companies that received weaker recommendations than in the preceding year. In 1976, as discussed in the October 1977 issue of the *Forum*, Best resumed the use of letter ratings.

Best long had a monopoly in rating insurance companies. In the 1980s, however, three major rating firms that assign ratings to corporate bonds began assigning ratings to insurance companies. Today the four major firms that assign ratings to insurance companies are A. M. Best Company, Fitch Ratings, Moody's Investors Service, and Standard & Poor's (S&P). All four of those firms have been designated by the Securities and Exchange Commission as Nationally Recognized Statistical Rating Organizations.

Nature of Ratings

A rating is not a statement of fact. Rather, a rating is an expression of opinion by a rating firm about the financial strength of an insurance company. The higher the rating, so the rating firm believes, the greater is the likelihood that the company will survive. The lower the rating, the greater is the likelihood that the company will fail.

Based on hindsight, observers sometimes criticize rating firms for what is perceived as tardiness in lowering the ratings of insurance companies with financial problems. On the other hand, insurance companies whose ratings are lowered sometimes criticize rating firms for undermining public confidence in their companies.

In the aftermath of the financial crash of 2008, some observers harshly criticized rating firms for underestimating the risks associated with collateralized debt obligations and mortgage backed securities, and for assigning high ratings to what later became known as "toxic" assets. I agreed with that criticism. However, with regard to the ratings of insurance companies, I think the rating firms generally have done a good job. Ratings are never perfect because no one has 20/20 foresight.

Rating Categories

The four major rating firms use letter ratings, but unfortunately their use of different lettering systems causes confusion. The current letter ratings used by the rating firms are shown in the box below. Secure ratings are sometimes called investment grade ratings. Vulnerable ratings are sometimes called below investment grade or junk ratings. The overwhelming majority of ratings assigned to life insurance companies are secure ratings. For example, the final tabulation of ratings in the *Forum*—in the September 2013 special ratings issue, which included ratings as of August 2, 2013—showed that Best assigned ratings to 888 life insurance companies, of which only 47 were assigned vulnerable ratings. The reason is simple: to assign ratings, a rating firm usually needs information

Best	Fitch	Moody's	S&P
Secure Ratings			
A++	AAA	Aaa	AAA
A+	AA+	Aa1	AA+
A	AA	Aa2	AA
A−	AA−	Aa3	AA−
B++	A+	A1	A+
B+	A	A2	A
	A−	A3	A−
	BBB+	Baa1	BBB+
	BBB	Baa2	BBB
	BBB−	Baa3	BBB−
Vulnerable Ratings			
B	BB+	Ba1	BB+
B-	BB	Ba2	BB
C++	BB−	Ba3	BB−
C+	B	B1	B
C	CCC	B2	CCC
C-	CC	B3	CC
D	C	Caa1	R
E		Caa2	
F		Caa3	
		Ca	

to supplement that found in publicly filed financial statements, and most companies that expect to receive a vulnerable rating decline to cooperate with the rating firms by providing the supplemental information. Consequently hundreds of life insurance companies are not rated by the rating firms. I recommend that consumers avoid buying life insurance from companies that are not rated.

Origin of the Special Ratings Issues

During the first 15 years of the *Forum,* I published various lists of the ratings assigned to life insurance companies by the rating firms. It was Executive Life's selective use of ratings that prompted me to start publishing annual special ratings issues.

In the late 1980s, as described in chapter 7, Executive Life was facing severe financial problems. Nonetheless the company continued to enjoy top ratings from Best and S&P. At the same time, the company was assigned a fifth-level rating by Moody's and a ninth-level rating by Duff & Phelps, the predecessor to Fitch Ratings. Executive Life heavily advertised and boasted about its top ratings from Best and S&P, but did not mention its significantly lower ratings by the other two major rating firms. I discussed the incident in the November 1988 issue.

After the Executive Life incident, I published some lists of ratings, but the 32-page September/October 1991 issue was the first full special ratings issue. It included all ratings assigned by the four major rating firms to all life insurance companies. The issue included an article describing the nature of ratings, discussing each of the four major rating firms, and explaining how to use the ratings. The issue also showed the ratings firms' descriptions of their rating categories.

The Watch Lists

The 1991 special ratings issue also included my first fully developed watch list. The companies included on the list were those with four or more abnormal Insurance Regulatory Information System (IRIS) ratios. Later the watch lists were modified to include companies with a vulnerable rating (as described earlier in this chapter) from at least one of the four major rating firms. Still later the watch lists were modified to include companies with low risk-based capital (RBC) ratios and companies with high ratios of surplus notes to total adjusted capital. Surplus notes, IRIS ratios, and RBC ratios are discussed in chapters 25, 30, and 31.

The Suggested Companies

Many rules of thumb may be constructed to help consumers choose a financially strong life insurance company. In the 1980s, when I first constructed a rule of thumb, I suggested that consumers choose a company that had received Best's top rating for ten consecutive years.

Later, when the other three major rating firms began assigning ratings to life insurance companies, I constructed a set of three rules of thumb. For example, in the September 2013 issue—the final special ratings issue—I suggested that consumers buy life insurance from companies with at least two high ratings from among the four rating firms. I defined the expression high ratings in three ways—one definition for extremely conservative consumers, a second definition for very conservative consumers, and a third definition for conservative consumers. The three definitions of high ratings are in the box at the right.

> *Extremely conservative*
> Best: A++
> Fitch: AAA, AA+
> Moody's: Aaa, Aa1
> S&P: AAA, AA+
>
> *Very conservative*
> Best: A++, A+
> Fitch: AAA, AA+, AA
> Moody's: Aaa, Aa1, Aa2
> S&P: AAA, AA+, AA
>
> *Conservative*
> Best: A++, A+, A
> Fitch: AAA, AA+, AA, AA−
> Moody's: Aaa, Aa1, Aa2, Aa3
> S&P: AAA, AA+, AA, AA−

In the September 2013 issue, there were 19 companies suggested for extremely conservative consumers. There were 38 companies suggested for very conservative consumers, consisting of the 19 companies for extremely conservative consumers and another 19 companies for very conservative consumers. There were 157 companies suggested for conservative consumers, consisting of the 38 companies for very conservative consumers and another 119 companies for conservative consumers. The 157 companies, grouped into the three categories, are listed in appendix C.

Other Troubling Incidents Involving Ratings

Over the years, in addition to the 1988 Executive Life incident, there have been other troubling incidents involving the improper use of ratings by insurance companies. For example, General American Life Insurance Company, in a 1989 press release about a mediocre rating by Moody's, distorted the language of Moody's press release about the rating. See the March 1990 issue.

Another example involved Guardian Life Insurance Company of America, which for many years advertised its top ratings from all four major rating firms. However, when Moody's lowered the company's rating by one notch in 1996, the company omitted the Moody's rating from its advertisements. See the June 1997 issue.

Blaming the Messenger

Earlier in this chapter I mentioned that companies whose ratings are lowered sometimes blame their troubles on rating firms. In 1999 a classic example of this phenomenon involved Missouri-based General American Life Insurance Company.

For several years General American issued funding agreements. They are essentially large certificates of deposit issued to large institutional investors. The investor may request a withdrawal at any time, without limit and without penalty, and the company has to honor the request within the withdrawal payment period. General American issued, to several large institutional investors, $5 billion of funding agreements that had withdrawal payment periods of only seven days.

In 1997 and 1998, Moody's expressed concern about such funding agreements. On March 5, 1999, Moody's lowered General American's rating one notch, citing the company's "significant exposure to funding agreements" with seven-day withdrawal payment periods. On July 30, Moody's lowered the rating another notch. On August 9, Moody's lowered the rating four more notches. At that point all the investors in the funding agreements filed withdrawal requests, and the company was not able to convert enough assets into cash to honor the withdrawal requests without incurring huge capital losses.

On August 10, the Missouri director of insurance, at General American's request, placed the company under a supervision order. On August 12, Moody's lowered the rating three more notches. On August 15, a story about the company appeared in the *St. Louis Post-Dispatch*. Edward Liddy, chairman and chief executive officer of the company, was quoted as making this comment to the reporter:

> How do we feel about Moody's? You run a family newspaper, don't you? I don't think you want to quote me on this.

I wrote about the General American case in the October 1999 issue of the *Forum*. There I said that blaming the messenger is not constructive, and I expressed the opinion that Moody's had acted properly.

Weiss Ratings

In 1989 Weiss Research, Inc. began publishing ratings. In 1990 I considered the possibility of publishing the Weiss ratings, but decided against it. In 1993 I reconsidered and decided to publish the Weiss ratings in the special ratings issues. I continued to publish the Weiss ratings for the next decade.

During the preparation of the September 2004 special ratings issue, I reconsidered the matter yet again and decided to stop publishing the Weiss ratings. In the February/March 2005 issue, I wrote an article explaining the three primary reasons for the decision. First, when I began publishing the Weiss ratings a decade earlier, I had hoped the ratings would achieve widespread recognition, but they had not. Second, the Weiss ratings were perceived as "tougher" than the ratings by the major rating firms, but I felt that the perception often was incorrect. Third, Weiss initially charged me no fee to publish the ratings, but later started charging me a fee, and by 2004 the fee had escalated to the point that I would have had to increase the price of the special ratings issue; I did not want to do that. In the same February/March 2005 issue, I wrote a second article responding to the questions and comments that I received from readers about the decision to omit the Weiss ratings. In retrospect I believe that it was the correct decision.

Best's Lawsuit

In chapter 3 I said the only lawsuit in which I was a defendant was a copyright infringement lawsuit filed by A. M. Best Company. In November 1993 Best filed the lawsuit in federal court in New Jersey.

Best said its ratings were "copyrighted and trademarked material." I said the ratings were in the public domain.

In January 1995 Best entered into a stipulation of dismissal. In the March/April 1995 issue of the *Forum* I published a joint statement from Best and me describing in detail the events that had led to the lawsuit. I agreed to enter into the stipulation of dismissal and agreed not to publish Best's ratings without authorization. In 2000 I entered into an agreement with Best and resumed publication of its ratings in the September 2000 special ratings issue.

Issues Mentioned in This Chapter

January 1974, October 1977, November 1988, March 1990, September/October 1991, March/April 1995, June 1997, October 1999, September 2000, February/March 2005, and September 2013.

23

Transfers of Policies between Companies

$\mathcal{I}$n 1989 several extraordinary cases started a regulatory firestorm and caused me to write 29 articles in the *Forum* over the next 18 years. The subject, in a nutshell, is the transfer of blocks of insurance policies from one insurance company to another and the question of whether the transfers are made with the consent of the owners of the transferred policies.

The Underlying Issue

When an insurance company decides to stop selling a certain type of insurance, the policies the company previously issued usually prohibit the company from canceling the policies or otherwise discontinuing them. Yet the company may want to wash its hands of those previously issued policies. To do so, the company may seek to transfer the block of previously issued policies to another insurance company.

The Creditor-Debtor Relationship

An insurance policy is a legal contract. The contractual relationship between the owner of a policy and the insurance company that issued the policy is that of creditor (lender) and debtor (borrower); that is, the policyholder is the creditor and the insurance company is the debtor. Stated another way, an insurance company, when it issues an insurance policy, makes certain promises to the policyholder, and the policyholder is entitled to have those promises kept.

The Loan Contract Analogy

Consider an analogy. Bob borrows money from a bank. Bob and the bank enter into a loan contract. The bank lends the money to Bob, and Bob promises to repay the money on specified dates over a specified period of time with a specified amount of interest. The contractual relationship between the bank and Bob is that of creditor and debtor; that is, the bank is the creditor and Bob is the debtor.

Now suppose Bob, after entering into the loan contract with the bank, enters into a separate contract with his friend Jim. Under the separate contract, Jim promises to take over Bob's obligations to the bank. After Bob enters into the separate contract with Jim, here is the text of the "good-bye and good luck" notification letter Bob sends to the bank:

> Effective immediately, my obligations to you have been taken over by [Jim's name and address]. You have no recourse to me in the event of Jim's failure to meet his obligations to you.

Thus Bob seeks to relieve himself of his obligations to the bank by transferring those obligations to Jim. From a legal standpoint, however, this type of transfer can be effective only when the creditor consents to the transfer. In other words, it is necessary for the bank to consent to substituting Jim in place of Bob as the debtor under the original loan contract. Such a substitution of a debtor is called a novation.

Positive versus Negative Consent

A crucial question relating to a novation is the manner in which the creditor consents to the novation. Consent can be given in many ways. For purposes of this discussion, however, it is necessary to distinguish between only two ways of giving consent: positive consent and negative (or implied) consent.

Positive consent occurs when the creditor signs a form granting permission to complete the novation. Negative consent occurs when the creditor does nothing and is deemed to have consented to the completion of the novation.

Consider Bob's previously mentioned notification letter to the bank. If positive consent is given, the bank would consent in writing to the novation. The bank might be willing to consent after investigating Jim's financial condition, perhaps in a manner similar to the bank's investigation of Bob's financial condition before the bank loaned Bob the money in the first place. On the other hand, for one reason or another, the bank might not be willing to consent to the novation, in which event Bob's attempted transfer would not occur; that is, Bob would remain obligated to the bank under the original loan contract.

The First Pyramid Case

The first case about which I wrote involved an annuity rather than an insurance policy. In 1989 Adams (not his real name) sent me an incredible correspondence file.

In February 1983 Adams bought a single-premium deferred annuity from Arkansas-based First Pyramid Life Insurance Company of America. The single premium was $91,000. First Pyramid had a rating of B+ from A. M. Best Company at the time. Starting in 1984 Best no longer rated First Pyramid.

In November 1986 Adams received a letter and a certificate notifying him that the annuity had been transferred in October 1986 to First Pyramid's parent company, Kansas-based Security Benefit Life Insurance Company. The letter emphasized Security Benefit's A+ rating from Best. I was surprised Adams had not been asked for his consent to the transfer.

In April 1987 the annuity was transferred again—from Security Benefit to Life Assurance Company of Pennsylvania. The file contained no notification letter, so I did not know whether Adams had been informed of the transfer. Nor did I know whether Adams had been informed that Life of Pennsylvania had a rating of B+ from Best. I was again surprised Adams had not been asked for his consent to the transfer.

In June 1988 Adams received a letter and a certificate notifying him the annuity had been transferred yet again—from Life of Pennsylvania to Arizona-based Diamond Benefits Life Insurance Company. Adams was told the transfer was effective in December 1987, six months prior to the letter. In recent years Diamond Benefits was not rated by Best, and that fact was not mentioned in the letter. By this time, I was very surprised by the entire sequence of events, but the worst was yet to come.

In January 1989 Adams received a letter from the receivership office of Diamond Benefits. The letter made six points: (1) the cash value of the annuity was $124,000, (2) Diamond Benefits was insolvent, (3) the Arizona director of insurance was the receiver, (4) the transfer was under investigation, (5) all transactions relating to the annuity were "pended," and (6) "We will attempt to keep you fully advised as events become known concerning your policy and its coverage."

I wrote to the president of Life of Pennsylvania and asked some questions about the situation. On the advice of his attorney, and probably because of the ongoing investigation by the receiver, the president declined to answer the questions. The First Pyramid case is discussed in the October 1989 and January 1991 issues.

The Penn Mutual Case

I also received an incredible correspondence file from Baker (not his real name). In 1963 he bought a noncancellable and guaranteed renewable disability insurance policy from Pennsylvania-based Penn Mutual Life Insurance Company. In the 1970s Penn Mutual stopped issuing disability insurance. Until 1986, however, Penn Mutual continued to administer the block of previously issued policies by sending premium notices, accepting premium payments, receiving disability claims, paying disability benefits, and handling the other administrative details associated with the policies.

In 1986 Baker received a letter notifying him his policy had been transferred to Illinois-based Benefit Trust Life Insurance Company. The letter did not mention that Penn Mutual had an

A+ rating from Best and that Benefit Trust had an A rating. The letter said the change in location of the policy's administration did not alter any of the policy provisions. I was surprised Baker had not been asked for his consent to the transfer.

In 1988, in response to his inquiries, Baker received a letter from an actuary at Penn Mutual. The actuary said Penn Mutual's expertise in disability insurance had "dissipated," and the company felt it was better for both Penn Mutual and its disability insurance policyholders to transfer the previously issued policies to a company with a "greater presence" in the disability insurance market. The actuary spoke highly of Benefit Trust, but he did not mention the companies' ratings. Then the actuary made an astonishing statement. He said that Benefit Trust had taken total control of the policies and the obligations under them, and that Penn Mutual had no further obligations under the policies. The actuary made no mention of the need for Baker's consent to complete the novation.

I wrote to Penn Mutual's chief executive officer and asked what would happen in the event of Benefit Trust's insolvency. This astounding response came from an executive vice president: "Policyholders would have no recourse to Penn Mutual for satisfaction of their claims in the event of Benefit Trust's insolvency." Again there was no mention of the need for Baker's consent to complete the novation. The Penn Mutual case is discussed in the October 1989 and December 1989 issues.

The Ohio State Life Case

I also received an incredible correspondence file from Charles (not his real name). He owned a disability income insurance policy issued by Ohio State Life Insurance Company. In March 1989 he received a letter from the company notifying him, "effective immediately," the policy had been transferred to Texas-based Lone Star Life Insurance Company. The letter did not mention Ohio State's A+ rating from Best or Lone Star's C+ rating from Best.

However, the letter did allude to consent. The letter said the payment of a premium by Charles to Lone Star and/or the receipt by Charles of any disability insurance benefits from Lone Star "shall constitute and evidence your unqualified acceptance of Lone Star as the substituted insurer...." The letter did not say what Charles should do if he did not want to consent to the novation. The implication was that, if Charles did not want to consent to the novation, he could refrain from paying the next premium due on the policy and in that manner terminate his disability insurance protection. The Ohio State case is discussed in the October 1989 issue.

The Struggle for Reform

In the December 1989 issue I reported on yet another case, and on the fact that the New York Department of Insurance was involved in the Penn Mutual case. I sent my October 1989 and December 1989 articles to the regulators of all the states. Some regulators expressed interest and invited me to submit specific suggestions. I then developed a reform proposal that was built around positive consent.

The National Association of Insurance Commissioners (NAIC) decided to appoint a study group of insurance regulators to explore the subject of policy transfers. The study group was chaired by James Hanson, a senior official in the Illinois Department of Insurance.

The NAIC study group decided to appoint an advisory committee. I wrote to Hanson expressing a willingness to serve on the advisory committee. Despite the fact that my articles had generated the regulators' interest in the subject, Hanson responded that I was not going to be appointed to the advisory committee. Hanson probably did not want me to serve on the committee because I had expressed my strongly held belief that positive consent is essential to a valid transfer.

Jim Long, the North Carolina insurance commissioner, was president of the NAIC at the time. He was aware of my lawsuit against his North Carolina predecessor, John Ingram, discussed in chapter 5. I wrote to Long and explained the situation. A few days later I received a telephone call from Hanson, who said I had been appointed to the advisory committee. I have no knowledge of the content of what may have been a colorful telephone conversation between Long and Hanson.

On February 28, 1991, at a meeting of the nine-member advisory committee (eight insurance company representatives and me), the advisory committee voted 8 to 1 in favor of negative consent. The dissenting vote was mine. The advisory committee prepared a report containing a proposed model law built around negative consent. I prepared a minority report containing a proposed model law built around positive consent. My proposal is in the May 1991 issue.

For more than two years thereafter, I hammered away with further articles. Based on a 2007 tabulation, ten states had adopted the committee's model built around negative consent, another ten states had adopted at least some rules built around negative consent, and the remaining states had no rules.

The Mechanics of a Transfer

All the advisory committee members agreed that the owners of the transferred policies must be notified of the transfer. Also, all agreed that consent was necessary. Where we differed was on the form of consent. An explanation of the mechanics of a transfer of a block of policies is necessary to have an understanding of the views of the eight advisory committee members who voted in favor of negative consent.

The transfer of a block of policies is accomplished through a reinsurance agreement between the company transferring the policies (the transferor) and the company receiving the transfer of the policies (the transferee). Also, there is an administration agreement between the transferor and the transferee under which the transferee sends premium notices, accepts premium payments, receives claims, pays benefits, and handles other administrative details relating to all the transferred policies.

With regard to policies owned by policyholders who consent to the transfer, the transferor is relieved of its obligations to the policyholders. The transferee not only continues to administer the policies but also assumes full responsibility for the obligations under the policies.

By contrast, with regard to policies owned by policyholders who do *not* consent to the transfer, the transferee continues to administer the policies but *the transferor remains contingently obligated* under the policies. Although the transferee continues to administer the policies, the transferor remains obligated under the policies in the event that the transferee becomes financially unable to honor the obligations under the policies.

The eight insurance company representatives on the advisory committee said using positive consent would thwart the purpose of the transfer, which was to allow the transferor to wash its hands of the transferred policies. They believed that, in most if not all transfers, a large majority of the policyholders—perhaps more than 90 percent—would fail to respond to the notification letter. In other words, they believed that, if positive consent were used, only a few policyholders would consent and the overwhelming majority would be deemed to have *not* consented to the novation. On the other hand, they believed that, if negative consent were used, the overwhelming majority would be deemed to have consented to the novation.

I agreed to some extent with the beliefs of the insurance company representatives. However, I believed that a well-written notification letter that explained the implications of the transfer would attract the attention of a substantial percentage of the policyholders, and that consequently the percentage responding would be significantly enlarged.

Furthermore, I felt that a well-written notification letter would describe clearly the advantages and disadvantages of the transfer from the viewpoint of the policyholder. For that reason, I believed that a substantial percentage of policyholders would consent if the transfer were in their best interest, and that a substantial percentage would not consent if the transfer were not in their best interest. In other words, policyholders should be told the truth about the transfer and have the opportunity to act in their own best interest.

The other advisory committee members and I also disagreed on the extent of the disclosures that should be made in the notification letter. I favored strong disclosure requirements, while some favored minimal disclosure requirements. For example, I favored disclosure of all the financial strength ratings (including explanations of the ratings) assigned to the transferor and the transferee by the four major rating firms, but others viewed such disclosure as excessive.

The Constitutional Issue

When the NAIC working group received the advisory committee's majority draft of the proposed model law built around negative consent, Hanson was worried about whether a state law built around negative consent would survive a challenge under the U.S. Constitution. Hanson asked the advisory committee to obtain a legal opinion. Patrick Carmody, an actuary at Mutual of Omaha Insurance Company, chaired the advisory committee. Donald Greene of the law firm of LeBoeuf, Lamb, Leiby & MacRae was a member of the advisory committee. Carmody asked Greene to write a legal opinion. Here is the final sentence of Greene's lengthy opinion letter:

> For the reasons set forth above, we are of the opinion that the implied consent provision of the proposed Model Act would withstand a challenge based upon the United States Constitution.

I asked David Vladeck, an expert on constitutional law and a member of Public Citizen Litigation Group, a public interest law firm, to review Greene's legal opinion. (Vladeck had been my attorney in my lawsuit against the North Carolina insurance commissioner, as described in chapter 5.) Vladeck's lengthy memorandum included this paragraph:

> Having carefully reviewed the [Greene] letter and the authorities it discusses, I do not believe that the analysis set forth in the letter is persuasive. For the reasons discussed below, it is far from clear that an implied consent provision would pass muster under either the Due Process or Contract Clauses of the Constitution.

To my knowledge, neither Hanson nor the NAIC took the slightest interest in Vladeck's opinion. In other words, they apparently decided to rely on Greene's self-serving opinion. Greene's legal opinion and Vladeck's memorandum are in the August 1992 issue.

The Crown Life Case

In 1993 Crown Life Insurance Company (Regina, Saskatchewan) transferred its U.S. disability insurance business to Texas-based Lone Star Life Insurance Company. The transfer was a classic example of the nondisclosure of material information to the owners of the transferred policies. Here I mention only three areas of nondisclosure.

First, under Canadian rules, a company planning to make a transfer was required to announce publicly in advance its intent to apply for approval of the transfer. The announcement had to appear in the *Canada Gazette*, which is for public announcements and is not seen routinely by members of the public, and in a newspaper of general circulation. For the latter, Crown Life cleverly selected *The Leader-Post*, a daily newspaper in Regina, despite the facts that all the policyholders lived in the U.S. and that few if any of them would see the Regina newspaper.

Second, neither the notification letter from a senior vice president of Crown Life nor the letter of greeting from the chief executive officer of Lone Star Life disclosed that Crown Life had an A+ rating by A. M. Best and that Lone Star had a rating of B–. Nor were the ratings disclosed in the transfer certificates or other materials sent to the policyholders.

Third, under Canadian rules, the transferor must obtain a report from an independent actuary. Crown Life obtained a report from Alan Brereton of the Toronto office of Ecker Partners, an actuarial consulting firm. Crown Life fought to keep the report secret, but I obtained it through a request pursuant to Canada's Access to Information Act. When I saw the report, it was obvious why Crown Life was anxious to keep it secret. The report, in a section about the effect on policyholders, included this profoundly disturbing sentence:

> Crown Life has stated it is unwilling to continue its support of this line [its disability insurance business in the U.S.], and with its move to Regina [from Toronto], it is potentially unable to continue its support at least at reasonable cost.

The Crown Life case is discussed in the August 1993 issue. I included in the article the following plain English translation of what Crown Life was really saying:

> We at Crown Life made solemn contractual promises to those U.S. residents to whom we sold disability insurance policies. We have now made the strategic decision to focus our efforts in other areas, and to move our headquarters from Toronto to Regina. It would be inconvenient and expensive to honor our promises under those policies. For those reasons, we are unwilling to honor those promises.

The TIAA Case

Teachers Insurance and Annuity Association of America (TIAA) and its affiliate, College Retirement Equities Fund (CREF), which are based in New York, cater primarily to academicians and senior administrators of colleges and universities. TIAA is a large, highly regarded company with perennial top ratings from the major rating firms, except for recent one-notch downgrades by Standard & Poor's and Moody's Investors Service. TIAA's biggest business is in retirement plans, but it has long offered life insurance.

Around 1990 TIAA began offering individual long-term care insurance. By the fall of 2003 it had 46,000 long-term care insurance policyholders, but had not become a major player in the long-term care insurance business.

In November 2003 I received a telephone call from a long-time academic colleague at another university. He was angry. He said that he had purchased a long-term care insurance policy from TIAA some years earlier, and that he had chosen TIAA because of its stellar reputation for fair treatment of its policyholders in such areas as pricing and claims handling. He said he had just received a letter from TIAA saying that it was getting out of the long-term care insurance business and that it had sold its existing block of policies to Metropolitan Life Insurance Company, a major company based in New York.

In response to my question, my colleague said TIAA actually used the word "sold." I knew the word was wrong, because I knew TIAA must have transferred the policies to Metropolitan solely for administration and could not escape its obligations under the policies without obtaining the consent of the policyholders. I asked my colleague to send me a copy of the notification letter. Within the next few days, I received similar irate calls from academic colleagues at other universities. Out of that incident grew major articles in the March/April 2004, December 2005, and June 2007 issues of the *Forum*.

My Statement to New York

Because TIAA and Metropolitan were both domiciled in New York, I knew the transfer of the long-term care insurance policies would be subject to the approval of the New York Department of Insurance. I submitted a formal statement to the Department suggesting that the Department impose five requirements as conditions for approving the transfer. Here is a summary of my suggested requirements:

> (1) Each policyholder should be given thorough disclosure of the consequences of consenting to the elimination of TIAA's obligations under his or her policy.
> (2) Positive consent should be required from each policyholder who consents to the elimination of TIAA's obligations under his or her policy.
> (3) Compensation should be paid to each policyholder who consents to the elimination of TIAA's obligations under his or her policy.
> (4) TIAA should retain final authority for claim denials, claim settlements, and claim terminations relating to each policyholder who does not consent to the elimination of TIAA's obligations under his or her policy.
> (5) All policyholders should be covered by a single set of contracts between TIAA and Metropolitan.

I sent TIAA a courtesy copy of the statement when I submitted it to the Department, but TIAA did not reciprocate. I had to obtain TIAA's response through a request pursuant to the New York Freedom of Information Law (FOIL). TIAA's response was from Bertram Scott, an executive vice president.

On item 1, TIAA essentially agreed. However, I had serious doubts that TIAA would make adequate disclosures to the policyholders.

On item 2, TIAA said that it would follow New York rules, which are based on negative consent, and that no states require positive consent. I later learned that two states—Minnesota by law and Washington State by insurance department regulation—had positive consent requirements. I also later learned that Metropolitan never tried to obtain consent from any of the policyholders in those two states.

On item 3, TIAA disagreed vigorously. I had made the suggestion because I felt that the transfer was disadvantageous to policyholders, and that any policyholder who nonetheless consented to the transfer should be provided with compensation for doing so.

On items 4 and 5, TIAA essentially agreed. I had suggested item 5 because I was aware of another case where one set of contracts applied to New York policyholders and a different set of contracts applied to policyholders in other states.

TIAA's response prompted me to submit a follow-up statement to the Department. I elaborated on some of the points and discussed two additional matters. I am not aware of the extent, if any, to which my statements affected the outcome of the approval process, but I know negative consent was used and no compensation was paid to policyholders who consented to the transfer.

The Department approved the transfer in May 2004. I had difficulty obtaining relevant documents, but eventually obtained some of them through FOIL requests. It was not until 2007 that Metropolitan finally began trying to obtain consent from policyholders to complete the novations. I do not know the final results of those efforts.

My Aborted CREF Resolution

I was not a TIAA long-term care insurance policyholder, but I owned (and still own) TIAA life insurance and CREF annuities. I wanted to warn TIAA long-term care insurance policyholders about the consequences of ignoring the notification and thereby consenting to the novation by default. I knew of no way to communicate directly with my fellow TIAA-CREF policyholders, but I hatched an idea.

CREF is regulated by the Securities and Exchange Commission (SEC) and sometimes includes a few participant resolutions in its proxy statements. TIAA is not regulated by the SEC and does not include resolutions in its proxies. However, I was certain that virtually all of TIAA's long-term care insurance policyholders owned CREF annuities.

I prepared a resolution to be included in CREF's proxy for the June 2004 annual meeting. The "whereas" paragraphs of my proposed resolution described the implications of consenting to the novation. The operative paragraph called for limiting the arrangement to a transfer solely for administration, with TIAA retaining the contingent liability.

I submitted the resolution to CREF, which wrote to the SEC and gave five reasons why my resolution should be omitted from the proxy. I wrote to the SEC responding to each of the reasons. The SEC wrote to CREF focusing on one of the five reasons: the "5 percent rule," under which a resolution may be omitted from the proxy when the subject matter relates to only a small part of the company's total business. Thus my resolution was omitted from the proxy because long-term care insurance was only a small part of TIAA-CREF's total business.

The Bottom Line

My efforts on behalf of the owners of policies transferred from one insurance company to another were not entirely successful. Although rules now exist in some states regarding transfers, many policyholders are still being victimized by inadequate procedures. Perhaps some day an enterprising attorney will challenge the constitutionality of state rules allow-

ing insurance companies to wash their hands of solemn promises the companies made to policyholders without obtaining
the informed, positive consent of those policyholders.

Issues Mentioned in This Chapter

October 1989, December 1989, January 1991, May 1991,
August 1992, August 1993, March/April 2004, December 2005,
and June 2007.

24

Compensation of Insurance Executives

*O*ver almost the entire life of the *Forum* I reported on the annual compensation of highly paid insurance company executives. In this chapter I discuss what happened along the way. In terms of access to data I experienced some victories and some setbacks.

Data for 1974

It all began with an article in the October 1975 issue about executive compensation in 1974. I selected the five largest mutual life insurance companies as measured by assets: Prudential Insurance Company of America, Metropolitan Life Insurance Company, Equitable Life Assurance Society of the United States, New York Life Insurance Company, and John Hancock Mutual Life Insurance Company.

I chose to focus on large mutual companies for two reasons. First, most major shareholder-owned (stock) companies were part of publicly owned firms that filed compensation data with the Securities and Exchange Commission (SEC), and therefore the data were considered easily available. Second, compensation data for mutual companies were filed only with the states and the data were considered not easily available.

I assembled the data from "Schedule G" in the annual financial statements that were filed with state insurance regulators.

I showed for each company the number of executives in each of eight categories: the lowest category was $30,000 to $39,999, and the highest category was $100,000 and over. The five mutual companies combined had 3,205 executives in the eight categories. I showed names, job titles, and compensation of those in the highest category.

Data for 1975-1982

Readers expressed considerable interest. Over the next eight years I showed similar data. During that period I expanded to the ten largest and later the 15 largest mutual life insurance companies. Also, I raised the threshold from $100,000 to $125,000, then $150,000, then $175,000, then $200,000, and then $225,000.

Data for 1982-1986

In 1983 I began looking at more mutual companies. I also began looking at stock companies after a mutual company executive jokingly suggested I should start including data for stock companies. At the same time I began looking at SEC filings by stock companies. I showed 1982 data for about 100 additional individuals and about 50 additional companies. Over the next four years I continued publishing data for mutual companies and stock companies based on data from Schedule G and the SEC. During that period I raised the threshold to $300,000, and then $350,000.

The Setback of 1986

Each year the National Association of Insurance Commissioners (NAIC) promulgates the annual financial statement form that must be used by life insurance companies. There has never been anything comparable to Schedule G in the annual statement form for property insurance companies. As mentioned, one of my sources was Schedule G in the life insurance company statements.

In 1986 the NAIC abruptly deleted from the statement form the portion of Schedule G showing executive compensation data. There were no public hearings or public debate about the action. I learned later that the action was taken at the request of Theodore Bausher, a senior official in the Pennsylvania Insurance Department. I corresponded on the matter with several regulators. James Hanson, a senior official in the Illinois Department of Insurance, explained that "the information served little purpose for financial analysis and surveillance" and that "other reporting mechanisms have supplanted the need for it." He acknowledged that "the public, especially agents or producers, found the schedule interesting," but "their interest was not germane to financial regulation."

The effect of the action was to overturn an 80-year tradition of executive compensation disclosure dating back to legislation enacted in New York State following the Hughes-Armstrong Committee's investigation of the life insurance business in 1905. The investigation uncovered, among many other things, serious abuses in executive compensation, including nepotism. However, instead of recommending compensation restrictions, the committee recommended full public disclosure—often referred to as "sunshine"—and the concept was reflected in the executive compensation disclosure law that was enacted in New York State in 1906.

I believe that the impetus for eliminating the data from the annual statement came from life insurance companies, and that the companies' effort grew out of the displeasure of some executives who were unhappy about being named in my tabulations. I have no evidence to support those beliefs, but I think the regulators would not have taken the action without being pushed into it. I discussed the incident in the January 1987 issue of the *Forum*.

The New York Department of Insurance was not able to go along with the NAIC and eliminate the executive compensation data from Schedule G. The reason was that New York still had the executive compensation disclosure law, which after its enactment in 1906 was amended several times to increase the disclosure threshold. Thus the Department thereafter required life insurance companies doing business in the state to file Schedule G as part of the "New York Supplement" to the NAIC annual statement form. However, companies not doing business in New York were relieved of filing compensation data with state insurance regulators. My sole sources of data then became Schedule G in the New York Supplement and filings with the SEC by publicly owned stock companies.

Data for 1987-1999

For the next 13 years I continued to publish compensation data using data from New York and the SEC. In 1988 I also began using data from the Nebraska Department of Insurance. Nebraska has long had an executive compensation disclosure law that was enacted a few years after the revelations by the Hughes-Armstrong Committee in New York. The Nebraska law applies not only to mutual life insurance companies, but also to stock life insurance companies and property insurance companies doing business in Nebraska.

I raised the threshold to $400,000, then $500,000, then $600,000, and then $700,000. In 1992 I lowered the threshold to $500,000 and left it there for four years. In 1996 I lowered the threshold to $350,000. I raised it back to $500,000 in 1997 and then $600,000 in 1999.

Despite the generally increasing thresholds, the numbers of companies and individuals shown in the tabulations continued to expand. I did not attempt to explain the reason for the increasing numbers of companies and individuals, but I felt it was a reflection of rapidly increasing levels of compensation of insurance executives. In 1999, even without data from New York (for reasons discussed in the next section of this chapter), there were 222 companies and 1,035 individuals in the tabulation, and the compensation figures continued to escalate.

The Setback of 2000

In November 1999, in accordance with my usual practice, I submitted a request to the New York Department pursuant to the New York Freedom of Information Law (FOIL). I asked for all the Schedule Gs, which were part of the New York Supplement to be filed March 1, 2000. For several years I had been receiving the documents routinely in April. In 2000, when I had heard nothing by May 1, I called the Department to inquire about the status of my request.

I was astounded to learn that the Department was preparing to black out the names of all but the directors and three top officers of each company. When I asked for an explanation, an attorney in the Department said I would have to submit a FOIL request. I did so immediately, and received the file on May 13. It revealed a three-month, secret campaign waged by New York-based Equitable and New Jersey-based Prudential.

The file included a February 22 letter to Neil Levin, the New York superintendent of insurance, from Michael Hegarty, president and chief operating officer of Equitable. Hegarty said the Association of Current and Former Equitable Agents had posted on its website the entire 1998 Schedule G compensation exhibits of Equitable, Metropolitan Life Insurance Company, Mutual Life Insurance Company of New York, and Prudential.

The file revealed close relationships between Equitable executives and Department officials. For example, there was a February 25 "Dear Kevin" letter from Wendy Cooper, senior vice president and associate general counsel of Equitable, to Kevin Rampe, senior deputy superintendent of insurance and general counsel of the Department. Before joining Equitable, Cooper was first deputy superintendent of insurance and served at one point as acting superintendent of insurance.

Cooper enclosed with her February 25 letter a February 23 legal memorandum prepared on behalf of Equitable by Elizabeth Moore and Deborah Shapiro of the firm of Nixon Peabody, and by Wolcott Dunham and John Dembeck of the firm of Debevoise & Plimpton. They said public disclosure of the data was a violation of FOIL, despite the fact that the data had been disclosed routinely ever since FOIL was enacted in 1974 and even before FOIL existed. They cited FOIL's exemption from disclosure for information which, if released, would constitute an "unwarranted invasion of personal privacy." Cooper asked the Department to black out the names of all but the directors and the three top officers. In his April 19 reply to Cooper, Rampe concluded that "public disclosure of the names of employees (other than the directors, trustees or senior officers)...is prohibited as an unwarranted invasion of personal privacy...."

Prudential's March 3 letter to Rampe was from Thomas Faist of the firm of Bogdan & Faist. He asked that the public be denied access to Schedule G in its entirety based on three FOIL exemptions: "unwarranted invasion of personal privacy," "trade secrets," and information which, if disclosed, "would endanger the life or safety of any person." In her April 19 reply to Faist, Sally Geisel, an attorney in the Department, rejected the trade secrets argument and the endangerment argument, but she accepted the privacy argument.

I was as astonished by the procedure as by the result. The file contained no legal arguments from parties who would have favored continued disclosure. The reason was the total secrecy surrounding the move. I could not believe that a state agency, by administrative action, could terminate a 94-year-old and legally required disclosure regime without public notice and without a request for public comment.

I received no data from New York in time for my July 2000 issue. Thus the data shown there were from Nebraska and the SEC only. I later submitted to the Department a revised FOIL request seeking names, job titles, and amounts of compensation only for those who in 1999 received $600,000 or more (my then current threshold). The Department denied my request in part by blacking out the names of all but the directors and the three top officers of each company.

In July 2000 my attorney filed on my behalf an administrative appeal of the Department's partial denial of my FOIL request. The Department took the position that the blacked-out information fell within FOIL's exemption relating to unwarranted invasion of personal privacy. We took the position that the very purpose of the executive compensation disclosure law was to make the information available to the public. The Department denied our administrative appeal.

In December 2000 my attorney filed on my behalf in state court a petition for judicial review of the Department's partial denial of my FOIL request. The attorney general of New York, on behalf of the Department, opposed our petition. The Life Insurance Council of New York (LICONY), an association of life insurance companies doing business in New York, intervened and opposed our petition.

In September 2001 the judge ordered the Department to honor my request for the 1999 data—including names, and with the $600,000 threshold—within 30 days of his order. The Department took five months to comply with the order. I eventually published a belated update based on the 1999 New York data. I discussed the setback of 2000 and the 2001 court order in the July 2000 and November 2001 issues.

A Tragic Side Note

As mentioned earlier, Neil Levin was the New York superintendent of insurance at the time of the Department's action in 2000. He resigned in March 2001 and was appointed executive director of the Port Authority of New York and New Jersey by the governors of the two states. The Authority had its executive offices on the 68th floor in the north tower of the World Trade Center. On September 11 Levin was attending a breakfast meeting at the Windows on the World restaurant on the top floor when the first airliner struck the tower. At that moment, he reportedly was speaking on his cell phone with his executive assistant and said: "What was that?" Levin died five days before his 47th birthday.

Data for 2000-2007

For the next eight years, I continued publishing executive compensation data from my three sources. After the 2000 action, and after the litigation, there were delays in publishing the New York data not only for 1999 but also for 2000 and 2001. Prior to publishing the 2002 data, I published the data in a single large table. When there were figures for the same person from more than one of my three sources, and when the figures differed, I published the largest figure. Beginning with the 2002 data, I began publishing three tables of data, one for each of my three sources, and continued with that practice through the 2012 data. For 2004 data I raised the threshold to $750,000, and for 2006 data to $1 million.

A Temporary Victory in 2007

On February 20, 2007, in my routine FOIL request to the Department for the 2006 data, I asked for the Schedule Gs with no names blacked out. The Department at that time was under new management, and I felt the time was right to ask the Department to reverse the July 2000 administrative action. I enclosed an explanatory memorandum.

The Department, without informing me, sent my request to LICONY. Moore of Nixon Peabody prepared a March 28 legal memorandum on behalf of LICONY arguing that my request should be denied. On June 13, in a lengthy legal memorandum, the Department informed LICONY that, effective June 25, the Department "will return to its prior and longstanding practice of producing Schedule G records without redaction of names." I was unaware of any of these developments until after the fact, when I saw the documents through a FOIL request. I discussed the Department's change of position in the October 2007 issue.

The Setback of 2008

LICONY was enraged by the Department's 2007 rescission of its 2000 administrative action. LICONY quietly arranged for bills to be introduced in each house of the New York legislature in the spring of 2008 to decimate the 102-year-old compensation disclosure law. I say quietly because I was unaware of the existence of the bills, on which there had been no debate, no hearings, and no publicity, until I received a tip from a "Deep Throat" informer after the proposed legislation had sailed through both houses and had been sent to Governor David Paterson for his signature. I rushed a package of material to the governor and asked him to veto the amendment, but he signed it into law.

The amendment required life insurance companies doing business in New York to disclose (1) names and compensation of directors, (2) names, job titles, and compensation of the chief executive officer and the next four highest compensated employees, (3) names, job titles, and compensation of the next five highest compensated employees, and (4) job titles and compensation, *but not the names*, of other employees below the top ten but whose compensation exceeded $750,000. Those requirements meant that, in large companies, there would be many highly paid executives whose job titles and compensation would be disclosed but whose names would be blacked out. I discussed the setback of 2008 in the October 2008 issue.

Data for 2008-2012

For the final five years of my tabulations, I retained the $1 million threshold. I presented 2008 data in the July 2009 issue. I indicated "name not disclosed" for each individual who received compensation of at least $1 million but whose name was blacked out in accordance with the newly amended law. In the New York section of the tabulation of the 2008 data, I also presented 2007 data in a separate table showing name, job title, and amount for each individual who received compensation of at least $1 million. The 2007 data showed all the names because the 2007 data had been filed before the newly amended law took effect. By comparing the 2007 and 2008 data, a careful reader can identify some individuals whose names were blacked out in the 2008 data.

I presented 2009 data and 2010 data in the July 2010 and July 2011 issues. I showed job title and amount, and indicated "name not disclosed" for each individual who received compensation of at least $1 million and whose name was blacked out. Here again a careful reader can identify some individuals by referring back to the 2007 data in the July 2009 issue.

I presented 2011 data in the July 2012 issue, and 2012 data in the July 2013 issue. In those two issues, for each individual who received compensation of at least $1 million, I showed only the number of names blacked out by each company. For example, in the 2012 data shown in the July 2013 issue, there were 674 individuals with compensation of at least $1 million, but only

272 were identified. The names of the other 402 were blacked out. The following companies had these numbers of individuals for whom the names were blacked out:

Aetna Life Ins Co	148
AXA Equitable Life Ins Co	6
Connecticut General Life	2
Guardian Life Ins Co	1
Massachusetts Mutual Life	11
Metropolitan Life Ins Co	70
New York Life Ins Co	28
Penn Mutual Life Ins Co	3
Phoenix Life Ins Co	3
Principal Life Ins Co	14
Prudential Ins Co of America	103
Teachers Ins & Annuity Assn	13

My final tabulation of executive compensation was in the July 2013 issue. It showed that 66 individuals received total compensation of $10 million or more in 2012. Their names, amounts, and company affiliations are in appendix D.

The Compensation Trend

A glimpse at the trend of top executive compensation in the insurance business over the period from 1974 to 2012 may be obtained by listing the highest compensated individual shown in my tabulation each year. The list showing the name, amount, and company affiliation of each individual is in appendix E.

A Temporary Victory in Nebraska in 2014

On Friday, March 21, 2014, I received an unexpected telephone call from Paul Hammel, a reporter at the *Omaha World-Herald*. He said a bill had been introduced in January 2014 in the Nebraska legislature to repeal Nebraska's century-old executive compensation disclosure law. The call was my first knowledge of the repeal effort.

On Sunday, March 23, the newspaper published Hammel's lengthy article, which was entitled "Texans target Nebraska law requiring insurance firms to disclose top executives' pay." The article ran prominently; it began at the top of the front page of the newspaper's second section and continued on the second page of that section.

Behind the repeal effort was United Services Automobile Association (USAA), a large Texas-based company that caters to current and former members of the military and their families. USAA paid $50,000 to Mueller Robak, a legal and lobbying firm whose office is one block from the Nebraska state capitol building in Lincoln.

Spearheading the repeal effort was William McCartney, senior vice president and associate general counsel of USAA. Ironically, he was director of insurance in Nebraska from 1987 to 1994, where he had lived with the Nebraska executive compensation disclosure law. During a discussion of the repeal effort, he said he never liked the law. He served as president of the NAIC in 1992.

I reported the repeal effort in blog no. 39 (April 7, 2014) and discussed USAA's executive compensation. Because USAA is a private company, it does not file with the SEC. Nor does it file with the New York Department, because only a small subsidiary operates there and the compensation allocated to the subsidiary is trivial. USAA's executive compensation exhibits filed with the Nebraska Department of Insurance each year contain this notice in italicized, boldface, solid capital letters:

NOTICE: THIS INFORMATION IS PROPRIETARY AND CONFIDENTIAL. DO NOT FILE WITH ANNUAL STATEMENT OR IN ANY OTHER PUBLICLY ACCESSIBLE FILE OR DOCUMENT.

The Nebraska disclosure law contains no provision permitting the Department to maintain confidentiality for the executive compensation data. Therefore the Department provides the information to anyone who requests it pursuant to the Nebraska public records law. I presented in blog no. 39 all the 2011, 2012, and 2013 data filed in Nebraska by USAA and its subsidiaries that operate in Nebraska. Josue Robles, Jr., the chief executive officer of USAA, received $6.5 million in 2011, $10.5 million in 2012, and $7.4 million in 2013. McCartney received $399,156 in 2012; no data were shown for him in 2011 or 2013.

I reported in blog no. 40 (April 11, 2014) that the repeal bill was scheduled to die when the legislature adjourned. The bill did in fact die. Thus the Nebraska executive compensation disclosure law survived the 2014 repeal effort, at least until some future session of the legislature.

Issues and Blog Items Mentioned in This Chapter

October 1975, January 1987, July 2000, November 2001, October 2007, October 2008, July 2009, July 2010, July 2011, July 2012, and July 2013, and blog nos. 39 (April 7, 2014) and 40 (April 11, 2014).

25

Surplus Notes

*D*uring the first two decades of the *Forum* I made occasional references to what are called surplus notes in most states. They are called contribution certificates in California and surplus debentures in Texas. The most significant references in those early days were in some of my articles about the financial condition of Executive Life Insurance Company, as discussed in chapter 7. In 1993, two years after the collapse of Executive Life, surplus notes became a topic of major attention for me, for reasons explained in this chapter.

What Is a Surplus Note?

I have referred to a surplus note as a bizarre financial instrument and as an accountant's nightmare. A surplus note is a promissory note that represents debt; that is, an insurance company issuing a surplus note thereby borrows money from the purchaser of the surplus note. The money received from the purchaser increases the insurance company's assets. However, unlike an ordinary promissory note, issuing a surplus note does not require the insurance company to establish a liability. Consequently the surplus note increases the insurance company's net worth, since net worth is the company's assets minus its liabilities.

A surplus note increases an insurance company's net worth because state insurance laws allowing the issuance of surplus notes say the insurance company is not required to establish a liability in connection with the issuance of a surplus note. The original purpose of such laws was to provide a mechanism through which mutual insurance companies, which do not have shareholders, may increase their net worth from external sources. The early laws were enacted many years ago because of the dire financial condition of some mutual insurance companies at the time. Some of the laws have been amended, after effective lobbying by stock (shareholder-owned) insurance companies, and now allow stock insurance companies to issue surplus notes even though stock companies can increase their net worth by selling shares to investors.

State surplus note laws say an insurance company is allowed to issue a surplus note only with the prior approval of the insurance commissioner in the insurance company's state of domicile. The laws also say payments of interest and repayments of principal on a surplus note are allowed only with the prior approval of the insurance commissioner.

A surplus note does not provide permanent net worth because the issuing insurance company promises to repay the borrowed money. However, the theory behind the laws is that a surplus note is treated appropriately as part of an insurance company's net worth because the surplus note is subordinated to all the company's other liabilities, and because interest payments and principal repayments on a surplus note are made only when the company is in satisfactory financial condition as determined by the insurance commissioner. As discussed later, I believe that the theory is open to question.

Podunk Mutual

An anecdote illustrates the original purpose of surplus notes. Paul is the president and chief executive officer of Podunk Mutual Life Insurance Company, a small, fictional company with inadequate net worth. Indeed, the company is perilously close to financial collapse.

Mary is Paul's mother-in-law. She wants Podunk to survive because she wants Paul to remain employed for the sake of her daughter and the grandchildren. Mary is willing to put $1 million into Podunk to increase its net worth, but a mechanism is needed. Podunk cannot increase its net worth by issuing shares of stock to Mary in exchange for the $1 million because a mutual insurance company has no shares of stock and no shareholders. Nor can Podunk increase its net worth by issuing an ordinary promissory note to Mary in exchange for the $1 million because issuing an ordinary promissory note would increase Podunk's assets and liabilities but would not increase its net worth.

Enter the surplus note, an instrument that is allowed under the surplus note law in Podunk's state of domicile. With the prior approval of the insurance commissioner there, Podunk can issue a surplus note to Mary in exchange for the $1 million. Although the surplus note would be evidence of debt, the law says Podunk is not required to establish a liability. Thus Podunk's issuance of a $1 million surplus note would increase Podunk's assets by $1 million and would increase Podunk's net worth by $1 million.

The Tax Angle

As will be seen, income tax considerations now play a major role in the decisions of insurance companies to issue surplus notes. The key point is that interest payments on a surplus note are treated in the same manner as interest on debt and therefore are deductible by the insurance company. On the other hand, if interest payments on a surplus note were treated in the same manner as cash dividends paid on shares of stock, the interest payments would not be deductible by the insurance company.

A surplus note is often described as tax effective. I think it is more accurate to describe a surplus note as providing the issuing insurance company with a subsidy from U.S. taxpayers.

The situation has not been ignored by the Internal Revenue Service (IRS). Several court cases addressed the question of whether interest payments on a surplus note should be treated as interest on debt and therefore deductible, as argued by the insurance companies, or whether those interest payments should be treated as cash dividends paid on shares of stock and therefore nondeductible, as argued by the IRS. I think the cases could have gone either way, but the courts decided the cases in favor of the insurance companies.

I think those court decisions are regrettable for three reasons. First, the decisions provide insurance companies with an advantage over competitors in the financial services business. Second, the decisions cause those competitors to push for enactment of similar laws to level the playing field, thereby shifting to other taxpayers the burden of paying for vital government services. Third, the decisions tempt insurance company executives to borrow money and thereby threaten the long-term financial strength of insurance companies.

Traditional Surplus Notes

As mentioned above, surplus notes originally were designed to be issued by mutual insurance companies that were in poor financial condition. Indeed, the very existence of a surplus note in an insurance company's financial statement was a red flag indicating that the insurance company was in financial trouble. A surplus note issued by a mutual insurance company in poor financial condition is called a traditional surplus note.

Intercorporate Surplus Notes

Surplus notes sometimes are used to transfer funds from one member of an insurance company group to another member of the group. For example, an insurance company may issue a surplus note to its parent company in exchange for funds provided to the insurance company by the parent company. Such surplus notes played a prominent role at Executive Life Insurance Company, as discussed in chapter 7. A surplus note issued by one member of an insurance company group to another member of the group is called an intercorporate surplus note.

Investor Surplus Notes

In April 1993 Prudential Insurance Company of America (Newark, NJ) became the first financially strong insurance company to issue a surplus note to sophisticated investors through

a private offering. Prudential issued a $300 million, 10-year sur-
plus note at an annual interest rate of 6.875 percent. A surplus
note issued to sophisticated investors through a private offering
is called an investor surplus note.

I was surprised by the issuance of a surplus note by a financially strong insurance company. Also, I expected that other
financially strong insurance companies would promptly copy
Prudential's action.

Therefore I called a Prudential senior officer I knew and
asked for an explanation. He said he would call back in an hour,
and he did so. He said two company executives wanted to come
to Indiana to meet with me personally rather than discuss the
matter by telephone or letter. I agreed to the meeting. The reason for the unusual nature of the response was clear: the company was concerned that I would view its issuance of a surplus
note as a sign of financial weakness.

In our meeting the executives said Prudential issued the
surplus note for two reasons. First, they cited court rulings that
interest payments on a surplus note are deductible for income
tax purposes in the same manner as interest payments on debt.
Second, they said the company created a voluntary employee
benefit association (VEBA) to provide post-retirement medical
and other benefits for certain unionized employees. The company used the $296 million of net proceeds from the surplus
note offering to prefund the VEBA. The prefunding generated
about $100 million of income tax savings for the company in
1993. The executives emphasized that the company was not in
any kind of financial difficulty.

Goldman, Sachs & Co. was Prudential's adviser on the surplus note offering and the VEBA project. Prudential submitted
to the New Jersey insurance commissioner a Goldman report
that included an interesting chart. It showed that 62 percent of
the initial contribution to the VEBA came from Prudential and
that the other 38 percent came from the IRS. Goldman could
have said the 38 percent came from other taxpayers.

The New Jersey surplus note law allowed the issuance of a surplus note only for a few specified purposes, none of which struck

me as applicable in this case. I therefore wrote to the insurance commissioner inquiring about the authority to allow the issuance of a surplus note in the Prudential case. I received a lengthly and reasonable response from Asutosh Chakrabarti, the New Jersey commissioner's chief actuary.

The Revolution of 1993

As I expected, Prudential's action was copied in a wave of surplus note offerings by financially strong insurance companies. In October 1993 Metropolitan Life Insurance Company (New York, NY) issued two surplus notes. One was a $400 million, 10-year surplus note at an annual interest rate of 6.3 percent. The other was a $300 million, 30-year surplus note at an annual interest rate of 7.45 percent. The net proceeds of $691 million were to be used "for general corporate purposes, including the conduct of [Metropolitan Life's] business." The New York insurance superintendent authorized the issuance of the surplus notes under the New York surplus note law.

In November 1993 Massachusetts Mutual Life Insurance Company (Springfield, MA) issued a $250 million, 30-year surplus note at an annual interest rate of 7.625 percent. The net proceeds of $246 million were to be used "for general corporate purposes." This sentence was in the confidential private offering circular: "In Massachusetts, there is no statute that specifically authorizes the issuance of surplus notes or addresses their accounting treatment or repayment terms." Since the offering circular said nothing further on the matter, I wrote to the Massachusetts insurance commissioner inquiring about the authority for approving issuance of the surplus note. In response, an attorney in the Division of Insurance said "there are no existing public documents which address this question." Later I wrote again. In March 1994 I received this letter from the deputy commissioner and general counsel of the Division:

> The Division has broad supervisory powers over insurance companies doing business in Massachusetts. This is especially true of those insurers domiciled in the Common-

wealth. The Division's chief responsibility is the protection of both policyholders and the public, and the Massachusetts General Court has granted the Division broad statutory authority over the financial condition and transactions of our domestic insurers, including the obligation to monitor and to periodically examine their financial status.

Approval of surplus note transactions by Massachusetts domestic insurers is within the General Court's broad grant of authority to the Division and is consistent with the legislative charge.

In response I asked the Division's deputy commissioner for the precise language of the "broad grant of authority" and the "legislative charge." I received no reply.

In December 1993 New York Life Insurance Company (New York, NY) issued two surplus notes. One was a $150 million, 10-year surplus note at an annual interest rate of 6.4 percent. The other was a $300 million, 30-year surplus note at an annual interest rate of 7.5 percent.

The flurry of surplus note offerings that followed Prudential's action is discussed in my February 1994 issue. Also, the subsequent "reshuffling of capital" through surplus notes issued by insurance companies and purchased by other insurance companies is discussed in the September 1994 issue. By the end of 1994 surplus notes were a heavily used financial instrument. Life insurance companies had issued a total of $6.6 billion of surplus notes, in contrast to only $400 million at the end of 1981. Among the many strong life insurance companies that issued large amounts of surplus notes, in addition to the four already mentioned, were General American Life Insurance Company, John Hancock Mutual Life Insurance Company, Mutual Life Insurance Company of New York, National Life Insurance Company (VT), New England Mutual Life Insurance Company, Northwestern National Life Insurance Company, Ohio National Life Insurance Company, Pacific Mutual Life Insurance Company, Principal Mutual Life Insurance Company, Security Life of Denver Insurance Company, and Sun Life Assurance Company of Canada (U.S.).

After the emergence of the surplus note as a popular financial instrument, I began publishing every year in the *Forum* a tabulation of all insurance companies with appreciable amounts of surplus notes outstanding at the end of the previous year. In my final tabulation, in the August 2013 issue, I reported that life insurance companies had $28 billion of surplus notes outstanding at the end of 2012, or 5 percent of the industry's net worth, and that property insurance companies had $14 billion of surplus notes outstanding, or 2 percent of the industry's net worth.

Maturities of Surplus Notes

Prudential's first surplus note matured in ten years. Subsequent surplus notes issued by Prudential and other companies had longer maturities, often 20 or 30 years. At the extreme, Liberty Mutual Insurance Company and Lumbermens Mutual Casualty Company issued 100-year surplus notes. In recent years most maturities have not exceeded 30 years.

Ratings of Surplus Notes

Although traditional and intercorporate surplus notes are not rated, investor surplus notes are rated. For a highly rated insurance company, surplus notes usually are rated two notches below the company's financial strength rating. For example, a company with financial strength ratings of AA+ by Standard & Poor's and Aa1 by Moody's Investors Service usually receives ratings of AA– and Aa3 on a surplus note. For a lower-rated company, a surplus note usually is rated at least three notches below the financial strength rating.

The Disasters

In recent years, regulators have found it necessary to take the disastrous step of denying some insurance companies permission to pay interest on surplus notes. One notable case was Lumbermens Mutual Casualty Company, one of the companies that had received permission to issue a 100-year surplus note only a few years earlier. The Lumbermens incident is discussed in the November 2003 issue.

Another notable case was Atlantic Mutual Insurance Company. The company was later taken over by its state insurance regulator. The Atlantic Mutual incident is discussed in the March/April 2007 issue.

Still another notable case was Shenandoah Life Insurance Company, which also had to be taken over by its regulator. Later the regulator arranged for the company to be sold to United Prosperity Life Insurance Company, and an existing $20 million surplus note became a roadblock to completion of the sale. Ultimately the unfortunate surplus note investors were forced to accept $4 million in exchange for the $20 million surplus note, thus taking a $16 million loss. In other words, the surplus note investors were forced to make a $16 million uncompensated contribution to Shenandoah on top of the $60 million United Prosperity paid to acquire the company. The Shenandoah case is discussed in the August 2012 issue.

The Last Holdouts

New York-based Teachers Insurance and Annuity Association of America (TIAA) and Wisconsin-based Northwestern Mutual Life Insurance Company long held top ratings for financial strength. They were the last major holdouts against the tidal wave of surplus note offerings following the 1993 revolution inspired by Prudential. I thought TIAA and Northwestern would never issue surplus notes, but I was wrong.

In December 2009 TIAA issued $2 billion of 30-year surplus notes at an annual interest rate of 6.85 percent. In March 2010 Northwestern issued $1.75 billion of 30-year surplus notes at an annual interest rate of 6.063 percent. The net proceeds were for general corporate purposes. The TIAA and Northwestern surplus notes are discussed in the August 2010 issue.

Northwestern has a large field force to which the company had long promoted the absence of debt in its financial statements. Thus the company needed to address the concerns of its field force about the company's massive departure from tradition. A newsletter for the field force contained an edited segment of a conversation between a company executive and a member of the field force. The executive said the company had an "opportunity" to obtain "access" to net worth, the company had no plans to use the funds for any specific purpose, the company might want to have additional net worth on hand if the economy went through another event similar to what happened in September 2008 through March 2009, interest rates were as low as they probably will go, the company should be able to invest the funds at a rate equal to or higher than the after-tax cost of the funds, it is better to borrow when funds are not needed, and the company concluded that "accessing" the net worth was in the best interest of the policyholders.

I am not persuaded. Surplus notes are tempting because they increase net worth and enjoy income tax advantages. However, they are also addictive. There can be no assurance that the company will be able to keep the funds invested at an interest rate higher than the company is paying for the funds, there can be no assurance that the company will be able to refinance the surplus notes at maturity on favorable terms, and repaying the borrowed money will decrease the company's net worth.

In September 2014 TIAA issued another $2 billion of surplus notes: $1.65 billion of 30-year surplus notes at an annual interest rate of 4.90 percent and $350 million of 40-year surplus notes at an annual fixed-to-floating interest rate of 4.375 percent. The net proceeds of the new surplus notes were for general corporate purposes and to fund a portion of the cost of acquiring Nuveen Investments, Inc., a diversified investment management company, for $6.25 billion. Moody's responded by lowering its Aaa top rating of TIAA one notch to Aa1. A. M. Best, Fitch Ratings, and Standard & Poor's did not lower their ratings of TIAA. I wrote about TIAA's new issuance of surplus notes in blog no. 68 (September 22, 2014).

My Watch Lists

As discussed in chapter 22, for many years I published in the special ratings issues watch lists of life insurance companies with a vulnerable financial strength rating from at least one major rating firm. I also included in the watch lists each company whose surplus notes were large relative to the company's total adjusted capital. (Total adjusted capital, which is similar to net worth, is discussed in chapter 31.) In the September 2013 special ratings issue, for example, I showed 26 companies whose ratios of surplus notes to total adjusted capital were at least 50 percent.

The Bottom Line

Those responsible for issuing surplus notes are insurance company executives who decide to issue the surplus notes and state insurance regulators who grant permission to issue the surplus notes. Those executives and regulators will be long gone when the consequences of issuing the surplus notes will have to be faced, especially where maturity dates are more than ten years in the future. Thus surplus notes are a classic example of a WWNBA transaction: We Will Not Be Around.

Issues and a Blog Item Mentioned in This Chapter

February 1994, September 1994, November 2003, March/April 2007, August 2010, August 2012, August 2013, and September 2013, and blog no. 68 (September 22, 2014).

26

The Demutualization Wave

$\mathcal{T}$he two primary corporate forms of organization in the insurance business are mutual insurance companies and stock insurance companies. A few insurance companies operate under other organizational forms, but they are beyond the scope of the discussion in this chapter.

Definitions

A mutual insurance company, at least in theory, is owned by its policyholders and operates for the exclusive benefit of its policyholders. A mutual company has no stock and no stockholders. It is difficult if not impossible for the policyholders of a mutual company to exercise effective control over the company, and there can be no assurance that the company is operated for the exclusive benefit of the policyholders.

A stock insurance company, at least in theory, is owned by its stockholders and operates for the exclusive benefit of its stockholders. It is difficult if not impossible for the stockholders to exercise effective control over the company, and there can be no assurance that the company is operated for the exclusive benefit of the stockholders.

In some stock insurance companies, policyholders with participating (dividend-paying) insurance policies have certain limited rights. This matter is discussed in my book entitled *Participating Life Insurance Sold by Stock Companies*, which is mentioned in chapter 3.

Most states have laws allowing an insurance company to convert from one form of organization to another. The conversion of a stock company into a mutual company is called a mutualization. The conversion of a mutual company into a stock company is called a demutualization. Also, in recent years some states have enacted laws allowing a mutual company to change its form of corporate organization by creating a mutual holding company (MHC).

Mutualizations

A century ago mutualizations were fairly common in the insurance business, but in modern times they have been rare. A mutualization requires the approval of the insurance regulator in the state where the company is located for regulatory purposes, and also requires the approval of the stockholders. The stock company buys the stock from the stockholders, retires the stock, and becomes a mutual company.

One purpose of a mutualization is to prevent a change in the ownership of the company through the sale of stock. One such case, completed in 1974, was the mutualization of Farmers and Traders Life Insurance Company (Syracuse, NY).

Some mutualizations were prompted by the exposure of scandals in which the management of a stock company engaged in improper behavior. A classic example was the prominent newspaper coverage of the lurid activities—some of them involving the frivolous use of company funds—engaged in by the management of Equitable Life Assurance Society of the United States late in the 19th century. Those activities were a major factor leading to the famous Hughes-Armstrong investigation of the life insurance business in New York in 1905. Equitable adopted a mutualization plan in 1917, and acquired the last of the stock to complete the mutualization in 1925.

Demutualizations

In a demutualization, a mutual company buys out the ownership interests of the policyholders. A demutualization requires the approval of the insurance regulator in the state where the company is located for regulatory purposes, and also requires the approval of the policyholders. Demutualization is a complex process involving these steps:

- A new stock company—a "holding company"—is created.
- The holding company raises money through an initial offering of stock to the public or by issuing stock to a single outside investor. When money is raised from a single outside investor, the demutualization is "sponsored" by the investor.
- The holding company buys out the ownership interests of the policyholders by paying them cash and/or giving them stock in the holding company.
- The former mutual company becomes a stock company, all its stock is owned by the holding company, and its name is changed, if necessary, to remove the word "mutual."

I first wrote about this type of reorganization about 50 years ago, when it had never been done and therefore had no name. In what I thought was the coining of a logical word parallel to mutualization, I called it stockization. When it started happening in the 1980s, it was called demutualization. So much for my ability to coin a word.

There were a few demutualizations in the 1980s, such as Union Mutual Life Insurance Company (Portland, ME). The first major demutualization was completed in 1992 by the previously mentioned Equitable, which had completed its mutualization in 1925. In the late 1980s Equitable was facing serious financial problems and needed a large infusion of funds.

I have no recollection of whether surplus notes were given serious consideration as a method for raising funds. Because of Equitable's financial problems, I doubt that surplus notes could have been issued in sufficiently large amounts and under reasonable terms, or that the issuance of surplus notes would have been approved by Equitable's regulator. Also, as discussed in chapter 25, investor surplus notes did not come on the scene until what I called the revolution of 1993.

The insurance law in New York State, where Equitable is located for regulatory purposes, at the time did not provide for demutualization. Thus Equitable had to lobby for enactment of the legislation, and did so successfully. Equitable completed the demutualization under the sponsorship of AXA, a large French company that infused $1 billion into Equitable. In its new stock form, Equitable became a subsidiary of AXA and changed its name to AXA Equitable Life Insurance Company. Later it became AXA Life Insurance Company.

The Demutualization Wave

During the final decade of the 20th century and the first decade of the 21st, a demutualization wave swept the life insurance industry in the U.S. and Canada. This partial list of demutualizations includes many large companies: Canada Life Assurance Company, General American Life Insurance Company, John Hancock Mutual Life Insurance Company, Manufacturers Life Insurance Company (Canada), Metropolitan Life Insurance Company, Midland Mutual Life Insurance Company, Mutual Life Assurance Company of Canada, Mutual Life Insurance Company of New York, New England Mutual Life Insurance Company, Phoenix Home Life Mutual Insurance Company, Principal Mutual Life Insurance Company, Provident Mutual Life Insurance Company of Philadelphia, Prudential Insurance Company of America, Standard Insurance Company (Oregon), and Sun Life Assurance Company of Canada.

The arguments offered by demutualizing life insurance companies were that the stock form of organization gave the companies access to capital markets, made it easier to acquire other companies because the acquisitions could be made with stock of the holding company rather than cash, allowed life insurance companies to acquire banks and other financial services companies to offer consumers one-stop shopping to meet their needs for financial services, and allowed the companies to diversify through the acquisition of companies outside the life insurance business. Here is what I said at the time about the assertion that consumers wanted one-stop shopping to meet their needs for financial services:

Nonsense! I do not think consumers are anxious to buy insurance from banks or securities brokers or have insurance companies perform banking services. I do not think consumers are demanding anything other than honest and fair treatment. Those who say financial services integration is in the best interests of consumers are those who stand to make money in the process.

I was referring to many categories of individuals who make money in the process. The demutualizing company's top officers receive stock and stock options in addition to enhanced compensation. The demutualizing company's directors receive stock and stock options. Investment bankers are paid for handling the stock offerings. Consulting actuaries are paid to make the calculations of the amounts to be paid to the policyholders. Attorneys are paid to draft the many legal documents that are needed. I heard about a seminar for mutual company officers where the first topic on the agenda was how they could benefit financially from a demutualization. Here is how I described the advice consultants were giving to officers and directors of mutual companies:

You've got to demutualize so you will be able to use stock as acquisition currency. Everybody is doing it, and you will be left behind if you do not do it. And by the way, if you do it, there will be plenty of stock options and other goodies in it for you.

Thus the individuals who make the decision to demutualize have a conflict of interest because they are in a position to receive major financial benefits from the reorganization. One example was David F. D'Alessandro, the chief executive officer of John Hancock Mutual Life Insurance Company, which demutualized in 2000. He received compensation of $1.8 million in 1999, $3.1 million in 2000, $8.1 million in 2001, and $21.7 million in 2002. Those figures do not include the financial bonanza he received when John Hancock was later acquired by Manufacturers Life Insurance Company.

Another example was Robert W. Kloss, chief executive officer of Provident Mutual Life Insurance Company of Philadelphia, which demutualized in 2002 under the sponsorship of Nationwide Corporation. He received compensation of $1.8 million in 2000, $3.0 million in 2001, $1.8 million in 2002, and $17.9 million in severance benefits when he left the company after the demutualization. See the August 2002 issue.

The Unclaimed Property Problem

Since a demutualization involves obtaining the approval of the policyholders and buying out their ownership interests, the policyholders have to be contacted. Therein lies a problem, because many policyholders have not been contacted for many years. For example, many policyholders have paid-up policies requiring no further premiums, no premium notices are mailed to them, and mailing lists are outdated. When John Hancock mailed its demutualization packages to its millions of eligible policyholders, about 400,000 reportedly were returned as undeliverable. Prudential reportedly had lost contact with 2.7 million eligible policyholders.

Not only were the companies unable to obtain the approval of the lost policyholders, but also the companies could not deliver the stock or cash to which the lost policyholders were entitled. The problem attracted the attention of state officials responsible for administering state unclaimed property laws (or escheat laws), under which businesses are required to turn over to the state all property that remains unclaimed for a certain number of years. See the November 2010 issue.

The Fairness Issue

In a demutualization the company retains the services of an outside actuarial consulting firm to determine the amount that should be distributed to the policyholders in exchange for giving up their ownership interests in the mutual company. The objective is for the demutualization plan and the formula for the distribution to each policyholder to be "fair."

In the policyholder information statement mailed to policyholders with the company's request for the policyholder's vote to approve or disapprove the demutualization plan, the company expresses the opinion that the plan is fair. The actuarial firm retained by the company expresses the opinion that the plan is fair. The investment banking firm retained by the company expresses the opinion that the plan is fair. The state insurance regulator where the company is located for regulatory purposes expresses the opinion that the plan is fair.

The policyholder has no choice but to accept these opinions. The policyholder who asks for details is told they involve confidential and proprietary information. In other words, the details are in a black box.

As mentioned previously, policyholders receive distributions in the form of stock and/or cash. The distribution to each policyholder is the sum of a fixed component and a variable component. The fixed component is paid to each policyholder irrespective of the size and type of policy held by the policyholder. The variable component depends upon the size and type of policy. When I was writing about demutualizations, I often received letters from agents who complained about strange discrepancies among their policyholders in terms of the number of shares allocated to them in the variable component of the demutualization distribution. My first article about this phenomenon, in the May 1999 issue, related to Standard Insurance Company (Portland, OR). The second article, in the December 1999 issue, related to John Hancock. Here a few of the John Hancock examples, with the data altered to prevent identification without changing the relationships:

- Zero variable shares of stock for a $10 million second-to-die life insurance policy issued in 1992.
- 92 variable shares of stock for a $100,000 term life insurance policy issued in 1994.
- 62 variable shares of stock for a $250,000 cash-value life insurance policy issued in 1992.
- 1,352 variable shares of stock for a $250,000 cash-value life insurance policy issued in 1992.

The Canadian Approach

The demutualizations in the U.S. and Canada differed in one major respect. In Canada, each demutualizing company disclosed in its policyholder information statement the formula for determining the number of shares of stock allocated to each policyholder.

Here is an example from the August 1999 issue. Consider a policyholder of Mutual Life Assurance Company of Canada with a policy in force for 15 years, a death benefit of $100,000, and a cash value of $20,000. First, he received 22 fixed shares. Second, he received two variable shares for each year of his relationship with the company, or 30 shares (15 × 2). Third, he received 49 variable shares for the death benefit (100,000 × .00048664896, rounded upward). Fourth, he received 248 variable shares for the cash value (20,000 × .01236, rounded upward). Thus he received 349 shares (22 + 30 + 49 + 248).

Taxation of Demutualization Distributions

The late Charles D. Ulrich, CPA, took a keen interest in the income tax treatment of demutualization distributions to policyholders. Early in 2003 he contacted me to say he felt that the treatment mentioned by the Internal Revenue Service (IRS) and by the demutualizing companies was wrong. After I reviewed the matter, I agreed with him. He and I both felt that the policyholder has a substantial basis in the demutualization distribution, although we did not necessarily agree on how the basis should be determined. My first article on the subject is in the June 2003 issue. In that article I described the IRS/company approach as follows:

> For the policyholder who receives stock, there is no immediate taxable income; however, when the stock is sold, the policyholder's basis in the stock is zero and the full amount received in the sale is a capital gain. For the policyholder who receives cash, the full amount received is taxed immediately as a capital gain. In either case, whether it is a long-term capital gain or a short-term capital gain depends on when the

policyholder first acquired an ownership interest in the company; because the typical policyholder purchased his or her first policy in the company more than one year before the distribution, the amount received in most instances is a long-term capital gain. I call the tax treatment described by the IRS and the companies the "zero basis approach."

The IRS justified the zero basis approach by citing a pair of revenue rulings it had adopted in the early 1970s that had nothing to do with demutualization. Indeed, those revenue rulings were issued long before the first demutualization occurred, and long before the word had been coined. Moreover, revenue rulings do not have the force of law.

Nonetheless the companies went along with the zero basis approach. I think the companies agreed to that approach under duress. A company must obtain a private letter ruling from the IRS that the demutualization will be treated as a tax-free reorganization, and probably decided to go along with the zero basis approach rather than argue for a more reasonable approach. In other words, one of the first demutualizing companies capitulated rather than fighting the IRS on behalf of its policyholders. I do not know which company was the first to capitulate, but once that happened, it became difficult for other companies to obtain approval of a more reasonable approach.

Thus the IRS's zero basis approach became the rule in all the demutualizations. The matter has been litigated in a few lawsuits filed by individual taxpayers who paid the capital gains taxes and claimed refunds. The results of the lawsuits favored the taxpayers, but the IRS dragged the cases out as long as possible. Even after losing those cases and finally honoring a few individual refund claims, the IRS continued to drag its feet on changing its approach. By now the statute of limitations has run out on many policyholders who paid capital gains taxes after receiving cash distributions and failed to file refund claims, and on many policyholders who paid capital gains taxes after selling the stock and failing to file refund claims. For those who did file timely refund claims, it is my understanding that the IRS has told them their claims remain pending until a final resolution of the matter. It is not clear what "final resolution" means, and I am not aware of any move to have Congress enact legislation to address the issue.

Meanwhile the IRS has made the subject into a moving target for taxpayers by repeatedly changing the Schedule D instructions, which are supposed to inform taxpayers about how to handle capital gains and losses. Here are key sentences in the 2012, 2013, and 2014 instructions relating to the demutualization of life insurance companies:

> 2012: Because the basis of your equity interest in the mutual company is considered to be zero, your basis in the stock received is zero.
>
> 2013: If you received cash in exchange for your equity interest, you may have to recognize a capital gain.
>
> 2014: If you received cash in exchange for your equity interest, you must recognize any capital gain.

The 2012 instructions mention the zero cost basis, but the 2013 and 2014 instructions do not. Also, there is no explanation of how to calculate the amount of the capital gain the taxpayer "may have to recognize" or "must recognize." Furthermore, there is no mention of the situation where the taxpayer receives stock at the time of the demutualization and later sells the stock. The insurance companies merely instruct taxpayers to consult their tax advisers, but the tax advisers receive no guidance on what to do. In short, the income taxation of demutualization distributions remains a disaster for taxpayers.

Mutual Holding Companies

In the late 1990s, during the demutualization wave, MHCs came on the scene as a purported alternative to demutualization. The promoters of the MHC conversion described it as a method by which to achieve the flexibility associated with the stock form of organization while avoiding the complexity of a demutualization and the cost of buying out the interests of the policyholders. When a mutual company creates an MHC, these things happen simultaneously:

- The mutual insurance company is transformed into a stock insurance company.
- An MHC is created.
- An intermediate holding company is created.
- The rights of the policyholders as owners of the former mutual insurance company are transferred to the MHC.
- The rights of the policyholders as customers remain with the former mutual insurance company, which is now a stock insurance company.

The intermediate holding company will own all the stock of the former mutual insurance company, which is now a stock insurance company. Also, the MHC will own at least a majority of the stock of the intermediate holding company.

Despite the glowing rhetoric of the promoters, an MHC organization is fraught with difficulties. From the viewpoint of the policyholders, the most important problem is that the policyholders receive no compensation for the loss of their ownership interests in the former mutual insurance company.

From the viewpoint of the company, although the promoters claimed the intermediate holding company would be able to issue stock and thereby facilitate acquisition of other companies inside and outside the insurance business, it did not work out that way. The intermediate holding companies in almost all instances were not able to sell stock because investors were not interested in investing in an organization where those investors as a group could never acquire majority control.

There are also subtle problems. For example, neither the MHC nor the intermediate holding company is an insurance company, so they are not subject to many of the laws and rules that apply to insurance companies. I learned from an insider at one MHC organization about the retired chief executive officer of a mutual insurance company who, in his capacity as an official of the new MHC, received a huge amount of compensation that was never disclosed because the MHC was not subject to the disclosure requirements imposed on insurance companies. I was never able to write effectively about the incident because there was no public information about the matter.

In the December 1997 issue I expressed the opinion that the MHC concept is fundamentally flawed and should not be allowed. I also said a mutual insurance company that wants the flexibility of a stock insurance company should demutualize.

The Provident Mutual Fiasco

In 1998 the board of directors of Provident Mutual Life Insurance Company of Philadelphia adopted a plan to reorganize through the creation of an MHC. I was a Provident policyholder because my former company, Continental American, was by then a part of Provident. Therefore I took more than a casual interest in developments.

I received Provident's letter to policyholders and its two-color, six-page flyer extolling the virtues of the MHC plan and asking the policyholders to approve the plan in the eventual voting process. I thereupon wrote a one-page letter to my fellow policyholders providing them with the other side of the story and urging them to vote against the plan. I sent my letter to the Pennsylvania Insurance Department with a request that the Department order Provident to send my letter to the policyholders. The Department denied my request. I discussed these developments in the May 1998 issue.

When the Department official denied my request, he brought to my attention the upcoming public hearing to be held in Philadelphia concerning the plan. I attended the hearing, which was a farce. I discussed the hearing in detail in the June 1998 issue.

In November 1998 the Department approved Provident's MHC plan. I discussed the approval in the January 1999 issue.

In December 1998 Provident sent a policyholder information statement to its policyholders and asked them to approve the plan. About 21 percent of the policyholders voted. About 89 percent of those voting approved the plan.

On February 11, 1999, in a stunning setback for Provident two days after completion of the voting, Stephen E. Levin, a Pennsylvania judge, handed down a preliminary injunction barring Provident from implementing the MHC plan "until after the court conducts a full hearing and issues an order to take such action." The injunction was issued in connection with a lawsuit brought by a group of Provident policyholders in Philadelphia. Here is the key paragraph in Judge Levin's ruling:

> We conclude that a preliminary injunction should issue because the Policyholder Information Statement omits material information, fails to fully and fairly address whether the Conversion is in the best interests of policyholders, is misleading on material facts and, taken as a whole, does not enable the policyholder to make an informed decision on whether to approve or disapprove the Plan. Thus, we determine, preliminarily, that policyholders did not have sufficient information to make an informed vote when they approved the Plan on February 9, 1999. Thus, the defendants should be enjoined from effectuating the Plan because it is not the product of an informed policyholder vote.

In March 1999 Judge Levin held a hearing on the preliminary injunction. In June 1999 he held a hearing on whether to make the injunction permanent. In September 1999, following Provident's unsuccessful appeal, he permanently enjoined the company from implementing the plan until the company met a list of conditions. Here are two key sentences in his ruling:

> We conclude that Provident's directors breached their duty of disclosure because they disseminated a policyholder information statement which unfairly described the Plan of Conversion, and therefore prevented policyholders from making an informed vote on the Plan. The only adequate remedy is to revise the Information Statement, redistribute the Information Statement containing the disclosures explained in this opinion and identified in the Court's decree nisi, and to have the policyholders vote again on the Plan of Conversion.

In October 1999 Provident scrapped its MHC plan. The credit goes to a small group of Provident policyholders who filed the lawsuit that led to the injunction. Credit also goes to Jason Adkins, who was one of their attorneys, and to David Schiff, former editor of *Schiff's Insurance Observer*. Adkins and Schiff were long-time vocal opponents of the MHC concept.

In August 2001 Provident and Nationwide Financial Services, Inc. (Columbus, OH) announced a plan for the sponsored demutualization of Provident and the subsequent acquisition of Provident by Nationwide Corporation. In December 2001 Provident's board of directors adopted the demutualization plan. In October 2002 Provident completed its demutualization and became Nationwide Life Insurance Company of America.

Issues Mentioned in This Chapter

December 1997, May 1998, June 1998, January 1999, May 1999, August 1999, December 1999, August 2002, June 2003, and November 2010.

27

Life Insurance
Policy Dividends

*A*s mentioned in chapter 2, as a teenager I was paying premiums on three small participating (dividend-paying) life insurance policies issued on my life by Equitable Life Assurance Society of the United States. Thus it was natural for me to be interested in the size of the dividends on those policies.

In my graduate studies at Penn, I learned some basics about life insurance dividend calculations. Later, when I sought to understand more fully how companies calculate dividends, I found that the companies almost without exception claim that the details of their dividend formulas are trade secrets and refuse to divulge information about the calculations.

The Three-Factor Method

My first major article about dividend calculations was published as the lead article in the March 1978 issue of *The Journal of Risk and Insurance.* I described the three-factor method, which involves the calculation of the three components of the dividend—the interest component, the mortality component, and the expense component. The sum of the three components is the dividend.

I was able to learn about the rudiments of the three-factor method from textbooks and actuarial materials. From publicly filed financial statements, I was able to learn about a few but not

274

all the numbers insurance companies use to arrive at each of the three components of the dividend. Thus I had to use hypothetical figures in the 1978 article to illustrate the calculations.

The elements of the interest component of the dividend are the reserve at the end of the policy year in question, the reserve interest rate used in calculating the reserve, and the dividend interest rate declared by the company for the policy year in question. The excess of the dividend interest rate over the reserve interest rate is multiplied by the reserve to calculate the interest component of the dividend.

The elements of the mortality component of the dividend are the reserve mortality rate used in calculating the reserve, the dividend mortality rate reflecting the company's mortality experience in the year in question, and the net amount at risk, which is the face amount of the policy minus the reserve for the year in question. The excess of the reserve mortality rate over the dividend mortality rate is multiplied by the net amount at risk to calculate the mortality component of the dividend.

The elements of the expense component of the dividend are the premium expense charge used in calculating the premium for the policy and the dividend expense charge reflecting the company's expense experience in the year in question. The excess of the premium expense charge over the dividend expense charge is the expense component of the dividend.

Some of the elements used in calculating the three components of the dividend are available in the policy or in public documents. Also, the dividend interest rate is sometimes available. However, the dividend mortality rate and the dividend expense charge are not available.

Each of the three components of the dividend may be positive or negative. Suppose a company uses a high dividend interest rate and therefore generates a large interest component of the dividend. However, the company may use a large dividend expense charge and therefore generate a large negative expense component. I mention this because some companies advertise high dividend interest rates while maintaining secrecy about their dividend expense charges.

My 1975 Correspondence with New York

To arrive at the dividend interest rate, most companies traditionally used the portfolio average method, under which the company uses the same dividend interest rate in calculating the dividends on all the company's policies. By April 1975, however, I was aware that some companies had begun using an investment year method, under which the company uses different dividend interest rates depending on when the premium money flows into the company. Investment year methods were already being used in the pension business.

I wrote to Alvin Alpert, chief of the life bureau of the New York Department of Insurance. I chose that Department for three reasons: (1) Equitable, which had issued my policies, was based in New York State for regulatory purposes; (2) I was a New York State resident when my policies were issued; and (3) the Department had a reputation for being the toughest in the U.S. in pushing for fair treatment of policyholders. I asked whether the Department had ever approved an investment year method for individual policies. In his thorough letter of response, Alpert said:

> To date no life insurance company using the investment year method has requested approval to use this method within the ordinary life branch. On a purely theoretical basis, there does not appear to be anything objectionable to such an approach. From a practical standpoint, any company attempting this would have a monstrous and costly task even with a new generation computer. A company would have to calculate separate investment year rates for each year it was using this method and each rate would have to be applied to a portion of the initial policy reserve for the current year. Because of the difficulties that would be encountered in examining the complex calculations of the interest contribution factor portion of the dividend and the possibility of errors and manipulation, if such an approach were ever adopted the [Life] Bureau would insist upon extensive safeguards and would possibly wish to review the feasibility of auditing the computer program.

The *Probe* Article

Probe was a feisty four-page semimonthly newsletter founded in the 1950s by Ralph Engelsman, general agent in New York City for Penn Mutual Life Insurance Company, and Halsey Josephson, general agent in New York City for Connecticut Mutual Life Insurance Company. After Engelsman died, Josephson carried on. After Josephson died, the newsletter went through many ownership changes and eventually bore no similarity to the newsletter that Engelsman and Josephson had created. The fate of *Probe* was a factor in my decision to end the *Forum* rather than turn it over to someone else.

In the January 1, 1976 issue of *Probe*, Josephson ran an article entitled "Good-bye Portfolio Rate and Mutuality." He mentioned a company's 1976 dividend scale announcement that "the scale recognizes that the rate of investment return is greater on funds that support recently issued policies than it is on funds supporting older ones."

In the article Josephson did not identify the company. I asked him for the name of the company. In an amazing coincidence, he said it was Equitable. It meant the dividends on my policies were going to be affected in a negative way because my policies were about 30 years old.

The Department's Follow-Up Letter

A few weeks later, Alpert sent me an unsolicited follow-up letter. He said Equitable had

> recently requested approval for a change in its investment year method filing, to allocate investment income within the ordinary life and individual annuity lines of business, in order to be able to use dividend interest rates, depending on policy year of issue. After a considerable amount of discussion, the company was granted an approval on a conditional basis. The approval was limited to one year, and furthermore, was subject to being withdrawn by this Department at any time, without notice, if it is determined that the method of investment income allocation is inequitable. With respect to the replacement problem, we were satisfied that the method

of determining the dividend interest rates would not encourage older policyholders to replace their policies.

Impact of Equitable's New Scale

Equitable's new dividend scale generated substantially increased dividends in new business sales illustrations, substantially increased dividends for policies issued in 1971 and later, somewhat larger dividends for policies issued from 1967 to 1970, and no change in dividends for policies (such as mine) issued prior to 1967. Also, for new business sales illustrations and for policies issued in 1971 and later, the dividend increases were greater for policies of $25,000 or more than for policies smaller than $25,000.

My 1976 Correspondence with Equitable

I wrote to Equitable, and an actuary explained the new dividend scale in general terms. He implied the change was consistent with the principles of equity, because the new scale "was developed after elaborate investment year calculations that show the rate of interest earned on funds that support policies issued in different issue years." Although the company actuary did not mention market considerations in his letter to me, the company's promotional material distributed to agents included these five points:

- A history-making change to reflect current investment yields in illustrating dividends, plus outstanding investment performance, combine to produce dramatic competitive gains.
- The greatest competitive advance is in the biggest and best market—the $25,000 and larger permanent insurance policies.
- Great news! Dramatically improved net insurance cost illustrations put Equitable in forefront of industry competitively.
- Illustrations of the already-popular Executive policy will make it virtually unbeatable in competition with similar policies.

- In the business insurance market, where competition is most keen, the new scale will allow higher illustrations on Split Dollar, Deferred Compensation, Sole Proprietor, Stock Redemption, Partnership Plans.

My Article

The April 1976 issue of the *Forum* carried an article entitled "Great News—Except for Equitable's Old Policyholders." It was the first in a series of articles on the subject, and in retrospect I think it was one of the most important articles published in the *Forum*. I said that Equitable's 1976 dividend scale was a major development in the life insurance business, that it was an expedient way to deal with temporary market conditions, and that it would come back to haunt the industry. The events that followed are discussed in detail in my October 1978 issue.

My FOIL Request and Appeals

I submitted to the New York Department of Insurance a request pursuant to the New York State Freedom of Information Law (FOIL). I asked for Equitable's application to the Department for permission to use an investment year method, and for the Department's approval of the application. The Department denied my request on the grounds that the documents contained information about the company's internal procedures, but suggested that I ask the company. I did so, and the company denied my request.

I submitted to the Department an administrative appeal of its denial of my FOIL request. I received no reply.

I submitted another administrative appeal, and sent a copy to the Committee on Public Access to Records (COPAR), a state agency that supervises the administration of FOIL. I received no reply from the Department, but COPAR told me the Department had denied my administrative appeal.

My Court Petition

I retained an attorney who agreed to represent me *pro bono.* He filed a petition in state court in New York asking the judge to order the Department to furnish the documents. We took the position that the public has a right to know how a state agency reaches decisions—in this instance a decision affecting millions of policyholders of a major mutual company—and that the public's right to such knowledge is at the heart of FOIL.

The Department responded to the petition by saying the requested documents were withheld under the FOIL exemption relating to trade secrets and other confidential financial information. After a hearing, the judge issued an order saying he was unable to determine whether the documents were confidential. He invited Equitable to present its views. Equitable then entered the case and took the same position the Department had taken.

The judge ordered the file to be turned over to him so that he could examine it in chambers. Later he ordered Equitable's attorney to divide the file into two parts—one part consisting of documents for which the company was seeking trade secret protection, and the second part consisting of documents for which the company was not seeking trade secret protection. The company's attorney made the division. The judge then ruled against us on the first part of the file, and we were not successful in subsequent efforts to obtain that part of the file.

The judge ruled in our favor, however, on the second part of the file, and we received it shortly thereafter. The documents prompted us to file additional FOIL requests for documents that were referred to in the released file, and those documents were released to us. Although I learned nothing significant about the technical aspects of the dividend calculations, the documents included several interesting items of information and allowed me to describe the chronology of the Department's approval of Equitable's application to use an investment year method.

Several Nuggets

The released portion of the file included several interesting nuggets. First, an Equitable memorandum said: "Many of our peer companies have been illustrating dividends on the investment year basis in one way or another, at least since 1969."

Attached was a list of the peer companies: Massachusetts Mutual Life Insurance Company, National Life Insurance Company (Vermont), State Mutual Life Assurance Company of America, Guardian Life Insurance Company of America, Prudential Insurance Company of America, Mutual Life Insurance Company of New York, and Bankers Life Company (Iowa).

Second, a letter from Equitable to the Department, after mentioning the peer companies, said: "We also feel that this development should be subject to full and open disclosure to our agents and the public." The sentence was ironic in view of Equitable's later refusal to disclose the details.

Third, an Equitable memorandum of law invoked the report of the Hughes-Armstrong Committee investigation of 1905, which did not recommend that the legislature establish the manner in which dividends should be calculated. Rather, the report recommended that companies be required to state their methods of computation to allow comparisons of methods and results. Thus Equitable cited the disclosure argument as a reason why government should not interfere with dividend determination methods, only to turn its back on disclosure after the change was approved.

Fourth, the same memorandum invoked the 1936 case of *Rhine v. New York Life* (273 N.Y.S. 1), which said that the company's method of apportioning its surplus is *prima facie* equitable, and that a complaining policyholder must prove it is not equitable. However, it is impossible for a policyholder to prove anything when the apportionment method is secret. Catch 22!

Chronology

The released documents shined considerable light on the chronology of the Department's approval process. As far back as the early 1960s, when it was seeking approval of an investment year method for its pension business, Equitable was not proposing to use the method for its individual business. The company gave three reasons in a 1961 memorandum: inducement to replacement, expense and difficulty of administration, and inappropriateness for level-premium policies.

Thirteen years later, despite advances in computer technology and major changes in the market interest rate situation, reservations about the investment year method were still being voiced by Equitable officials. An Equitable actuary was still negative about the idea at a meeting of the Society of Actuaries in 1974.

In July 1975 an Equitable actuary told the Department the company intended to move to an investment year method for individual policies in its 1976 dividend scale. Two weeks later, a Department actuary said the Department would not approve the change. Two more weeks later, the Equitable actuary explained more fully why the company was planning the move. Three more weeks later, the Department actuary again said the Department would not approve the change.

Over the next two months, at least two meetings were held involving Equitable and Department officials. In October 1975 Herbert Shyer, Equitable's top legal officer, wrote to Deputy Superintendent of Insurance Peter P. Smith, III and explained why the company felt it did not need the Department's approval to make the move.

In November 1975 First Deputy Superintendent of Insurance Michael Curan informed an Equitable actuary that the company's proposal was approved, subject to three conditions. The company was to submit additional material, and the company did so. The approval was subject to disapproval if the Department determined that the method was inequitable. The approval was limited to 1976, and the company was required to reapply for 1977.

In August 1976 an Equitable attorney informed Deputy Superintendent Smith of the company's intent to continue the 1976 scale into 1977, and asked whether the Department needed further information. In October 1976 the Department's chief actuary requested a substantial amount of additional information. One week later Equitable provided the additional information to the Department.

In January 1977, in a letter to an Equitable attorney, First Deputy Superintendent Curan said the matter required extensive actuarial study, the broad scope of the study prevented development of a definitive set of guidelines, and the Department did not object to continuing the 1976 scale into 1977, pending completion of the Department's study. Thus the approval for one year became a *de facto* permanent approval, because there has been no evidence of a Department study or definitive set of guidelines.

In short, when the Department approved the 1976 scale, it did not have in its files any information on which to base the approval. The questions that should have been asked prior to approval were not asked until October 1976, six months after the subject had achieved notoriety.

In the Department at the time, it was highly unusual for political appointees to overrule the permanent civil service staff. The decisions to approve Equitable's 1976 and 1977 dividend scales had the appearance of political decisions rather than soundly based regulatory decisions.

Although Equitable was a large and politically powerful financial institution, I was not able to determine precisely what kind of leverage Equitable used to get its way. One thing to consider, however, is that New York City was on the verge of bankruptcy in the 1970s, and it issued Municipal Acceptance Corporation (MAC) bonds. Financial institutions such as Equitable were strongly urged to buy MAC bonds to help the city avoid a financial catastrophe.

A Personal Note

Prior to the Equitable saga described above, I was oblivious to what was happening to the dividends on the Equitable policies issued on my life in the 1940s. In 1976, for example, the dividends on the three small policies combined increased by 1.5 percent. In 1977 they increased by 1.7 percent. Those increases seemed reasonable because of the gradually growing savings component in the policies. Until I saw the details in the documents later released to me, I had no idea that policies issued more recently were enjoying substantially increased dividends under the use of the investment year method.

Further Efforts

I tried over many years to learn how life insurance companies calculate policy dividends. For the most part, I was unsuccessful because most companies insisted the calculations were trade secrets and constituted proprietary information.

With regard to my own policies, I wrote letters to the companies from time to time. I would state the amount of the latest dividend and ask how that dividend was calculated. I would say I wanted to see the formula and the numbers the company had inserted into the formula. My wife wrote similar letters with regard to her policies, and some of my subscribers wrote similar letters with regard to their policies. Here are a few examples of the language used by the companies to avoid providing the requested information:

> Bankers Life (Iowa): Dividends are based upon the plan of insurance, the cost of maintaining records, the amount of death claims, and of course, upon the earnings of the Company for the year. Because the various factors are subject to change, no dividend is guaranteed.
>
> Continental American: The information concerning the formulas that were used in the determination of the dividends is not available. The amount of dividends payable in a particular year is based on Company experience for that year. The Board of Directors decides what the dividend scale will be each year and in 1971 they created a new dividend scale by which dividends would not increase in that year. As stated above, the dividend scale is calculated according to Company experience and that is the reason that a new dividend scale was adopted in 1971.
>
> Mutual Benefit Life: The dividend on the $5,000 policy was calculated by multiplying the dividend factor of $11.43 for the 34th policy year by the face amount expressed in thousands of dollars (5). [The method of calculating the figure of $11.43 was not shown.]
>
> Prudential: While this policy is in force other than as extended term insurance, the portion, if any, of the divisible surplus of the Company accruing upon the policy at each policy anniversary will be determined annually by the Board of

Directors, and will be credited to the policy as a dividend on such anniversary provided all premiums due hereunder have been paid in full to such anniversary and the insured is living at that time.

Availability of Dividend Data

I have explained that it is all but impossible to find out how life insurance companies calculate dividends. But that is not the only problem. It is also difficult to learn what dividends they actually pay.

When a company offers participating (dividend-paying) policies, it is common for the company to list so-called illustrated dividends. Those are the dividends used for sales purposes, but they are not guaranteed. As the years pass after a person buys a policy, the company credits to the policy so-called historical (sometimes called "actual") dividends.

For many years there was a publication called *Flitcraft Compend* assembled by a commercial publisher. It showed illustrated dividends on a few policy types at a few issue ages. It also showed historical dividends on a few policy types at a few issue ages for policies that had been issued ten or twenty years earlier. Aside from the incompleteness of the data, there was a serious problem. The publisher was at the mercy of the companies in terms of what data were provided. Many companies provided no data, and many companies provided data that had been rigged to make the companies look better than they deserved to look.

Eventually *Flitcraft Compend* was acquired by the A. M. Best Company, a firm that assigns financial strength ratings to insurance companies. Best published *Best's Flitcraft Compend* for many years, but halted publication after the 1994 edition. I think there were two primary reasons. First, Best was having increasing difficulty obtaining adequate cooperation from the companies. Second, the number of full-time life insurance agents was declining significantly, resulting in decreasing demand for the publication. In short, extensive information on dividends is not readily available in the public domain.

A Side Note

Peter P. Smith, III, who is mentioned in this chapter, seems to have been the first political appointee contacted by Equitable in its effort to win the Department's approval of the move to an investment year method for calculating policy dividends. Smith received his law degree from Villanova University in 1959. He began his legal career with the New York City firm of Shea & Gould. Smith worked in U.S. Senator Robert Kennedy's 1968 Presidential campaign and was with him in Los Angeles when he was assassinated. In 1975 Smith was appointed deputy superintendent of insurance in the New York Department of Insurance. In 1978 he was appointed general services commissioner of New York City. Shortly thereafter, he resigned and pleaded guilty to charges of having diverted $70,000 of Shea & Gould legal fees to his private account. He spent four months in prison and was disbarred. With his legal career at an end, he devoted the rest of his life to working for the poor, the homeless, and the victims of the HIV/AIDS epidemic. He died in 1992 at age 57 and was survived by two sisters.

Issues Mentioned in This Chapter

April 1976 and October 1978.

28

Agents' Contracts with Insurance Companies

U.S. Senator Philip Hart, who was mentioned in chapters 6 and 11, was the first member of Congress to champion the rights of life insurance consumers. In March 1974, in a speech to a life insurance audience, he discussed not only the need for rigorous price disclosure but also what I called "an emancipation proclamation for life insurance agents." That was the title of the lead article in the June 1974 issue of the *Forum*. It was the first of many articles about agents' contracts during the early years of the *Forum*.

Vulnerability of Agents

In that June 1974 article I mentioned the "NYLIC" agents' contract used by New York Life Insurance Company. The contract prohibited the agent from placing business with other companies, gave the company the right to terminate an agent's contract without cause, and provided that the agent would forfeit all future commissions if the contract was terminated in fewer than 20 years. Commissions "vest" after an agent's contract remains in effect for a certain length of time, meaning that the agent is entitled to those commissions even if the agent dies or leaves the company. Nonvested commissions are forfeited by an agent who dies or otherwise leaves the company. Vesting is important because commissions are paid not only on first-year premiums but also on premiums paid in a policy's subsequent years.

In the March 1975 issue of the *Forum* I cited some New York Life agent turnover data that Hart's staff had assembled. For example, the company recruited 3,508 new agents in 1967, and 3,119 of those agents (89 percent) had left the company by the end of 1972. These figures suggest that few agents complete the 20-year requirement for commission vesting under the NYLIC contract. In that article I showed comparable data for 20 other major life insurance companies.

In the September 1978 issue of the *Forum* I described the case of a successful agent who had entered into a contract with a general agent of New England Mutual Life Insurance Company. He placed most of his business with other companies, but he continuously met the minimum requirements to qualify for nonvested commissions. The arrangement continued on a satisfactory basis until his general agent, who was his supervisor, retired. Soon afterward, the person who replaced the general agent terminated the agent's contract, causing the agent to lose his nonvested commissions. In the September 1978 article I suggested that an agent's contract should distinguish between termination with cause and termination without cause, and that an agent terminated without cause should not forfeit nonvested commissions.

In the August 1979 issue I wrote about another dimension of the vulnerability of agents. A long-time agent of Equitable Life Assurance Society of the United States went with another company in order to offer his clients a plan not offered by Equitable. However, he sought to continue providing service to his Equitable clients. One of his clients signed an authorization letter to Equitable asking the company to send the agent certain information the agent needed to advise his client. Equitable sent the information directly to the client with a copy to a "servicing agent" designated by Equitable. The former Equitable agent wrote about the matter to Coy G. Eklund, Equitable's president and chief executive officer. Eklund wrote back explaining that "orphan" policyholders are assigned to "a competent Equitable

Agent," and that the company "cannot look to non-Equitable Agents." In other words, the agent in this case had to obtain the information from his client, and was also confronted with the possibility of competition from the new "servicing agent" for the loyalty of the client.

Posture of the NALU

In the October 1974 issue I reported on an agent who had entered into a contract with Sun Life Assurance Company of Canada in 1952. About 20 years later, he received a letter from the company with congratulations on his lengthy service. Shortly thereafter he received a letter terminating his agent's contract effective three days after his receipt of the termination letter. The company gave no reason for the termination. As a result of the termination, the agent forfeited his nonvested commissions and the company's contributions to his pension plan.

In the February 1975 issue I reported writing to C. Carney Smith, executive vice president of the National Association of Life Underwriters (NALU). With the Sun Life of Canada agent in mind, I asked Smith whether an NALU member could get help from NALU if the member felt victimized by a company. Smith did not answer the question directly, but implied the agent could get no help from NALU. Smith explained that NALU had entered into a settlement agreement with the National Labor Relations Board after the NALU had been accused of carrying on the functions of a labor union. According to Smith:

> The companies agreed not to recognize NALU as a collective bargaining representative, and NALU agreed that it would at no time engage in any of the activities reserved by law for labor organizations, such as dealing with employers concerning employee grievances, labor disputes, wages, rates of pay, hours of employment or conditions of work.

One of my final articles in the *Forum* about agents' contracts was in the July 2010 issue. An agent of Protective Life Insurance Company informed me that he had been subjected to a commission chargeback when his client died shortly after buying life insurance. Protective's contract calls for a full chargeback in the event of policy termination during the first six months after the policy was issued and a 50 percent chargeback in the event of termination during the second sixth months. Termination apparently includes termination by death. I can understand a chargeback if fraud was involved in the application, but I do not understand the logic of a chargeback in the absence of fraud. I sought an explanation from John E. Johns, chairman and chief executive officer of Protective. He did not respond to my letter.

A Provocative Telephone Conversation

In the September 1977 issue I reported on a lengthy telephone conversation that I had with a prominent life insurance agent. We discussed a wide range of topics, including my efforts to require companies to provide rigorous disclosure of price information to life insurance consumers. He said disclosure would not affect the market appreciably, because most consumers would not understand the information. I said the most profound impact of disclosure would be through providing the information to agents, most of whom were not aware of the huge price differences among companies. He disagreed. He said most agents are fully aware of price differences. He also said most agents who survive their first few years in the business and are still with companies that offer high-priced insurance are fully aware of the situation and have somehow convinced themselves to stay where they are.

He then explained his situation. He was a successful agent and had obtained his Chartered Life Underwriter (CLU) designation. He had taken the CLU professional pledge, which is based on the golden rule. When he first entered the business, he went with a company offering what he later found to be high-priced insurance. He occasionally placed business in companies offering low-priced insurance. He discovered to his discomfort that he would place business in a low-priced company when he was in competition on a case, and in his primary company when he had no competition. He was troubled by the apparent conflict between his activities and the CLU pledge, which he took seriously. He began to have difficulty sleeping. He finally threw in the towel and went with a low-priced company. The present value of the nonvested commissions he sacrificed when he terminated his contract with the high-priced company was well up in six figures, but he decided he could not continue selling high-priced insurance to his faithful clients.

Issues Mentioned in This Chapter

June 1974, October 1974, February 1975, March 1975, September 1977, September 1978, August 1979, and July 2010.

29

The Insurance Regulators

$\mathcal{I}$nsurance in the U.S. is regulated by the states rather than the federal government. How such a giant national business came to be regulated by the states may be explained as an historical accident.

Elizur Wright

Elizur Wright, a resident of Boston, found slavery appalling. By 1833 he had become a prominent and outspoken abolitionist. He was also a mathematician, and in 1844 he traveled to England on behalf of an American insurance company. In his autobiography, he said he attended a London literary breakfast, at which a prominent songwriter said that life insurance is "the greatest humbug in Christendom." Wright described himself as "thunderstruck," because he would not have made the dangerous ocean voyage if he did not have life insurance to protect his wife and five children who had remained at home in Boston.

The songwriter told Wright to "Go to the Royal Exchange Thursday afternoon at three o-clock, and you will see what I mean." Wright did so, and was shocked to see life insurance policies on the lives of elderly men auctioned off to speculators who, before bidding, examined the insured men closely. Insured men who needed money sold their policies to speculators because level-premium policies in those days did not contain what later were called nonforfeiture values. In other words, if the insured man simply discarded the policy, he would receive nothing, and would thereby forfeit the theoretical equity that he had built up by paying the level premiums. Wright likened the London market to slave auctions he had seen at home. He later said that, if he should become old, he "should not like to have a policy on my life in the hands of a man with the slightest pecuniary motive to wish me dead."

When Wright returned to the U.S., he lobbied for the creation of a governmental agency to regulate insurance companies. Because he lived in Boston, it was more convenient for him to direct his lobbying efforts at the Massachusetts legislature than the federal Congress. His efforts resulted in the creation of the Massachusetts Division of Insurance. In 1858 Wright became the Massachusetts insurance commissioner and the first insurance regulator in this country.

Wright fought for enactment of laws requiring insurance companies to include nonforfeiture values in level-premium policies. Originally the nonforfeiture laws required companies to include only paid-up insurance in level-premium policies, but later the laws required cash values as well.

Wright also secured enactment of other important laws for the protection of policyholders, and he became recognized in the U.S. as the "Father of Life Insurance." Even today he is remembered as the most feared regulator in the history of the U.S. insurance business. I wrote about Wright in the March 1989 issue of the *Forum*.

Speaking of fearsome insurance regulators, it is necessary to mention Herbert Denenberg, whose role in creating the *Forum* is described in chapter 1. In 1971 Governor Milton Shapp appointed Denenberg the Pennsylvania insurance commissioner. In that position Denenberg became the most famous, most feared, and most hated regulator in American insurance history, with the sole exception of Elizur Wright.

With Massachusetts regulating insurance under Elizur Wright, New York State did not want to be left behind. Its legislature created the New York Department of Insurance. Other states took similar action, and insurance regulation by the states was off and running.

Pushing for Federal Regulation

Those insurance companies operating in many states soon found it difficult if not impossible to comply with the dizzying differences in the requirements imposed by the various states. For example, each state developed its own financial statement form, and a company had to prepare a different financial statement in each state where the company did business. Laws and regulations not only differed but in some instances conflicted with one another; that is, to comply with one state's rules, a company would have to violate another state's rules. Therefore the companies sought to have the insurance business regulated by the federal government rather than the states.

For example, the companies supported the efforts of an agent in Virginia who refused to comply with a Virginia law requiring him to obtain a state license to sell insurance. He argued that insurance was commerce that should be regulated by the federal government rather than by the states. The case went all the way to the U.S. Supreme Court, which in 1868 handed down an infamous decision—in *Paul v. Virginia*—that insurance was not commerce and that the business was therefore a proper subject for regulation by the states.

Organizing the Regulators

The *Paul* decision was a body blow to the insurance companies. They responded with a successful effort to organize the state insurance commissioners into an organization named the National Convention of Insurance Commissioners. The first meeting of the Convention was in 1871, and the first order of business was the development of uniform financial statement forms the companies could complete and file in every state. The uniform statements became known as convention blanks. The Convention also encouraged enactment of similar laws and adoption of similar regulations in the various states.

In 1939 the Convention changed its name and became the National Association of Insurance Commissioners (NAIC). To this day, major functions of the NAIC are to develop uniform statement forms (now called association blanks), encourage enactment of similar laws, and encourage adoption of similar regulations in the various states.

Lobbying Congress

A series of Supreme Court decisions followed and were consistent with the *Paul* decision. However, in 1944, the Supreme Court—in *U.S. v. Southeastern Underwriters*—ruled that insurance was commerce. By then, the insurance companies had become accustomed to state regulation and wanted no part of federal regulation. The companies successfully lobbied Congress to pass the McCarran-Ferguson Act of 1945, which allowed the states to continue regulating the insurance business.

Problems Faced by Regulators

It is widely believed that there are serious shortcomings to state regulation of the giant insurance business. A number of reasons have been offered for the apparent inability of state insurance regulators to provide adequate protection to insurance consumers.

One argument is that the departments are not adequately funded and cannot hire adequate numbers of qualified personnel. That argument is reminiscent of my personal experience with a senior staff person in the Indiana Department of Insurance. I filed a complaint with the Department over certain sales material used by the A. L. Williams organization (ALW). I was sitting in the staff person's office when he told me the Department was prohibited from conducting an investigation without a complaint from a member of the public. I was infuriated by his implication that my knowledge of the subject matter disqualified me as a member of the public. I told him the Department had the authority to start an investigation based on evidence from any source, and I stormed out. The Department never conducted the investigation. ALW is discussed in chapter 5.

A variation on that argument is that insurance companies have enough political influence with state legislators to keep state insurance departments inadequately funded. Another variation on that argument is that a regulator is reluctant to take on an insurance company because the regulator will not have the resources to fight the company. The latter variation is reminiscent of an effort by the California Department of Insurance to take on ALW for certain alleged false and misleading representations. ALW was represented by a team of attorneys from a big Los Angeles firm, and the insurance company for which ALW was an agency was represented by a team of attorneys from a big San Francisco firm. The Department was represented by a single staff attorney who was overwhelmed during the four-day hearing before an administrative law judge. The incident is discussed in the December 1989 issue of the *Forum*.

Another argument is that insurance companies have built close relationships with insurance regulators and therefore are able to persuade the regulators to do the companies' bidding. A variation on that argument is that insurance companies have such lobbying clout in state legislatures that the companies are able to make sure the laws do not provide adequate regulatory weapons for the regulators. That variation is reminiscent of an incident involving Lincoln National Life Insurance Company (Fort Wayne, IN) and the Indiana insurance commissioner. In two consecutive years, the company filed sworn annual statements containing a significant error in an important exhibit. The commissioner fined the multi-billion dollar company a total of $1,000. When I asked the commissioner to explain the meaningless tap on the wrist, he said the law provided for a maximum fine of $500 for each such transgression. The incident was not sufficiently newsworthy to be mentioned in the media.

Another argument is that insurance regulators hold their positions only temporarily. Some serve at the pleasure of their governors, and each election exposes them to being booted out to make room for a political appointment by a new incoming governor. Some of the commissioners are elected, and they need to obtain political contributions from insurance companies and agents to support election campaigns.

A related argument is one I consider especially persuasive. When the regulator leaves office, he or she may want a high-paying job in the insurance business. This is sometimes referred to as the "revolving door" argument, and is reminiscent of an incident involving a regulator who had spoken out forcefully against the mutual holding company (MHC) concept. (See chapter 26.) However, when a company in his state requested his permission to form an MHC, he approved the request. He later explained privately that he expected to leave his regulatory position at a time when his children were about to enter college, and that he therefore would need a good high-paying job. He decided to approve the company's request because he feared that, if he denied the request, he would be unable to secure a job anywhere in the insurance business.

The Lack of Uniformity

Despite the efforts of the NAIC to promote uniformity among the states in insurance statement forms, insurance laws, and insurance regulations, major differences remain. A classic example of the lack of uniformity is that an individual regulator may permit a company based in that regulator's state to engage in certain practices that would not be permitted elsewhere. For example, Transamerica Life Insurance Company (Cedar Rapids, IA) was permitted by the Iowa insurance commissioner to employ two accounting practices that are not allowed under accounting rules adopted by the NAIC. As of the end of 2013, the combination of those two practices permitted in Iowa increased the company's net worth for regulatory purposes in all states by $4.2 billion—from $0.5 billion to $4.7 billion. See blog nos. 44 (April 22, 2014), 71 (November 6, 2014), 72 (November 12, 2014), and 73 (November 19, 2014).

These permitted practices produce a major lack of uniformity among the states in the quality of insurance regulation. They also pose a serious threat to the financial stability of insurance companies.

The NAIC

The funding and some of the activities of the NAIC have long been a matter of concern. In the March 1988 issue of the *Forum* I pointed out that data base fees paid by insurance companies were by far the largest single source of NAIC revenue—more than half the total revenue. Those fees were paid by insurance companies when they filed copies of their financial statements with the NAIC to allow the computation of the ratios that were part of the Insurance Regulatory Information System. See chapter 30.

Almost 20 percent of NAIC revenue—the second largest single source of revenue—came from publications and subscriptions. A related point I have found frustrating is that NAIC model laws and model regulations are not freely available to the public; rather, they must be purchased from the NAIC.

Since the beginning of state insurance regulation in the U.S., insurance companies filed their financial statements with state insurance departments, where the statements were freely available to members of the public. I occasionally took the 75-minute drive to the office of the Indiana Department of Insurance in Indianapolis to review the financial statements of some companies. I used to call ahead to ask that the needed statements be pulled before I arrived, thus saving time. In 2003, shortly after the statements were due to be filed, I made the usual call and was astounded to learn that the statements of companies not domiciled in Indiana were no longer being filed with the Indiana department. Soon thereafter I learned that almost 30 state insurance departments had told their out-of-state companies not to file the statements. I also learned that the action had been suggested by the NAIC, which had decided to relieve the states of the responsibility for making statements available to the public. In other words, members of the public could obtain the statements from the NAIC—for a fee. Worse yet, in order to obtain the statements from the NAIC, the member of the public had to agree to an elaborate three-page license arrangement that prohibited, among other things, commercial use of the data in the statements. Thus the NAIC ended the long tradition of free and ready public access to the financial statements of insurance companies, and took steps to convert what had been public information into private information. I discussed the situation in the October 2003 issue of the *Forum.*

The Question of Federal Regulation

I have often been asked whether I favor federal or state regulation of insurance. Until recent years I dodged the question by saying I am an insurance professor and not a political scientist. Recently, however, I have been dodging the question in a different way. I now say I simply do not know whether federal regulation of the insurance business would be an improvement on the existing system of state regulation.

The reason for my modified response is that I have seen evidence of important failures by federal regulators in other areas. One example is the failure of the federal regulatory system that led to the 2008 economic collapse. Another example is the failure of the federal regulatory system that led to serious problems affecting automobile safety, a failure that was not remedied until publication of Ralph Nader's landmark 1965 book. A third example, as discussed in chapter 20, is the failure of the federal regulatory system to protect retired military personnel and other retired federal employees from being victimized by the secondary market for retirement annuities.

Meanwhile recent developments raise questions about whether the state insurance regulatory system will destroy itself, thereby making federal regulation necessary. The system of permitted practices, mentioned earlier in this chapter, is an example of a race to the bottom as states do what they can to entice insurance companies to redomesticate (change the state of domicile for regulatory purposes) from one state to another, thereby leading to a dangerous weakening of the insurance regulatory system.

Issues and Blog Items Mentioned in This Chapter

March 1988, March 1989, December 1989, and October 2003, and blog nos. 44 (April 22, 2014), 71 (November 6, 2014), 72 (November 12, 2014), and 73 (November 19, 2014).

30

The Insurance Regulatory Information System

$\mathcal{I}$nsurance companies are subjected to periodic financial examinations by state insurance regulators, usually every three to five years. In 1972 the National Association of Insurance Commissioners (NAIC) created an early warning system. It was designed to identify insurance companies whose financial condition suggested they should receive regulatory attention sooner than the regularly scheduled examinations.

At the outset the system consisted of a series of ratios calculated each year from data in the annual statements of insurance companies. In 1977 the system was expanded to include analysis of the ratios by a team of financial examiners from various states. In 1979 the system was named the Insurance Regulatory Information System (IRIS).

The Nature of IRIS

IRIS has two phases. The first is called the statistical phase. It consists of a dozen or so ratios calculated from data in the companies' annual statements. For each ratio, there is a usual range of values. For example, one ratio is called "change in capital and surplus." If the sum of the capital and surplus at the end of the preceding year increases by more than 50 percent by the end of the current year, or decreases by more than 10 percent, the value of the ratio is considered unusual. It is not difficult to determine for any company how many of the ratios have unusual or abnormal values. The formulas for the statistical phase are shown in the June 1988 issue.

The second phase of IRIS is called the analytical phase. It is based on a review of the ratios with abnormal values by a team of financial examiners from various states. The team generally reviews each company that has four or more ratios with abnormal values, and determines whether the company should be accorded immediate regulatory attention, targeted regulatory attention, or no regulatory attention. NAIC materials say companies designated for immediate regulatory attention should be accorded the highest priority in the surveillance process. Targeted regulatory attention means the company should be accorded priority in the surveillance process. No regulatory attention means the company should not be accorded priority.

I first wrote about IRIS in the April 1985 issue. There I listed the 72 life-health insurance companies that had four or more ratios with abnormal values. A few companies expressed displeasure about being listed. One was Executive Life Insurance Company, whose problems are discussed in chapter 7. In subsequent years I continued to publish updated lists of companies that had four or more ratios with abnormal values.

Confidentiality

At first the NAIC strangely treated all the IRIS material— both the statistical and analytical phases—as confidential. I say strangely because the NAIC published a booklet showing the formulas for the ratios and the normal range of values for each ratio. The booklet also showed the page, line, and column number in the annual statement for each item in the formulas. Because companies file annual statements publicly with regulators, it was easy to calculate the ratios for each company and see which ratios had abnormal values.

The results of the analytical phase of IRIS were another matter. I understood why the NAIC wanted those results kept confidential, but I also felt that a strong case could be made for public access to the results of the analytical phase.

The Struggle for Access

Early in 1985 I wrote to all the state insurance departments seeking access to the IRIS data in accordance with their state laws governing access to public records. Some of those who responded expressed concern about disclosure of the requested data. Oregon, for example, expressed concern that "the responsibilities of regulators will be seriously impaired if we are unable to receive information that can be kept confidential." Florida granted partial access if I would travel to Tallahassee to obtain the information, but I decided against making the trip when the chief examiner was not able to tell me precisely what data I would be allowed to see. Indiana denied access, citing an exemption in the state's public records law, but shortly thereafter arranged for enactment of a law specifying that IRIS data were confidential. Kansas, Montana, and West Virginia initially granted access, but immediately reversed their positions after consultation with NAIC headquarters. All the other states either denied access to the data or did not respond to my request.

In August 1985 I filed a lawsuit in Montana because that state's constitution contains a strong right-to-know provision. A lower court judge granted me access to the IRIS data. However, the Montana insurance commissioner appealed the decision, and the Montana Supreme Court reversed the decision in a 4 to 2 split vote.

In April 1986 I filed a lawsuit in the District of Columbia, where the public records law resembles the federal Freedom of Information Act, and the NAIC intervened in the case. A lower court judge issued a court order granting me access to the IRIS data. Inexplicably, neither the District of Columbia insurance commissioner nor the NAIC appealed the decision. I then visited the commissioner's office and obtained all the IRIS data in accordance with the court order. The litigation is discussed in the August 1986 issue.

The data I obtained from the District of Columbia formed the basis for a blockbuster December 1987 issue. I listed each company and showed, for each of the years 1985, 1986, and 1987, whether the company was designated for immediate, targeted, or no regulatory attention. The results of the analytical phase of IRIS were of great interest to my readers. The reaction to the December 1987 issue is discussed in the January 1988 issue.

Edward J. Muhl, the Maryland commissioner of insurance, was the NAIC president at the time. John E. Washburn, the Illinois director of insurance, was the NAIC vice president. Three days before my December 1987 issue was published, they sent a form letter to individuals in the media referring to the court decision in the District of Columbia. They explained that a company may not be in financial trouble even though some of its IRIS ratios are abnormal. In the letter they did not emphasize the analytical phase of IRIS, which was the main thrust of my December 1987 issue. After the issue was published, I wrote to Muhl and Washburn and asked them to comment now that they had seen the contents of the issue. They did not respond.

I sought updated IRIS data the following year. However, I was not able to obtain the data because the NAIC had stopped providing the data to the District of Columbia.

Parental Guarantees

Immediately after publication of the December 1987 issue, I received a telephone call from Dennis Mullane, chief executive officer of Connecticut Mutual Life Insurance Company. I had known him for a long time. The call was prompted by the fact that CM Life Insurance Company, a Connecticut Mutual subsidiary, was shown as designated for immediate regulatory attention in 1985, 1986, and 1987. He said:

> Joe, surely you know Connecticut Mutual stands behind CM Life. If you had called me before publishing your article, I would have told you about our parental guarantee to CM Life.

I explained that there was no way I could have contacted the 1,455 companies listed in the issue. I asked him to send me a copy of the parental guarantee, and he did so.

Two other companies also contacted me. John Hancock Mutual Life Insurance Company provided its parental guarantee for John Hancock Variable Life Insurance Company, and Prudential Insurance Company of America provided its parental guarantee for Pruco Life Insurance Company.

That was my first knowledge of parental guarantees, as well as the conditions, time limits, and amount limits in such guarantees. I discussed the matter in the April 1988 issue, and reproduced the guarantees in full.

Later Developments

Although I was not able to publish updated tabulations of results of the analytical phase of IRIS listing company designations, I continued to publish lists of companies that had four or more ratios with abnormal values. The NAIC continued to treat the results of the analytical phase of IRIS as confidential, but eventually ended its confidential treatment of the results of the statistical phase. Indeed, the NAIC began publishing the results of the statistical phase.

In 1989 the NAIC restructured the designations in the analytical phase of IRIS. Instead of immediate regulatory attention, targeted regulatory attention, and no regulatory attention, the designations became first priority, second priority, third priority, and no priority.

Watch Lists

In the September 1989 issue, and for several years thereafter, I published annual watch lists of insurance companies based on the ratios in the statistical phase of IRIS. I showed the names of companies that had at least four ratios with abnormal values. In the first two such annual listings, I indicated the analytical phase designations the companies had received as reflected in the December 1987 issue.

In the November 1994 issue, I began publishing expanded watch lists based not only on IRIS ratios with abnormal values but also on low financial strength ratings assigned by one or more of the rating firms. For several years I continued publishing such lists as a part of the special ratings issues that are discussed in chapter 22. Finally, in the September 2006 special ratings issue, I based the watch list solely on low financial strength ratings assigned by one or more of the rating firms. I discontinued the use of IRIS ratios with abnormal values because I felt that the ratings were more reliable than the ratios.

Issues Mentioned in This Chapter

April 1985, August 1986, December 1987. January 1988, April 1988, June 1988, September 1989, November 1994, and September 2006.

31

Risk-Based Capital

$\mathcal{T}$he National Association of Insurance Commissioners (NAIC) adopted a risk-based capital model law for life insurance companies in 1992 and for property insurance companies in 1994. The models have been enacted by the states, and are landmarks in insurance regulation. For the most part, the laws replaced arbitrary, widely varying, often extremely small, and essentially meaningless minimum capital requirements.

Risk-Based Capital Ratios

A risk-based capital ratio is a comparison of two numbers and usually is expressed as a percentage. One number—the numerator—is total adjusted capital. It is the company's net worth (assets minus liabilities) with a few adjustments.

The other number—the denominator—is risk-based capital. It is the net worth the company theoretically should have in view of its operations. It is calculated by a complex formula that reflects some of the risks in the company's activities.

Suppose a company has total adjusted capital of $3 billion and risk-based capital of $1.5 billion. The risk-based capital ratio would be 200 percent, which is calculated by dividing $3 billion by $1.5 billion and expressing the quotient as a percentage.

Risk-Based Capital Levels

There are five risk-based capital levels. The levels are red flag level, company action level, regulatory action level, authorized control level, and mandatory control level. The levels are related to one another. Red flag level is 125 percent of company action level, regulatory action level is 75 percent of company action level, authorized control level is 50 percent of company action level, and mandatory control level is 35 percent of company action level.

Risk-Based Capital Zones

The five levels create six risk-based capital zones. In terms of risk-based capital ratios where the denominator in each case is company action level, here are the names of the zones:

Ratios (%)	Zone
125 and above	Adequate
100-124	Red flag
75-99	Company action
50-74	Regulatory action
35-49	Authorized control
Below 35	Mandatory control

The name of each zone indicates what happens when total adjusted capital is in that zone. When total adjusted capital is in the adequate zone, no action is needed. When total adjusted capital is in the red flag zone, the company must perform trend tests. When total adjusted capital is in the company action zone, the company must file a confidential risk-based capital report with the regulator. When total adjusted capital is in the regulatory action zone, the regulator may issue a corrective order. When total adjusted capital is in the authorized control zone, the regulator may but is not required to take over the company. When total adjusted capital is in the mandatory control zone, the regulator is required to take over the company.

Risk-Based Capital Data

The overwhelming majority of insurance companies are in the adequate zone; that is, they have risk-based capital ratios in excess of 125 percent of company action level. Based on year-end 2012 data, as shown in the August 2013 issue of the *Forum*, there were 1,189 life insurance companies in the adequate zone and 29 in the five lower zones combined. Here is the breakdown:

Zone	No. of Cos.
Adequate	1,189
Red flag	16
Company action	7
Regulatory action	1
Authorized control	2
Mandatory control	3

Confusion over the Ratio

In theory the denominator of a risk-based capital ratio can be any risk-based capital level, and people sometimes use different denominators. Those knowledgeable about the subject normally use company action level as the denominator. Unfortunately, however, the annual financial statement form promulgated each year by the NAIC does not require disclosure of a ratio. Rather, the form requires companies to disclose only two dollar amounts: total adjusted capital and authorized control level. I say unfortunately because the form implies that authorized control level is the denominator of the ratio.

Some background may be helpful. The risk-based capital system was developed in 1991 by some regulators and an advisory committee of insurance company representatives in the wake of the failures of several major insurance companies. One was Executive Life Insurance Company, which is discussed in chapter 7, and another was Mutual Benefit Life Insurance Company. Company action level was intended to be the basic level from which the other levels were derived. However, some insurance company executives feared that the total adjusted capital of a significant number of companies might be below company action level or only slightly above it. Therefore the regulators, who were afraid of political opposition to enactment of state risk-based capital laws, made a cosmetic change. They decided to use authorized control level (half the company action level) as the level from which the other levels were derived, and to require the companies to show in the annual statement only the total adjusted capital and the authorized control level.

When those numbers started appearing in the companies' annual statements, I began publishing risk-based capital data for major companies. I showed total adjusted capital, company action level (authorized control level times 2), and the risk-based capital ratio (total adjusted capital divided by company action level, with the quotient expressed as a percentage). I presented risk-based capital data every year, and explained that company action level was the denominator. My final tabulation was in the August 2013 issue.

Moody's Investors Service often mentions risk-based capital ratios, and uses company action level as the denominator. Many companies in filings with the Securities and Exchange Commission (SEC) use company action level as the denominator. Also, as indicated earlier, people knowledgeable about the risk-based capital system normally use company action level as the denominator.

Examples of the Confusion

A major article about the confusion is in the March/April 2004 issue of the *Forum*. What prompted the article was a press release and a filing with the SEC by what was then Conseco, Inc. (now CNO Financial Group, Inc.). In the press release, the company used company action level as the denominator, but did not indicate that company action level was the denominator. In an SEC filing, however, the company used authorized control level as the denominator, and indicated that authorized control level was the denominator.

I wrote to Conseco's chief executive officer. He responded that the company henceforth would consistently use company action level as the denominator. However, a company official later used authorized control level as the denominator in some testimony. When I explained the situation to him, including his chief executive officer's response to me, he nonetheless insisted the ratio he used in his testimony was appropriate.

On one occasion I received a letter from a knowledgeable consultant who said he could not understand why I persisted in using company action level as the denominator. I explained the situation to him. He did not respond, and I do not know whether he accepted my explanation.

To summarize, one thing is certain. Whenever a risk-based capital ratio is mentioned, it is essential to indicate what risk-based capital level was used as the denominator.

The Gag Rule

A poor relationship exists between risk-based capital ratios and financial strength ratings. For example, some companies with low ratings or no ratings have high risk-based capital ratios. Thus some companies and agents disadvantaged in the market by low ratings or no ratings may try to use risk-based capital ratios to suggest to unsuspecting consumers that the companies are financially strong. Thus the NAIC and many insurance companies are concerned about the potential misuse of risk-based capital ratios. However, instead of trying to educate people about risk-based capital ratios, the NAIC included in its model laws a strongly worded gag rule, which is now part of the risk-based capital laws in most states.

Proponents of the gag rule say the purpose is to prevent the deceptive use of risk-based capital data. However, that is not what the gag rule says. Rather, the gag rule prohibits insurance companies, insurance agents, and anyone else engaged in the insurance business from directly or indirectly disseminating risk-based capital data.

Insurance periodicals do not engage in the insurance business and presumably are exempt from the gag rule. (The *Forum* was an example.) However, an insurance company or insurance agent could be accused of violating the gag rule merely by telling a consumer that risk-based capital information exists and where to find it. I learned of an insurance agent who mentioned the existence of risk-based capital data in a proposal to a client and was officially threatened with the loss of his license.

The gag rule is ill-advised. It is not effective, because companies and agents who think they can use risk-based capital data to their advantage will find a way to do so. Moreover, it is not enforceable, because it is at odds with the First Amendment to the U.S. Constitution. At least one state—Oregon—repealed the gag rule on constitutional grounds.

An Exception to the Gag Rule

The risk-based capital gag rule provides an exception when a company needs to correct published risk-based capital figures that are erroneous. I experienced a situation of that kind with regard to New England Mutual Life Insurance Company.

In the November 1994 issue of the *Forum*, I published a watch list of companies based on the 1993 year-end data shown in the 1993 annual statements. Among the criteria that caused a company to be on the watch list was a risk-based capital ratio (with company action level as the denominator of the ratio) below 150 percent. I used that figure rather than the 125 percent red flag level because my discussion with one of the developers of the risk-based capital system convinced me the system had been weakened for political reasons.

New England Mutual was on the list because its risk-based capital ratio at the end of 1993 was 130 percent. The company announced to its field force that "Professor Belth has erroneously placed The New England on his insurer's watch list" and said with emphasis that "In fact, our [risk-based capital] ratio exceeds 150 percent and we should not be on his list."

When I asked the company about the matter, a vice president told me the company's risk-based capital ratio as of September 30, 1994, was 161 percent. When I asked how the company had accomplished that feat, he explained that the company had issued surplus notes and sold some real estate at a profit between the end of 1993 and September 30, 1994.

It needs to be emphasized that the only risk-based capital numbers in the public domain are the figures shown in the annual financial statement as of the end of the year. Because no risk-based capital numbers appear in quarterly financial statements, the figure of 130 percent that I used was correct.

Limitations of the Ratios

Risk-based capital ratios should not be used to rank insurance companies in terms of financial strength, for at least four reasons. First, risk-based capital ratios were not designed for the purpose of ranking companies. Rather, they were designed for the purpose of identifying weak companies. That is why I used them as one of the criteria for my watch lists.

Second, the risk-based capital formula does not reflect conservatism that may be used in computing a company's liabilities. For example, a company may use an interest rate lower than the maximum permitted rate, thus producing large reserve liabilities.

Third, the risk-based capital formula emphasizes asset risk. Thus a company with only highly rated bonds may have a small company action level (the denominator of the ratio) and therefore a high risk-based capital ratio. Yet the company's business strategy may be a risky one that could destroy the company quickly.

Fourth, risk-based capital ratios are vulnerable to manipulation. Various devices can be used to increase the numerator, decrease the denominator, or both—thus increasing a company's risk-based capital ratio—without making material changes in the company's risk profile. For example, surplus notes may be used to increase total adjusted capital (the numerator of the ratio) and thereby increase the ratio as New England Mutual did. Yet surplus notes are debt instruments that do not provide permanent net worth. See chapter 25.

In short, financial strength ratings are the primary and most reliable source of information about the financial strength of insurance companies. That is why I published special ratings issues, as discussed in chapter 22.

Issues Mentioned in This Chapter

November 1994, March/April 2004, and August 2013.

32

Conclusion

*F*rom the beginning of life insurance in the U.S. almost two centuries ago, the business has survived in the face of two fundamental obstacles and several self-inflicted problems that defy solution for political reasons. In this chapter I discuss the two fundamental obstacles and some self-inflicted problems.

Obstacle No. 1: The Procrastination Phenomenon

A fundamental obstacle is that the purchase of life insurance requires consumers to think about the unpleasant subject of their deaths and take action rather than procrastinate. As it is often said: "Life insurance is sold, not bought."

The significance of this obstacle is that life insurance companies must hire and train life insurance agents to seek out customers, persuade them to consider their obligations to their families, and persuade their customers to take action rather than "wait until next year." I call the latter the critical but difficult "anti-procrastination function" of life insurance agents.

The further significance of this obstacle is that a life insurance company must provide the agent with a strong financial incentive to engage in a difficult and often discouraging type of work. The agent usually is compensated by a large commission, which is often substantially more than half the first-year premium for the policy, when life insurance is sold. The commissions on the premiums paid in subsequent policy years usually are much smaller, often around 5 percent.

Life insurance is not the only area in which procrastination is a problem. For example, most people die without wills, even though they can still prepare wills when they are seriously ill, while they generally cannot buy life insurance when they are seriously ill. Most people die without wills because no one is compensated for performing the anti-procrastination function.

Obstacle No. 2: The Shape of the Mortality Curve

The second fundamental obstacle stems from the shape of the mortality rate curve. The probability of death generally is small when people are young, increases geometrically with age, and eventually reaches a certainty. The significance of this obstacle, unlike the situation in other areas of insurance, is that "natural" premiums to provide life insurance initially are small and increase geometrically with age, eventually becoming very large relative to the death benefit. Furthermore, premiums in the first policy year, when derived from relatively small natural premiums, do not generate enough money to compensate agents adequately for performing the functions referred to in the discussion of the first fundamental obstacle.

Life insurance companies try to deal with the problem in two ways. First, when they offer annual renewable term life insurance, in which premiums resemble natural premiums, they end the insurance protection at an age such as 65; by doing so, they avoid offering protection at a time when death rates would be very high and premiums therefore would be very large. Second, they construct "whole life" policies that pay the death benefit no matter when the insured person dies. The problem is that, while premiums for whole life policies usually are leveled out, thus building up cash values, the cash values are small or non-existent in the first one or two policy years mainly because of the large first-year commissions paid to the agents. One of the major reasons for the opposition of life insurance companies to rigorous price disclosure is their belief that it is necessary to conceal from customers the relatively high price of the life insurance protection in the first one or two policy years caused by the commissions and administrative expenses the companies incur to issue the policies. The companies believe that disclosing those relatively high prices would make it difficult to persuade people to buy life insurance.

The Short View

Life insurance policies are long-term contracts and the life insurance business is a long-term business. However, most leaders of the business, most regulators, and most lawmakers are unwilling to take the long-term view that is essential to the long-term survival of the business. Here are some examples: (1) the demutualization process that provides windfall benefits to the very insurance executives who make the decision to demutualize, (2) risky investment activities that are designed to enhance short-term financial results, (3) weakening of companies' financial strength through exotic reinsurance arrangements and the creation of phony assets, (4) weakening of companies' net worth through the issuance of surplus notes, (5) refusal to hire and train new life insurance agents in an effort to reduce expenses, and (6) transition away from the selling of life insurance and into the selling of annuities of dubious value.

Reverse Competition

Reverse competition has the effect of increasing rather than decreasing prices for consumers. The subject often is discussed in connection with credit life insurance, as mentioned in chapter 15. However, the concept applies also in companies' efforts to attract the business of high-producing life insurance agents. For example, companies often pay excessive commissions to attract the business of such agents, and the companies often engage in lax underwriting of policies. Such practices inevitably require policyholders to pay higher prices for life insurance protection.

The Evidence

The effect of the problems identified here is evidenced by troubling trends. Here are two examples: (1) a sharp drop in the number of individuals who consider themselves life insurance agents, as indicated by a sharp decline in membership in agent organizations; and (2) the sale of larger policies to fewer consumers, thus leaving more members of the middle class with little or no private life insurance protection.

The Focus on Secrecy

Finally, the life insurance business simply refuses to disclose the information needed to allow consumers to make intelligent decisions about their life insurance. This shortsighted nondisclosure approach may be illustrated by an anecdote.

About 30 years ago, I enjoyed a pleasant private dinner with a now-deceased friend of mine who was a senior actuary of a major life insurance company. The dinner took place several years after I had recommended rigorous disclosure of price and rate-of-return information to life insurance buyers and policyholders. It was also several years after my legal battle with the North Carolina insurance commissioner over the activities of the A. L. Williams organization, after the shelving of the controversial Federal Trade Commission staff report, after the shelving of the controversial National Association of Insurance Commissioners task force report, after I had given up on my efforts to achieve rigorous disclosure for the benefit of life insurance consumers, and before the collapse of Executive Life.

I asked my friend this threshold question: "Do you think the life insurance business would survive if rigorous disclosure along the lines of what I recommended were mandated by law or regulation?" His answer was a simple "No."

My dinner companion was a thoughtful and highly professional person, and I found his answer profoundly disturbing. First, I told him I disagreed with him. Second, I expressed my belief that the life insurance business would not only survive but would be strengthened and improved by the adoption of rigorous disclosure requirements. Third, I expressed my belief that any business built on the nondisclosure of information that is vital to its customers will not survive—and will not deserve to survive—over the long term. I still hold those beliefs today.

Acknowledgments

*H*alf a century before the creation of the State of Israel, my grandparents uprooted themselves from their Eastern European homes and braved the Atlantic Ocean voyage so that they and their descendants could live in America. My parents instilled in me certain values that have stood me in good stead during my entire life. My wife Marjorie (Marge) has been my constant companion and greatest support. Our children Ann, Michael (Mike), and Jeffrey (Jeff); our daughters-in-law Jeanne and Sandra (Sandy); our grandchildren, Rachel, Rebecca, Caleb, and Alan; and our stepgrandson Whitney Swain are a source of great pride and inspiration to us.

Our daughter Ann has been a stalwart helper. She was business manager of the *Forum* for many years, kept my computer functioning, handled the tabulations in the *Forum*, read the manuscript of this memoir, and offered excellent suggestions.

Our son Jeff helped for many years as circulation and list manager of the *Forum*. He designed and typeset this memoir using InDesign. He became proficient with that program while creating his award-winning book, *Butterflies of Indiana: A Field Guide* (Indiana University Press, 2013).

My first cousin Irene (Renie) Wolpin has been like the sister I never had. Her mother was my mother's late sister, Polaire Share. Renie and her mother lived in our house for a time while the head of their household, the late William Share, M.D., was serving in the U.S. Army during World War II.

I have been fortunate to have many wonderful friends. The late Dan Mays McGill was my mentor and confidant for more than 50 years. The late John Douglas Long was my colleague and faithful supporter for more than 40 years.

Travis Pritchett, Joan Schmit, and Harold (Skip) Skipper have long been my closest friends in the insurance academic community. On top of everything else they have done for me, they organized a celebration (described in this memoir) in my honor when I ended publication of the *Forum* after 40 years. They also read the manuscript for this memoir, offered excellent suggestions, and wrote the foreword.

Elizabeth Fleming copyedited the initial typeset version of this memoir. The late Herbert Sim played an important role in my life, as described in this memoir. David Schiff and Alastair Rickard, founders and longtime editors of *Schiff's Insurance Observer* and *The Canadian Journal of Life Insurance,* respectively, have been sources of inspiration. Alan Press, who served for many years as general agent in New York City for Guardian Life Insurance Company of America, has been my closest friend in the insurance business.

I am grateful to many *Forum* readers who suggested topics, to those who contributed articles under their own names or coauthored articles with me, and to those who helped in other ways. An alphabetical list of significant contributors is shown below. Sadly, many of them are no longer with us. Some of those listed are mentioned elsewhere in this memoir. I apologize to those inadvertently omitted from the list.

Jason Adkins, Theodore Affleck, Eugene Anderson, James Ballew, Scott Barrett, Laurence Barton, Eric Berg, Scott Berlin, Bart Bertero, Philip Bieluch, John Biggs, Birny Birnbaum, Roger Bixby, James Blatt, Lois Braunlin, William Braunlin, Keith Buckley, Alan Buerger, John Calagna, Richard Cardwell, William Carmello, Charlene Christopher, Glenn Daily, Mark DeBofsky, Robert DeFillippo, Herbert Denenberg, Timothy Dillon, Robert Dineen, Jack Dolan, John Dorfman, Steven Dryer, Gary Duncan, Tammy Ewbank, Barbara Farrington, Francis Ferguson, Haswell Franklin, Daniel Gardner, Andrew Gold, Peter Gould,

Chris Grimes, Dale Gustafson, Lloyd Hall, Jon Hanson, William Harman, Robert Harmon, Jan Hayden, J. Edward Hedges, James Hunt, Robert Hunter, Paul Ingrassia, Fred Joseph, Halsey Josephson, Barton Kaufman, John Keith, Spencer Kimball, William Koenig, Alan Konrad, James Lacey, Bongjoo Lee, Stephan Leimberg, Claire Lenz, E. J. Leverett, Cheyeh Lin, Michael Lovendusky, Philip Loy, Mark Lucius, Robert Maloney, Kevin Marti, Joseph Masella, Robert May, Larry Mayewski, Daniel McCarthy, Brian McTigue, Paul Mills, Ernest Moorhead, Alan Morrison, Milton Moskowitz, Ralph Nader, Charles Neumeyer, David Nelson, Irving Pfeffer, Richard Phillips, George Pinnell, Harry Privette, Debbie Purcell, Jane Bryant Quinn, Robert Riegel, Stephen Robertson, Lawrence J. Rybka, Leslie Scism, John Cary Sims, Arthur Snyder III, Joel Steinberg, Larry Stern, Richard Stewart, Thomas Tierney, Frederick Townsend, Charles Ulrich, Therese Vaughan, David Vladeck, George Vlahakis, William Wallace, William Warfel, Samuel Weese, Thomas Weiss, William Werfelman, Ernest Whichard, Matthew Will, Walter Williams, Tad Wilson, Brian Wolfman, Gloria Wolk, and Roy Woodall.

I assume full responsibility for the contents of this memoir, and for any errors that may remain.

Appendix A

Prices and Rates of Return

*T*his appendix shows the formula for calculating the yearly price per $1,000 of the protection component and the formula for calculating the yearly rate of return on the savings component in cash-value life insurance policies.

Formula for Yearly Price

$$YPT = \frac{(P + CVP)(1 + ayrr) - CV - D}{(F - CV)(.001)}$$

where

YPT is yearly price per $1,000 of protection
P is annual premium payable at beginning of year ($2,500)
CVP is cash value at end of preceding year ($15,000)
ayrr is assumed yearly rate of return on savings (3%)
CV is cash value at end of year ($17,000)
D is dividend payable at end of year ($500)
F is amount payable on death during year ($100,000)

Example using values shown above for each item:

$$YPT = \frac{(\$2,500 + \$15,000)(1 + .03) - \$17,000 - \$500}{(\$100,000 - \$17,000)(.001)} = \$6.33$$

Formula for Yearly Rate of Return

$$YRR = \frac{CV + D + (aypt)(F - CV)(.001)}{P + CVP} - 1$$

where

YRR is yearly rate of return on savings
CV is cash value at end of year ($17,000)
D is dividend payable at end of year ($500)
aypt is assumed yearly price per $1,000 of protection ($5)
F is amount payable on death during year ($100,000)
P is annual premium payable at beginning of year ($2,500)
CVP is cash value at end of preceding year ($15,000)

Example using values shown above for each item:

$$YRR = \frac{\$17{,}000 + \$500 + (5)(\$100{,}000 - \$17{,}000)(.001)}{\$2{,}500 + \$15{,}000} - 1$$

$$= 1.0237 - 1$$
$$= .0237$$
$$= 2.37\%$$

Appendix B
Annual Percentage Rates

$\mathcal{T}$his appendix, mentioned in chapter 8, is divided into three sections. Section 1 below shows a family of formulas to estimate annual percentage rates (APRs) associated with fractional (modal) premium charges. Sections 2 and 3 are on the next three pages.

Section 1

Semiannual: $\quad APR = \dfrac{200\,(2S - A)}{A - S}$

Quarterly: $\quad APR = \dfrac{1200\,(4Q - A)}{5A - 2Q}$

Monthly: $\quad APR = \dfrac{3600\,(12M - A)}{13A + 42M}$

where

APR is annual percentage rate expressed as a percentage
A is annual premium
S is semiannual premium
Q is quarterly premium
M is monthly premium

Section 2

This section shows a table to estimate APRs. Divide the fractional premium by the annual premium. Express the quotient as a decimal. Find the ratio in the table below. Read the APR to the right of the ratio. Interpolate as necessary.

Semiannual		Quarterly		Monthly	
Ratio	APR (%)	Ratio	APR (%)	Ratio	APR(%)
0.500	0.0	0.250	0.0	0.08333	0.0
0.502	1.6	0.252	2.1	0.0835	0.4
0.504	3.2	0.254	4.3	0.0840	1.7
0.506	4.9	0.256	6.4	0.0845	3.0
0.508	6.5	0.258	8.6	0.0850	4.3
0.510	8.2	0.260	10.7	0.0855	5.6
0.512	9.8	0.262	12.9	0.0860	6.9
0.514	11.5	0.264	15.0	0.0865	8.2
0.516	13.2	0.266	17.2	0.0870	9.5
0.518	14.9	0.268	19.4	0.0875	10.8
0.520	16.7	0.270	21.5	0.0880	12.1
0.522	18.4	0.272	23.7	0.0885	13.4
0.524	20.2	0.274	25.9	0.0890	14.6
0.526	21.9	0.276	28.1	0.0895	15.9
0.528	23.7	0.278	30.3	0.0900	17.2
0.530	25.5	0.280	32.5	0.0905	18.4
0.532	27.4	0.282	34.7	0.0910	19.7
0.534	29.2	0.284	36.9	0.0915	21.0
0.536	31.0	0.286	39.1	0.0920	22.2
0.538	32.9	0.288	41.3	0.0925	23.5
0.540	34.8	0.290	43.6	0.0930	24.7
0.542	36.7	0.292	45.8	0.0935	26.0
0.544	38.6	0.294	48.0	0.0940	27.2
0.546	40.5	0.296	50.3	0.0945	28.5
0.548	42.5	0.298	52.5	0.0950	29.7
0.550	44.4	0.300	54.8	0.0955	31.0
0.552	46.4	0.302	57.1	0.0960	32.2
0.554	48.4	0.304	59.3	0.0965	33.4
0.556	50.5	0.306	61.6	0.0970	34.7
0.558	52.5	0.308	63.9	0.0975	35.9
0.560	54.5	0.310	66.2	0.0980	37.1
0.562	56.6	0.312	68.5	0.0985	38.4
0.564	58.7	0.314	70.8	0.0990	39.6
0.566	60.8	0.316	73.1	0.0995	40.8
0.568	63.0	0.318	75.4	0.1000	42.0

Section 3

This section shows results from using the APR calculator on our website (www.theinsuranceforum.com). The input page that comes up when you click on "APR Calculator" on our website is shown below. I keyed in the annual premium of $1,525.50, the semiannual premium of $793.26, the quarterly premium of $404.26, and the monthly premium of $144.92. Note that dollar signs and commas must be omitted.

The results page that comes up after clicking "Calculate" on the input page is shown on the next page. It shows the APRs and the dollar costs of the fractional premium charges. It also provides some general guidance on APRs.

APR Calculator for Fractional (Modal) Premiums

When premiums are paid more often than once a year, the insurance company usually adds extra charges. This calculator shows the extra charges per year expressed as an annual percentage rate (APR) and in dollars. Click here for a detailed description of this APR calculator.

Instructions:

1. Key in the Annual Premium, without dollar signs and without commas.
2. Key in the Fractional Premiums, without dollar signs and without commas, in which you are interested.
3. Click Calculate.

Annual Premium	1525.50
Fractional Premiums	
Semiannual	793.26
Quarterly	404.26
Monthly	144.92
Calculate	

APR Calculator for Fractional (Modal) Premiums

Calculation Results

Premiums Entered		Extra Charges	
		APR	Dollars
Annual	$1525.50		
Semiannual	$793.26	16.7%	$61.02
Quarterly	$404.26	16.1%	$91.54
Monthly	$144.92	29.7%	$213.54

Make a new calculation   Edit your data

Note: If the results seem strange, double-check the figures you keyed in and recalculate. Be sure you omitted dollar signs and commas. If the results still seem strange, contact us.

General Guidance on the APR:

An APR below 5% is very low.
An APR between 5% and 10% is low.
An APR between 10% and 15% is moderate.
An APR between 15% and 20% is fairly high.
An APR between 20% and 25% is high.
An APR between 25% and 30% is very high.
An APR above 30% is extremely high.

Appendix C

Strong Life Insurance Companies

$\mathcal{T}$his appendix presents three lists of life insurance companies shown in the September 2013 special ratings issue of the *Forum* as having high financial strength ratings from at least two of the four major rating firms. Chapter 22 explains the three definitions of high ratings used to create the lists. The first alphabetical list is for consumers who are extremely conservative from the standpoint of financial strength, the second is for consumers who are very conservative, and the third is for consumers who are conservative. Company names are abbreviated, and the state where each company is domiciled for regulatory purposes is shown in parentheses (CN stands for Canada). *See the copyright notice at the bottom of page 329.*

Extremely Conservative

Berkshire Hathaway L (NE)
Berkshire LIC Amer (MA)
CM Life Ins Co (CT)
General Re Life Corp (CT)
Guardian Ins & Annuity (DE)
Guardian Life Ins Co (NY)
Knights of Columbus (CT)
Massachusetts Mutual (MA)
MML Bay State Life (CT)
New York L Ins & Ann (DE)

New York Life Ins Co (NY)
Northwestern LTC Ins (WI)
Northwestern Mutual (WI)
State Farm Life & Acc (IL)
State Farm Life Ins Co (IL)
Teachers Ins & Annuity (NY)
TIAA-CREF Life Ins (NY)
USAA Life Ins Co (TX)
USAA Life Ins Co NY (NY)

Very Conservative

Canada Life Asr Co (CN)
Canada Life Asr Co US (MI)
Columbus Life Ins Co (OH)
Great-West Life & Ann (CO)
Great-West Life & Ann (NY)
Great-West Life Asr (CN)
Great-West Life US Br (MI)
HCC Life Ins Co (IN)
Integrity Life Ins Co (OH)
Jackson National Life (MI)

Jackson National L NY (NY)
Lafayette Life Ins Co (OH)
London Life Ins Co (CN)
National Integrity Life (NY)
Perico Life Ins Co (DE)
Thrivent Financial Luth (WI)
Thrivent Life Ins Co (MN)
Western-Southern L Asr (OH)
Western & Southern L I (OH)

Conservative

Aetna Health CA (CA)
Aetna Health Inc (FL)
Aetna Health Inc (NJ)
Aetna Health Inc (NY)
Aetna Health Inc (PA)
Aetna Health Inc (TX)
Aetna Life Ins Co (CT)
Allianz Life Ins NY (NY)
Allianz Life N Amer (MN)
American Family L Asr (NE)
American Family L Asr (NY)
American Income Life (IN)
American United Life (IN)
Anthem B C L&H Ins (CA)
Anthem Health Plans (CT)
Anthem Health Plans KY (KY)
Anthem Health Plans ME (ME)
Anthem Health Plans NH (NH)
Anthem Health Plans VA (VA)
Anthem Ins Cos Inc (IN)
AXA Equitable L&Ann (CO)
AXA Equitable Life (NY)
Banner Life Ins Co (MD)
Blue Cross Blue Shield (GA)
Blue Cross Blue Shield HC (GA)
Blue Cross California (CA)
Combined Ins Co Amer (IL)
Combined Life Ins NY (NY)

Community Ins Co (OH)
CSI Life Ins Co (NE)
Empire HlthChoice Asr (NY)
Empire HlthChoice HMO (NY)
First MetLife Investors (NY)
General American Life (MO)
Globe Life & Acc Ins (NE)
Golden Rule Ins Co (IN)
Hannover Life Reasr Am (FL)
Health Care Svc Corp (IL)
Health Plan Nevada (NV)
HealthKeepers Inc (VA)
Healthy Alliance Life (MO)
HMO Missouri (MO)
John Hancock L&H Ins (MA)
John Hancock Life NY (NY)
John Hancock Life USA (MI)
Liberty National Life (NE)
Lincoln Life & Ann NY (NY)
Lincoln National Life (IN)
Manufacturers Life (CN)
Matthew Thornton Hlth (NH)
MetLife Ins Co CT (CT)
MetLife Investors Ins (MO)
MetLife Investors USA (DE)
Metropolitan Life Ins (NY)
Metropolitan Tower L (DE)
Minnesota Life Ins Co (MN)

Conservative (continued)

Monumental Life Ins (IA)
MONY Life Ins Co (NY)
MONY Life Ins Co Am (AZ)
Munich American Re (GA)
Mutual of America Life (NY)
New England Life Ins (MA)
Ohio National Life Asr (OH)
Ohio National Life Ins (OH)
Oxford Health Ins Inc (NY)
Oxford Health Plans (NY)
PacifiCare Life & Health (IN)
PacifiCare of Arizona (AZ)
Penn Ins & Annuity Co (DE)
Penn Mutual Life Ins (PA)
Primerica Life Ins Co (MA)
Principal Life Ins Co (IA)
Principal National Life (IA)
Protective Life & Ann (AL)
Protective Life Ins Co (TN)
Pruco Life Ins Co (AZ)
Pruco Life Ins Co NJ (NJ)
Prudential Annuities Life (CT)
Prudential Ins Co Amer (NJ)
Prudential Retirement (CT)
RGA Reins Co (MO)
RiverSource Life (MN)
RiverSource Life NY (NY)
Rocky Mountain Hosp (CO)
Securian Life Ins Co (MN)
Sierra Health & Life (CA)
State Life Ins Co (IN)
Stonebridge Life Ins Co (VT)

Sun Life Asr CN (CN)
Sun Life Asr CN US Br (MI)
Sun Life & Hlth Ins US (CT)
Swiss Re L&H America (CT)
Transamerica Advisors (AR)
Transamerica Advisors (NY)
Transamerica Fin Life (NY)
Transmerica Life (IA)
UHC of California (CA)
UnitedHealthcare AL (AL)
UnitedHealthcare AZ (AZ)
UnitedHealthcare FL (FL)
UnitedHealthcare GA (GA)
UnitedHealthcare IL (IL)
UnitedHealthcare KY (KY)
UnitedHealthcare Mdwst (MO)
UnitedHealthcare NC (NC)
UnitedHealthcare NewEng (RI)
UnitedHealthcare NY (NY)
UnitedHealthcare OH (OH)
UnitedHealthcare TX (TX)
UnitedHealthcare WI (WI)
UnitedHealthcare Benefits (TX)
UnitedHealthcare Ins (CT)
UnitedHealthcare Ins (IL)
UnitedHealthcare Ins (NY)
UnitedHealthcare Pl Rvr V (IL)
US Financial Life Ins (OH)
West Coast Life Ins Co (NE)
Western Reserve Life (OH)
William Penn Life NY (NY)

Appendix D

Ten Million Dollar Club

*T*his appendix presents an alphabetical list of the 66 insurance executives who were shown in the July 2013 issue of the *Forum* as having received total compensation of $10 million or more in 2012. In those instances where figures differed for an individual among our three sources—the Securities and Exchange Commission, the Nebraska Department of Insurance, and the New York Department of Financial Services—the list below shows the largest figure. Amounts and company affiliations are indicated. For further details, including names, amounts, and company affiliations of executives who received total compensation of $1 million or more in 2012, see the July 2013 issue.

Name	Amount	Company
Daniel Amos	$27,459,047	AFLAC Inc
Albert Annexstad	29,703,030	Federated Mutual
Edward Baird	14,585,666	Prudential Financial
Albert Benchimol	22,674,021	AXIS Capital
Robert Benmosche	10,573,910	American Intl Group
William R Berkley	31,296,780	W R Berkley Corp
Mark Bertolini	37,278,315	Aetna Inc
Angela Braly	32,133,277	WellPoint Inc
Joseph Brandon	17,056,019	Alleghany Corp
Michael Browne	24,314,176	Nationwide Mutual
Scott Carmilani	15,889,027	Allied World Assurance
William Casazza	12,086,481	Aetna Inc

Name	Amount	Company
Gregory Case	$12,723,070	Aon plc
C Edward Chaplin	10,726,506	MBIA Inc
John Charman	18,883,583	AXIS Capital
Laura Ciavola	13,302,277	UnitedHealth Group
David Cordani	12,881,495	CIGNA Corp
James Cracchiolo	17,828,431	Ameriprise Financial
Roger Crandall	20,885,066	Massachusetts Mutual
Christa Davies	11,392,949	Aon plc
Brian Duperreault	17,008,351	Marsh & McLennan
William Fallon	10,726,506	MBIA Inc
John Finnegan	13,887,842	Chubb Corp
Jay Fishman	24,099,921	Travelers Inc
William Foley II	14,992,067	Fidelity National
Dominic Frederico	13,363,715	Assured Guaranty
Herbert Fritch	10,734,543	CIGNA Corp
Jay Gellert	10,160,381	Health Net Inc
Daniel Glaser	10,217,538	Marsh & McLennan
Dennis Glass	11,342,213	Lincoln National Corp
Mitchell Graye	10,555,013	Great-West Life
Evan Greenberg	15,556,512	ACE Ltd
Mark Grier	19,857,570	Prudential Financial
Donald Guloien	10,445,702	Manulife Financial
Patricia Hall	17,465,275	Health Care Service
Stephen Hemsley	13,887,455	UnitedHealth Group
Duane Hercules	11,567,558	Philadelphia Indemnity
Constantine Iordanou	10,400,653	Arch Capital Group
Steven Kandarian	13,669,011	MetLife Inc
Elwood Lassiter	39,982,016	Alleghany Group
Theodore Mathas	10,484,850	New York Life
Margaret McCarthy	12,252,637	Aetna Inc
Liam McGee	11,157,261	Hartford Financial
Michael Mirt	16,381,226	CIGNA Corp
Robert Moody	15,744,244	American National
Thomas Motamed	10,647,714	CNA Financial Corp
Thomas Nerney	13,004,420	Berkshire Hathaway
Olza Nicely	12,148,254	Berkshire Hathaway
S Ramakrishnan	13,372,933	UnitedHealth Group
Glenn Renwick	16,584,987	Progressive Corp

Name	Amount	Company
Josue Robles Jr	$10,485,017	USAA Group
Mete Sahin	13,292,743	UnitedHealth Group
Gerald Scott	11,572,693	Philadelphia Indemnity
Paul Serini	19,328,320	UnitedHealth Group
Joseph Spruiell	13,258,130	UnitedHealth Group
John Strangfeld	30,693,655	Prudential Financial
Joseph Taranto	27,914,888	Everest Re Group
Thomas Watjen	13,811,307	Unum Group
Ronald Williams	56,670,401	Aetna Inc
Thomas Wilson	17,058,555	Allstate Corp
Jay Wintrob	12,194,251	American Intl Group
Allen Wise	11,967,573	Coventry Health Care
Elease Wright	20,424,321	Aetna Inc
Larry Zimpleman	10,609,725	Principal Financial
Joseph Zubretsky	21,852,367	Aetna Inc
Barry Zyskind	18,120,917	AmTrust Financial

Appendix E

Highest Paid Executive
Each Year

*T*his appendix shows the name, amount, and company affiliation of the highest paid insurance executive in each year from 1974 through 2012, based on data in the *Forum*. In those instances where figures differed for an individual among our three sources—the Securities and Exchange Commission, the Nebraska Department of Insurance, and the New York Department of Financial Services—the list shows the largest figure.

Year	Name	Amount	Company
1974	Donald MacNaughton $	351,923	Prudential Ins Co
1975	Donald MacNaughton	375,000	Prudential Ins Co
1976	Donald MacNaughton	440,908	Prudential Ins Co
1977	Donald MacNaughton	431,249	Prudential Ins Co
1978	William Kelly	526,698	Phoenix Mutual
1979	Richard Shinn	443,333	Metropolitan Life
1980	Robert Beck	507,760	Prudential Ins Co
1981	Coy Eklund	594,794	Equitable Life (NY)
1982	Carl Lindner	1,611,900	American Financial
1983	E G Fitts	1,750,000	Gulf United Corp
1984	Carl Lindner	1,904,600	American Financial
1985	John Amos	2,010,754	AFLAC Inc
1986	Carl Lindner	4,189,000	American Financial
1987	Carl Lindner	10,902,000	American Financial
1988	Carl Lindner	11,440,000	American Financial

Year	Name	Amount	Company
1989	Saul Steinberg	$ 6,265,000	Reliance Group
1990	Saul Steinberg	6,314,000	Reliance Group
1991	Saul Steinberg	6,035,000	Reliance Group
1992	Ronald Walker	12,479,000	American Financial
1993	Robert Greenhill	23,947,761	Travelers Inc
1994	Maurice Greenberg	12,083,080	American Intl Group
1995	Robert Greenhill	34,733,447	Travelers Inc
1996	John Powell	20,689,543	American Travellers
1997	Daniel Amos	21,823,433	AFLAC Inc
1998	Eli Broad	71,407,646	SunAmerica Life
1999	Jay Wintrob	55,299,653	American Intl Group
2000	Stephen Hilbert	77,065,287	Conseco Inc
2001	Eli Broad	48,174,739	SunAmerica Life
2002	Eli Broad	23,201,528	SunAmerica Life
2003	Leonard Schaeffer	37,629,181	Unicare Life & Health
2004	Thomas Geiser	50,743,161	Unicare Life & Health
2005	William Foley II	38,327,301	Fidelity National
2006	William Foley II	170,360,725	Fidelity National
2007	John Rowe	116,594,618	Aetna Inc
2008	Edmund Kelly	53,263,025	Liberty Mutual
2009	Edmund Kelly	50,062,372	Liberty Mutual
2010	Ronald Williams	54,524,112	Aetna Inc
2011	John Rowe	81,980,330	Aetna Inc
2012	Ronald Williams	56,670,401	Aetna Inc

Glossary

Accumulation Period: The period between the purchase of an annuity and the beginning of the payments. In an immediate annuity, the accumulation period is one time period.

Age Clause: *See* Misstatement-of-Age Clause.

Annuitant: A person who receives an annuity.

Annuitization: The conversion of an accumulation into an annuity. It usually occurs at the beginning of the liquidation period of the annuity.

Annuity: A series of payments—annually, semiannually, quarterly, or monthly—to liquidate a principal sum. Each payment is partly interest and partly a return of principal. Also means a contract providing an annuity.

Annuity Certain: An annuity in which payments are made for a specified number of years or to a specified age. Payments are not contingent upon the survival of the annuitant, and a beneficiary receives any payments that remain after the death of the annuitant.

Any Occupation: A definition of disability that means inability of an insured to perform the duties of any occupation.

Any Occupation for Which Suited: A definition of disability that means inability of an insured to perform the duties of the insured's own occupation or the duties of any other gainful occupation for which the insured is suited as a result of the insured's education, training, experience, and prior earnings.

Beneficiary: A person or entity designated in a policy to receive a death benefit upon the death of an insured.

Benefit Amount: The amount of each benefit payment during a disability.

Benefit Period: The maximum period—usually expressed in years—over which disability benefits are paid.

Cash Surrender Value: *See* Cash Value.

Cash Value: An amount paid by an insurance company to a policyholder when a policyholder surrenders a policy. *Also called* Cash Surrender Value or Savings Component.

Cash-Value Policy: A policy that builds cash values.

Coinsurance Percentage: The percentage of medical expenses the policyholder must pay in a medical insurance policy.

Continuance Clause: A clause in a policy showing the extent to which a policyholder has the right to continue a policy and whether the insurance company has the right to increase premiums. Used in disability, medical, and long-term care insurance policies.

Convertibility: A provision of a term policy that allows the policyholder to convert the policy into a cash-value policy without evidence of insurability.

Death Benefit: An amount paid by an insurance company to a beneficiary upon the death of an insured. *Also called* Face Amount.

Deductible: The amount a policyholder has to pay before beginning to receive benefits from a medical insurance policy.

Deferred Annuity: An annuity in which the first payment is made more than one time period after the annuity is purchased. The first payment may be made at a specified age or after a specified number of years.

Disability: Inability of an insured to perform occupational duties because of an illness or injury.

Disability Insurance: A policy providing benefits when the insured is unable to work because of an illness or an injury.

Dividend: An amount paid by an insurance company to a policyholder, usually once a year. Usually viewed as a refund of a portion of the premiums previously paid.

Dividend Expense Charge: An expense charge used in calculating the dividend on a life insurance policy.

Dividend Interest Rate: An interest rate used in calculating the dividend on a life insurance policy.

Dividend Mortality Rate: A mortality rate used in calculating the dividend on a life insurance policy.

Elimination Period: The period of time—usually expressed in days—between the beginning of a disability and the beginning of benefit payments. *Also called* Waiting Period.

Equity Index Annuity: *See* Index Annuity.

Evidence of Insurability: The health of the insured and other factors that are used by an insurance company in determining whether to issue a policy and, if so, what premiums will be charged.

Expense Charge: An amount that represents expenses and is used in calculating a premium.

Face Amount: *See* Death Benefit.

Fixed Annuity: An annuity in which the payments are stated in dollars. The assets backing the annuity are invested in debt instruments such as bonds and mortgages.

Fixed Index Annuity: An oxymoron created for an index annuity in an effort to prevent its classification as a security for regulatory purposes.

Flexible-Premium Annuity: A periodic-premium annuity in which the annuitant determines the amount and timing of each premium.

Fractional Premium Charges: Extra charges imposed on consumers by insurance companies for the privilege of paying premiums more frequently than once a year. *Also called* Modal Premium Charges.

Fractional Premiums: Premiums paid more frequently than once a year, usually semiannually, quarterly, or monthly. *Also called* Modal Premiums.

Grace Period Clause: A clause in a policy that says the policy remains in effect if a premium is paid late, usually for up to 31 days.

Guaranteed Renewable: A continuance clause that says a

policyholder has the right to keep the policy until a specified age and the insurance company has the right to increase the premiums for classes of policies but does not have the right to single out a policy for an increase. Used in disability, medical, and long-term care insurance policies.

Illustrated Dividends: A list used in sales illustrations showing nonguaranteed dividends to be paid in the future.

Immediate Annuity: An annuity in which the first payment is made one time period after the annuity is purchased. For example, in an annuity providing for monthly payments, the first payment is made one month after purchase.

Index Annuity: An annuity, not yet classified as a security for regulatory purposes, whose value is loosely related to an index such as the Standard & Poor's 500 index. *Also called* Equity Index Annuity.

Insurance Company: A company that issues the policy and promises to carry out the terms of the policy.

Insured: The person on whose life a policy is based, and whose death triggers a death benefit, or, in the case of health insurance, the person whose illness, injury, or need for long-term care triggers a benefit.

Interest: The price paid for the use of money. *Also called* Time Value of Money.

Interest Rate: The rate paid for the use of money, expressed as a percentage or as a decimal.

Investment Year Method: A method for calculating a dividend on a life insurance policy based on returns reflecting the timing of a company's receipt of premiums.

Joint Life Annuity: An annuity in which the payments are made jointly to two annuitants while they are alive and stop when one of the annuitants dies.

Joint-and-Survivor Life Annuity: An annuity in which the payments are made jointly to two annuitants while they are alive and stop when the surviving annuitant dies. Each payment to the surviving annuitant may be the same as, or a fraction of, each payment that was made jointly.

Lapse: Discontinuance of a policy by the policyholder.

Life Annuity: An annuity in which each payment is contingent upon the survival of the annuitant.

Liquidation Period: The period over which the annuity payments liquidate the principal. The liquidation period of a life annuity is the annuitant's lifetime. The liquidation period of an annuity certain is the period over which the annuity payments are made.

Loan Clause: A clause in a life insurance policy providing that a policyholder may borrow at interest from an insurance company. Any unpaid loan, together with unpaid interest, reduces the death benefit or the cash value.

Long-Term Care Insurance: A policy providing benefits when the insured needs long-term care.

Medical Insurance: A policy providing benefits when the insured incurs medical expenses.

Misstatement-of-Age Clause: A policy provision calling for an adjustment of the death benefit when the age of the insured is misstated in the policy. *Also called* Age Clause.

Modal Premium Charges: *See* Fractional Premium Charges.

Modal Premiums: *See* Fractional Premiums.

Mortality Rate: A probability of death (usually within one year), expressed as a decimal.

Net Amount at Risk: *See* Protection Component.

Noncancellable: A continuance clause saying a policyholder has the right to keep the policy until a specified age and the insurance company does not have the right to increase the premiums. Sometimes called "noncancellable and guaranteed renewable," and generally used in a disability policy.

Nonparticipating Policy: A policy that does not provide for dividends.

Own Occupation: A definition of disability that refers to the inability of an insured to perform the duties of the insured's own occupation.

Partial Disability: Inability of an insured to perform some occupational duties.

Participating Policy: A policy that provides for dividends.

Periodic-Premium Annuity: A deferred annuity purchased

with annual, semiannual, quarterly, or monthly premiums.

Policy: A contract between a policyholder and an insurance company providing for a benefit when an insured dies, is disabled, incurs medical expenses, or needs long-term care.

Policyholder: A person or entity possessing incidents of ownership of a policy, such as the right to designate the beneficiary, the right to surrender the policy, the right to receive dividends, and the right to assign the policy to another person or entity. *Also called* Policyowner.

Policyowner: *See* Policyholder.

Portfolio Average Method: A method for calculating the dividend on a life insurance policy based on returns from the company's entire investment portfolio.

Premium: An amount paid by a policyholder to an insurance company for the policy. The premium is usually paid annually, semiannually, quarterly, or monthly.

Premium Payer: The person or entity that pays the premium to the insurance company.

Protection Component: The difference between the death benefit and the cash value of a life insurance policy. *Also called* Net Amount at Risk.

Pure Life Annuity: A life annuity in which the payments stop when the annuitant dies. It may be pure only during the accumulation period, only during the liquidation period, or during both periods.

Refund Life Annuity: A life annuity in which the payments are for a specified period and thereafter are contingent upon the survival of the annuitant. An example is a life annuity with ten years certain; if the annuitant dies before receiving payments for ten years, the beneficiary receives payments for the remainder of the ten years.

Reinstatement Clause: A policy provision that shows the conditions to be met in order to put a policy back into effect after the policy has lapsed.

Reinsurance Company: A company with which an insurance company enters into a reinsurance contract to relieve the insurance company of certain liabilities.

Renewability: A provision in a term policy that shows how long the policy can be held without the insured having to show evidence of insurability.

Renewable at Company Option: A continuance clause saying an insurance company has the right to terminate the policy at any time. Used in some disability and medical policies.

Reserve: A liability of an insurance company.

Reserve Interest Rate: An interest rate used in calculating the reserves of a life insurance company.

Savings component: *See* Cash Value.

Settlement Option: A clause in a life insurance policy that allows a policyholder or a beneficiary to receive a benefit in installments rather than in one sum.

Single-Premium Annuity: An immediate annuity or deferred annuity purchased with one premium.

Term Policy: A policy that provides protection for a limited period, has premiums that may increase periodically, and builds little or no cash value.

Time Value of Money: *See* Interest.

Total Disability: Inability of an insured to perform any occupational duties.

Universal Life Insurance: A type of cash-value life insurance that provides for flexible premiums, divides the policy into its protection and savings components, and has cash values that depend upon the amount of the premiums that have been paid on the policy.

Variable Annuity: An annuity, classified as a security for regulatory purposes, in which the payments are stated in units. The company assets backing the annuity are invested in equity instruments such as stocks. The value of a unit is determined from time to time based on the value of the assets backing the annuity.

Variable Life: A type of policy, classified as a security for regulatory purposes, in which the company assets backing the policy are invested in equity instruments such as stocks, and in which the cash value and death benefit are based on the value of the assets backing the policy.

Waiting Period: *See* Elimination Period.

Waiver-of-Premium Clause: A policy provision that relieves the policyholder from premiums during a disability.

Yearly Price per $1,000 of Protection Component: A price for one year for each $1,000 of protection in a life insurance policy.

Yearly Rate of Return on Savings Component: A rate of return for one year on the savings component of a life insurance policy, usually expressed as a percentage or as a decimal.

Index

About the Author

Joseph M. Belth is professor emeritus of insurance in the Kelley School of Business at Indiana University. He is the author of several books and many journal articles. He founded *The Insurance Forum* and was its editor for its entire 40 years of existence. He received a George Polk Award for the *Forum* and many other important awards for his writings. He and his wife Marjorie live near Bloomington, Indiana.